CAREERS FOR

BOOKWORMS
& Other
Literary Types

VGM Careers for You Series

CAREERS

F O R

BOOKWORMS
& Other
Literary Types

Marjorie Eberts
Margaret Gisler

VGM Career Horizons
a division of *NTC Publishing Group*
Lincolnwood, Illinois USA

Dedication

To Patty White, our favorite bookworm, who reads books, hoards books, and keeps them as friends forever.

Library of Congress Cataloging-in-Publication Data

Eberts, Marjorie.
   Careers for bookworms & other literary types / Marjorie Eberts,
Margaret Gisler.

     p. cm.
     ISBN 0-8442-8618-4
     1. Book industries and trade—Vocational guidance. 2. Publishers
and publishing—Vocational guidance. 3. Information science-
-Vocational guidance. 4. Library science—Vocational guidance.
5. Research—Vocational guidance. I. Gisler, Margaret. II. Title.
III. Title: Careers for bookworms and other literary types.
Z278.E25   1990
381'.45002'023—dc20   90-32570
                                                   CIP

Published by VGM Career Horizons, a division of NTC Publishing Group.
© 1990 by NTC Publishing Group, 4255 West Touhy Avenue,
Lincolnwood (Chicago), Illinois 60646-1975 U.S.A.
All rights reserved. No part of this book may be reproduced, stored
in a retrieval system, or transmitted in any form or by any means,
electronic, mechanical, photocopying, recording or otherwise, without
the prior permission of NTC Publishing Group.
Manufactured in the United States of America.

Contents

About the Authors

Marjorie Eberts and Margaret Gisler have been writing professionally for eleven years. They are prolific free-lance authors with over fifty books in print. Their writing is usually in the field of education. The two authors have written textbooks, beginning readers, and study skills books for schoolchildren. They have also written a speech book for adults, career books, a college preparation handbook, and three volumes on the history of an army facility.

Besides writing books, the two authors have a syndicated education column, "Dear Teacher," which appears in newspapers throughout the country. Eberts and Gisler also give advice on educational issues in speeches, at workshops, and on television.

Writing this book was a special pleasure for Eberts and Gisler as they are decidedly bookworms. Investigating the many careers that require reading on-the-job let them spend hours reading—their favorite avocation.

Eberts is a graduate of Stanford University, and Gisler is a graduate of Ball State and Butler Universities. Both received their specialist degrees in education from Butler University. The two authors are also former teachers with over twenty years of teaching experience between them.

Acknowledgments

Some bookworms have jobs that let them spend considerable time reading. We would especially like to thank the following dedicated bookworms for providing us with information about their careers:

KATHY BARNARD	Indianapolis-Marion County Public Library
SUE ELLEN BLOMBERG	Howard J. Rubenstein Associates
CLAIRE BOLTON	World Book
ANNE BRAND	MGM/UA
RICHARD BREADY	World Book
ROGER BROOKS	Legislative Auditor's Office, Minnesota
L. T. BROWN	*Indianapolis News*
STEVE BUSHOUSE	Butler University
CHRIS CAIRO	Indianapolis-Marion County Public Library
BILL CARNES	United States Army Finance Corps
MARGARET CARNEY	Harlequin Books
AL CARP	International Multifoods
BETSY CAUFIELD	*Indianapolis Star and News*
THOMAS COCHRUN	WTHR, Indianapolis
PATRICK COLEMAN	Minnesota Historical Society
HELEN M. CORRALES	Hoover Institution
ELIZABETH CRAWFORD	Indianapolis-Marion County Public Library

LEIGH DAVIS	*Saturday Evening Post*
WILLIAM DEJOHN	University of Minnesota
KIM DURR	Postal Instant Press
DON ELLER	Mosely Securities Corporation
JOHN W. ELLWOOD	University of Minnesota
SUE ENGLEDOW	Clay Junior High School
SANDY ERICKSON	Vick Ramos
TIM ERICKSON	University of Wisconsin
SARA EVANS	University of Minnesota
JACQUELINE FISCHER	Indianapolis-Marion County Public Library
SANDY FITZGERALD	*Indianapolis Star and News*
JUDY GALBRAITH	Free Spirit
DENECE GILBERT	
VALISKA GREGORY	Free-lance Book Reviewer
STANLEY GREIGG	Congressional Budget Office
FRED GRISSONI	American Printing House for the Blind
FRAN HAGEBOECK	Mohawk Trails Elementary School
DAWN HALL	*Indianapolis Star and News*
NORMAN HARBERGER	Sibson Harberger
BETH HARRIS	Associated Press
TOM HATCH	Modern Curriculum Press
DENNIS HETZEL	*Capital Times*
DEIDRE HOUCEK	Marketing Research Corporation of America
RHONDA HUNNICUTT	Carmel Clay Public Library
KAREN ZACK INGEBRETSEN	World Book
JAYE ISLER	Literary Guild
JOAN JOHNSTON	Stanford University
JACK HUGHES	Mosely Securities Corporation
FELICE KNARR	Roncalli High School
GREG KNIPE	Walden Books
FRANK KNOUREK	General Mills
JOAN KOLIAS	Hudson Institute

RANDY KORNFIELD	MGM/UA
VALERIE KOUTNIK	Screenwriter
CYNTHIA KROOS	Villa Holidays
JOHN LEVINE	Dorsey and Whitney
MAUREEN M. LIEBENSON	World Book
DAVID MACANALLY	WTHR, Indianapolis
BARBARA EVANS MARKUSON	Indiana Cooperative Library Services Authority
SHIRLEY MULLIN	Kids Ink
NANCY MULVANEY	The American Society of Indexers
MARGARET MYERS	American Library Association
ROBERT NELSON	The Lilly Laboratory for Clinical Research
TERRI NELSON	International Multifoods
MOLLY PARSONS	A.C. Nielsen
JANET PETERSON	World Book
JEFF PIGEON	WIBC, Indianapolis
ROSEMARY PIPER	Hudson Institute
STEVE RIES	Barnes and Thornburg
PAUL RHUNQUIST	Library of Congress
JILL SANSONE	Book of the Month Club
JULIE G. SEDKY	County Nat/West/Washington Analysis Group
EVELYN SIMPSON	Carmel Clay Public Library
TED SLATE	Newsweek
BEN STROUT	WTHR, Indianapolis
BILL WEPLER	Indiana State Museum
HERBERT S. WHITE	Indiana University
JOHN WILLIAMS	House Research Department, Minnesota
DAVE WOOD	Minneapolis Star Tribune
DICK WOLFSIE	WTHR, Indianapolis
ROBERT O. ZELENY	World Book

Foreword

Working with words can be a very fullfilling—and sometimes frustrating—way to make a living. The work can be difficult, and the pay is often low. But the reward is in the work itself—reading, researching, editing, and otherwise working with words.

Some people are inextricably drawn to words, whether in books, songs, magazines, films, or any other form. These people pursue their love for words in schools, at home, in libraries, at poetry readings, and many other places. Yet, most word lovers at one time or another dream of having a job that will pay them to pursue their passion. It is for these dreamers that this book has been written.

Careers for Bookworms contains useful advice for people who want jobs involving lots of reading, research, even a little writing. Some of the workplaces covered include libraries, publishing houses, film studios, government agencies, think tanks, corporations, bookstores, and schools. You will also read actual case histories of people who currently work in these areas, what they like and don't like about their jobs, how they got where they are, and what advice they have for people like you who are just starting out.

This book is the first in a series for people who wish to turn their personal interests into careers. Other books will soon be available for people whose passions are sports, travel, the outdoors, and helping others. We hope this book helps bookworms everywhere realize their dreams of finding jobs and careers that let them wallow in the world of words!

The Editors
VGM Career Horizons

CHAPTER ONE

Jobs for Bookworms

D o you love books passionately, excessively, and unreasonably?
Are you unable to resist the attraction of books when you are
near hundreds or thousands of them? Are books the magnets
that draw you into bookstores and libraries? Do you enjoy taking a loaded
wallet into a bookstore to acquire its treasures? Are you moved by
excitement when you see a new book? Have you successfully resisted the
lure of television to remain curled in your chair reading? If so, then you
are a confirmed bookworm; and more than likely "book" is your favorite
four letter word.

Bookworms are a special breed. Once they have felt the magnetic pull
of books, their lives are changed forever. Bookworms want to spend as
many waking minutes as they can with the printed word. This includes
sharing meals with books, reading while going to work, and having the
secure feeling at the end of the day of falling to sleep with a book in their
hands.

Wherever bookworms live, their habitat is filled with books. Every
room is cluttered with books. They are on coffee tables, countertops,
bookshelves, window ledges, and even stacked on the floor. Nightstands
by beds are filled with books. Throughout a bookworm's home, favorites
are resting in prominent places so they can easily be picked up and reread.

Young bookworms have more books than toys, games, puzzles, or
dolls. Teenagers who are bookworms struggle to school carrying bags full
of books to cram in their lockers which are already overloaded with
books. Their cars look like bookmobiles.

Even though they have read hundreds of books and handled thousands
more, their passion for the printed word never cools. The longer bookworms live with books, the more the magnetism of books draws them to

read more and more titles. They enjoy relaxing with books, shopping for books, collecting books, and working with books. Unfortunately, very few bookworms have jobs which let them do considerable reading.

A Bookworm's Dream— Reading from 9 to 5

When bookworms read help wanted ads, they are always searching for jobs that will allow them to spend more of their time reading. The following ads would surely capture the attention of any bookworm:

ASSISTANT EDITOR   Outstanding opportunity to work for trade book publisher. Responsibilities include reading manuscripts for possible acquisition, making market studies, and editing young adult titles.

BOOKSTORE MANAGER   Independent bookstore seeks manager with retail book background to select and order books and manage operations.

RESEARCHER   Think tank wants intellectually curious person to read and summarize articles on the statehood movement in Puerto Rico.

CELEBRITY HELPER   Motion picture actress seeks person to read and answer fan mail.

READER   New audio cassette company seeks people with good reading voices to record current novels on tape.

This book is dedicated to helping all bookworms realize their dreams of finding jobs that will allow them to read on company time. Here is a bird's-eye view of some of the jobs that you will read about in this book.

Jobs in Libraries
Not a day passes in the life of anyone employed in a library without the opportunity to handle books and other reading material. Library jobs

offer bookworms direct physical contact with their most valued possessions—books. What's more, no competent employee can adequately serve library patrons without doing some reading on the job. Upon investigation bookworms will discover that jobs in a library offer far more challenges than checking books in and out.

Jobs with Book Publishers

The one thing that sets book publishing jobs apart from any others for bookworms is the opportunity to be part of creating a new book. And each step in the creation of that book involves working with the author's manuscript in some way. The manuscript must be acquired from the author, edited, copyedited, proofread, set in type, and sold. As the number of books printed each year increases, so do the number of jobs in publishing houses. The easiest way to discover the vast number of jobs that are available in publishing is to get your foot in the door by taking any kind of entry-level position that you can find.

Jobs at Magazines and Newspapers

Bookworms do not just burrow their noses in books. They read anything that is printed, including magazines and newspapers. Although many of the editorial jobs in magazines and newspapers are similar to those in book publishing, there are many additional jobs. Think about all the letters that magazines and newspapers receive; someone has to read them and deal with them. Then there are crossword puzzles to be created and wire service offerings and syndicated columns to be chosen.

Jobs in Glamour Industries

Just because a person loves to read is no reason to think that person would only want to work in a quiet atmosphere surrounded by books. There are glamorous jobs where bookworms can combine reading with a chance to hobnob with movie stars or even work closely with them. After all, someone has to be hired to read a superstar's mail and screen scripts to discover those which are exactly right for the star. And it's not just the movie industry, but also television, radio, and the theater that offer bookworms jobs with a touch of glamour.

Jobs in Education

You can't hold many jobs in the education world without doing considerable reading to increase your knowledge. Classroom teachers have to read textbooks and accompanying teacher's manuals, professional journals, and books and magazines to enrich the curriculum for their students. University professors have to read and research to get their doctorates. Then they have to keep reading and researching to publish scholarly works that will help them get tenure. Reading jobs in education are not confined to teaching; for example, someone has to read all the applications students make to colleges.

Jobs in Research

It's fair to say that researchers are readers. Imagine yourself rummaging through the stacks in a library trying to find books that trace the history of geraniums or the level of fashion-consciousness of the wives of Henry the Eighth. Such jobs may seem improbable, but they actually exist in the research job market. Jobs in research were traditionally found at universities. But now there are jobs with the government, businesses, and think tanks.

Jobs in the Public Sector

The government generates monumental amounts of paperwork. What is written is bound to be read, sorted, and stored by someone. Then there are all the letters that people write to government officials that have to be read and answered. Just think of the volume of mail that the patent and copyright offices receive each day. Senators and representatives need large numbers of people on their staffs who devote the majority of their time on the job to reading and answering constituent requests. The government at all levels abounds in jobs for bookworms. There are people searching for property titles on the local level and reading the president's mail on the national level.

Jobs in the Private Sector

With the explosion of information, it's essential for businesses to have employees who can find what they need to know. Bookworms are probably the perfect candidates for these jobs as information retrievers; however, they will need to be persistent and imaginative to find these jobs. Did you know that there are jobs on Wall Street, and in every brokerage house, for stockbrokers who must read in order to analyze the stock market? Were you aware that at most larger banks economists read about what is happening all over the world in order to give banking executives economic predictions about the future? Who do you think large corporations hire to handle information and complaint letters? The answer is readers, like you.

More Jobs for Readers

Bookworms tend to look for jobs that involve reading at places where books are traditionally found: libraries, schools, and publishing companies. While it is true that many jobs for readers are found in these places, there are less well-known jobs that still involve reading. However, it does take some investigation to discover these jobs. Bookworms may be perfect for jobs as translators, storytellers, genealogy researchers, and news clippers for individuals and companies. Then, of course, there is the almost perfect job for a true bookworm—being an author.

Job Qualifications

Bookworms speak frequently and eloquently about their love for books. They consider books not only as prized possessions but also as true friends. However, a love of books and reading is not sufficient qualification for many jobs that require a significant amount of reading. Education really counts. In many cases, it isn't even enough to have a bachelor's degree. Quite often a master's degree is a prerequisite for being considered for a position. And there are many jobs where holding double master's degrees or a doctorate would be helpful in getting a job.

Fortunately, bookworms tend to want to study and receive as much education as possible.

For Further Reading

On June 10, 1815, Thomas Jefferson wrote in a letter to John Adams, "I cannot live without books." This expresses perfectly the philosophy of all true bookworms. Bookworms should probably be familiar with the following books:

Booth, Richard, ed. *Book Collecting*. Florence, Ala.: House of Collectibles, 1976.

Chernow, Barbara A. and George A. Vallasi, eds. *The Reader's Adviser: A Layman's Guide to Literature*. New York: R. R. Bowker Company, 1986.

Fadiman, Clifton. *The Lifetime Reading Plan*. New York: Thomas Y. Cromwell Company, 1978.

Gilbar, Steven. *A Compendium of Lists, Quizzes, and Trivia about Books*. New York: Bell Publishing Company, 1981.

Haller, Margaret. *The Book Collector's Fact Book*. New York: Arco Publishing Company, 1976.

Jones, Charles E., ed. *The People You Meet and the Books You Read*. Harrisburg, Pa.: Executive Books, 1986.

Katz, Linda Sternberg and Bill Katz. *Writer's Choice*. Reston, Va.: Prentice Hall Company, 1983.

Parsons, Nicholas. *The Book of Literary Lists*. New York: Facts on File Publications, 1987.

Perrin, Noel. *A Reader's Delight*. Hanover, N.H.: University Press of New England, 1988.

Ward, Philip. *A Lifetime's Reading*. New York: Stein and Day Publishers, 1983.

CHAPTER TWO

Libraries
The Natural Habitat of Bookworms

Wh at better place is there for a bookworm to find a job than in a library! It seems ideal. Imagine working in a place where you are surrounded by thousands or even hundreds of thousands of books. If you are lucky enough to work in the Library of Congress, there will be at least 80 million books in 470 languages or dialects for you to peruse. You will even be able to find this book there because the Library of Congress tries to obtain copies of everything that is published in the United States. In 1988, over 50,000 new trade books like this one were added to the collection.

Today, there are over 100,000 libraries in the United States. The opportunities are almost endless for you to work in a library. Not only do these libraries employ over 150,000 librarians, there are jobs for almost 200,000 people as support staff.

If you decide to work in a library, you will be in good company. Aristotle is probably the first well-known librarian. He put together a collection of books for his school in Athens, founded in 347 B.C. Before that there were libraries of papyrus scrolls and clay tablets, so there were librarians as long ago as 2000 B.C. In the British Museum, you can actually see an ancient library of clay tablets which was organized by an Assyrian king in about 700 B.C.

Two famous colonial statesmen, Benjamin Franklin and Thomas Jefferson, were also librarians. Pinch-penny Franklin started a subscription library limiting its circulation to subscribers who had paid a yearly fee. Not only did Jefferson catalog and classify materials for the University of Virginia library, he had his own personal library of 10,000 books. After the first Library of Congress burned, Jefferson's collection became the nucleus of the Library of Congress.

Familiar figures in this century who were also librarians include J. Edgar Hoover, who worked at the Library of Congress while completing his law degree, and Mao Tse-tung, who was a library assistant at the Beijing University library. Mao carried periodicals to readers' tables and earned the same salary as a coolie.

Books are a librarian's major business. From 4,000 years ago until today, the focus of the·librarian's job is much the same. Librarians collect, organize, and make information available to people.

Taking a Good Look at the Workplace

When you choose to work as a librarian, it may not always be in a modern, comfortable, spacious environment. You may be driving around all day in a bookmobile, working next door to a laboratory with all its varied odors, or handing out books at a prison. There is a remarkable assortment of libraries in the United States, usually divided into these four categories: public, school, academic, and special.

But no matter whether a library is located at a zoo, in a law office, in a metropolitan area, or a small rural area; the librarian is the person who provides the essential services.

The Familiar Public Library

Bookworms are always familiar with the public libraries in their area. And there is no shortage of libraries for them to visit in the United States as there are about 15,000 public libraries. These libraries, which are usually supported locally, vary greatly in size. You can get lost in the huge New York Public Library with its eight million books or find yourself in a small one-room library within the Arctic Circle in Alaska. However, no matter where a library is or how large or small it is, a librarian is needed to serve its users.

Regardless of their size, all public libraries have the same mission of serving the people who use them. This means having at least a core of reference books for everyone in the community plus sections for children and adults. In some areas, libraries have special sections to meet the needs of that community. For example, the Detroit Public Library has a variety of materials on the history of the automobile.

Public libraries are no longer limited to traditional library buildings. In addition to roving bookmobiles, there are often services to retirement and nursing homes, jails, and hospitals.

School Libraries

The little old red schoolhouse did not have a library. Think back. Did your first school have a library or were there just books in the classroom? In recent years, more and more schools have put in libraries because teachers are asking their students to get information beyond what is in textbooks.

The contents of school libraries tie closely to what is being taught at the schools. Obviously, high school libraries have a far wider range of material than those in elementary, middle, or junior high schools. Because today's school libraries are also storehouses for films, filmstrips, recordings, and graphic materials; they are now usually called library media centers or just media centers.

Academic Libraries

"Where are you going?" one college student asks another. Not surprisingly, the answer often is "the library." Students go to the library to find information, to research, and to study at the large tables or special study carrels.

Not all academic libraries are the same. Community college libraries tend to cater to the needs of adult learners. College libraries will vary greatly in size and scope. However, because of library networks and interlibrary loans, students can obtain just about any book that they want. University libraries are usually the largest academic libraries. Many have very specialized collections on specific subjects. Within the gigantic University of California library system, there are collections devoted to subjects like citrus fruits, California history, and oceanography. At a large university, you may find many separate libraries devoted to specific subjects located all over the campus.

Because of the knowledge boom that began in the 1950's and continues today, there has been a real increase in library building to store all this information. There has also been a fantastic increase in the use of computers to find where all this information is stored.

Special Libraries

"Special" is the key word to use in describing special libraries. These libraries deal with specialized subjects like pharmacology, law, transportation, and medicine. They have users who want special information, like the federal requirements to be followed in removing asbestos or the best treatment for Parkinson's disease. Without these special libraries, people would find it impossible to keep up with the latest information in so many areas—especially in scientific fields. What follows is just a glimpse at some of the special libraries that exist, and all these libraries have jobs for librarians.

Government Libraries

The Library of Congress, the National Library of Medicine, and the Library of Agriculture are three government libraries that have developed such extensive collections that they are considered national libraries. Besides these three libraries, the government operates an amazing number of libraries.

Each branch of the armed services has technical, educational, and recreational libraries on a nationwide and worldwide basis. The navy even operates libraries on board ships. You will find libraries at Veterans Administration hospitals, the National Weather Services, the Patent and Trademark Office, the Environmental Protection Agency, and in every department of the government. In addition, there are state libraries. The list of government libraries is almost endless.

Business Libraries

When employees at a firm need special information, they can often find it in the company library. Special libraries can be found in businesses like the following ones:

banks

accounting firms

steel companies

public utilities

television stations

aeronautics firms

investment houses

newspapers

food processors

advertising agencies

research institutes

telephone companies

Science Libraries

The vast amount of scientific knowledge that is constantly being discovered, updated, and changed in scientific fields like nutrition, marine biology, botany, physiology, biochemistry, zoology, and the health sciences necessitates libraries in such places as the following:

chemical companies

cosmetic companies

medical schools

health centers

hospitals

petroleum refineries

mining firms

medical societies

space-oriented companies

pharmaceutical firms

Would You Really Like to Be a Librarian?

You won't become a millionaire as a librarian, but you may have the opportunity to do quite a bit of reading. Being a bookworm, this should please you. However, you should realize that relatively few librarians have the luxury of sitting down on the job and reading a book from cover-to-cover. Of course, there are exceptions like the bibliographer at the National Library of Congress who has spent forty years reading as he works on a bibliography of snow, ice, and permafrost.

The librarian sitting behind a desk at your local library is doing far more than reading as he or she spends a lot of time answering questions and helping patrons. But the librarian also has the chance to see new books coming into the library, to read reviews of books in an assigned area in order to find books to order, and to put together book lists. Some time may also be spent in scanning newspapers to update sources or to clip materials for various files.

Do You Have the Necessary Personal Qualifications?

Most library jobs require considerable versatility. However, there are certain qualities that most librarians share. Answer the following questions with a "yes" or a "no" to see if you possess most of these qualities.

		YES	NO
1.	Do you have a genuine love of books?	___	___
2.	Do you have a wide knowledge of books?	___	___
3.	Do you have the patience to keep searching until required materials are found?	___	___
4.	Do you have above average academic ability?	___	___
5.	Do you have a good memory?	___	___
6.	Do you possess intellectual curiosity?	___	___
7.	Do you have the ability to make decisions?	___	___

8. Do you have the ability to attend carefully
    to details?   ____   ____

9. Do you have the ability to be patient?   ____   ____

10. Do you have good oral and written
    communication skills?   ____   ____

11. Do you have the ability to adjust to new
    procedures?   ____   ____

12. Do you possess the knack of being tactful and
    courteous?   ____   ____

13. Do you have a desire for continuing education?   ____   ____

14. Do you have a genuine interest in helping
    people use libraries?   ____   ____

15. Do you have the ability to get along with all
    types of people?   ____   ____

Thinking about Your Qualifications

Even if you answered "yes" to all of the above questions, it does not mean
that you will be happy or successful in every library position. The
personal qualities that would make you an excellent indexer might not
make you an excellent children's librarian. In addition to the necessary
personal qualifications, prospective librarians need to realize that there
are considerable educational requirements for the position of professional librarian.

The Education of a Librarian

The amount of education needed to work in a library depends upon the
job that you want to hold. If you want to be a professional librarian, you
are going to have to obtain a master's degree in library science (M.L.S.).
This will take you at least a year; however, a two-year program is

becoming common. You will take basic courses in librarianship as well as advanced courses in such things as indexing, abstracting, cataloging, classification, administration, and automation.

Although there are a number of colleges that offer the M.L.S. degree, you will probably want to attend one that has a program accredited by the American Library Association. Admission to these programs isn't easy. Not only will you need good college grades and an acceptable score on the Graduate Record Examination, you may also need to have knowledge of a foreign language.

Librarians are quite an educated group. After obtaining an M.L.S., many take courses in continuing education throughout their careers. And librarians with specific goals often go on to get certificates for advanced study programs, master's degrees in different fields, or even doctorates in library science.

Schooling Required for a Professional Librarian

PUBLIC LIBRARIES   If you want a really high administrative post in a very large library, having a master's degree may not be enough. You may need to have a Ph.D. in library science.

SCHOOL LIBRARIES   If you like working with school-age children and are seriously considering being a school librarian, check the Department of Education's certification requirements in the state where you want to work. It may be enough to have a bachelor's degree in education plus courses in library science. More than likely, you will need to have a master's in educational media or library science.

ACADEMIC LIBRARIES   Librarians wishing to teach or hold top administrative posts will find it very helpful to have doctorate degrees.

SPECIAL LIBRARIES   Not only is a special librarian going to need an M.L.S., at least a bachelor's degree or possibly another master's degree is required in the special field.

Schooling Required for Library Technicians

Library technicians certainly don't need the years of education beyond high school that professional librarians do. In fact, it is even possible to get a position as a library technician with just a high school diploma. Many libraries, nevertheless, prefer technicians to have completed a two-year college program in library technology.

Librarians Talk about Their Work

Librarians love to read and feel that they need to read all the time because so much new material is constantly being published. However, most librarians can't read as much as they want because they have so many other things to do on their jobs. Librarians do manage to keep current with literature in their specific areas by relying on professional journals, book lists, and reviews.

The types of jobs librarians do are largely the same whether they are working in a public, school, academic, or special library. To give you a better picture of what librarians do, some librarians describe their work on the following pages.

Coordinator of Children's Services

A portable cart with at least 200 children's books sits by the desk of Chris Cairo, who is the coordinator of children's services at a major metropolitan library. Chris is a librarian who does a lot of reading, and she feels that most children's librarians also do considerable reading. The books on the cart are the ones the selectors at the main library and branch libraries wish to add to the library's collection. Chris will read the staff librarians' reviews on each of the books but only read 50 percent of the books from cover-to-cover. She reads the books to familiarize herself with the authors, illustrators, themes, and trends as well as to see which books the children's librarians in the library system want. She is responsible for ordering all the books for the metropolitan library system.

As coordinator of children's services, Chris also sets up various reading programs, supervises the creation of book lists on such subjects as "Reading Outloud," "Indians of North America," and "Toddler Tales." Another responsibility is supervising all the children's librarians in the system. Chris, who has always loved to read, even takes books home in the evening to read to her children.

Head Librarian at a Magazine

Ted Slate confessed that his first love was eating, but by the age of two he had developed a new love—books. As library director at *Newsweek*, he now gets paid to read—the thing that he most loves to do. And he supervises a staff of nineteen people who really read on the job.

Two staff members read and index the domestic edition and the three international editions of *Newsweek* in order to provide the date and page of *Newsweek* articles to people who call or write for information that previously appeared in the magazine. The indexers put subject tags on the stories so the stories can be retrieved easily.

Other staff members are librarians who spend their days researching information for the magazine's writers and reporters who must keep abreast of what is happening in the world. Each of these librarians is assigned a subject area or areas corresponding to the departments in the magazine. The librarian assigned to national affairs, for example, reads such things as White House releases, the *National Journal*, and *Congressional Quarterly* magazines, as well as a variety of daily newspapers to keep files in this area up-to-date.

Ted says you simply can't work on a news magazine without reading. What kind of a background do you have to have to get jobs like this? Ted has an undergraduate degree in history and master's degrees in both history/political science and library science. His reference librarians are college graduates with advanced degrees in library science; many have master's degrees in a variety of other specializations as well. How do you get these jobs? Most of the staff sent unsolicited résumés to the magazine.

Not only does Ted read on the job, he also has what he calls a books-and-magazines-in-progress program which he follows in his spare time. The program has him carrying a book in his briefcase to read traveling to and from the office, placing a book in each bathroom in his home, and having magazines by his bed.

Indexer and Abstractor in a Newspaper Library

"The job is reading!" according to Dawn Hall, an indexer and abstractor in the library of a large newspaper. "It's very concise, exact, and fast reading," she says. Her job as an indexer begins when she is assigned several pages of the newspaper to read carefully. She selects the stories the newspaper will want to keep on file. Then index marks are put on each story to indicate what the subject tags are. The stories are then clipped out of the paper and put in a stack for the abstractors.

As an abstractor, Dawn will read a newspaper story that has been indexed to get an idea of what it is about. Then she will determine the file heading which will be typed on an envelope. A brief summary of the article (the abstract) will then be typed under the file heading. After determining what the cross references will be, each cross reference is typed on a card as well as the abstract. The envelopes and cards are then ready for filing.

Dawn's background includes a degree in education and an M.L.S. However, some of her coworkers have B.A.'s in liberal arts, and some are just working on their college degrees. Dawn had worked at a small newspaper after college before she found this job through a want ad in the newspaper.

Reference Librarian in the Social Sciences Division

People think that librarians sit around reading for their pleasure, but this is a myth according to Kathy Barnard who works as a reference librarian in the social sciences division of a large public library. When you see her sitting at the desk, which is approximately 60 percent of her workday, much of her time is taken up in helping library patrons.

When she is not doing this, she is constantly scanning newspapers and general news magazines to update her assigned areas. For example, if she reads that a world leader has died, she will update the information in such references as *Statesman's Yearbook* or *Current Biography*. Kathy's job also requires her to read book reviews and to select new materials for an assigned area. When she is not at the desk, she is helping patrons find information by using indexes (both print and computer) and the library's on-line catalog, among other sources.

Reference Librarian in a Suburban Library

While working on her M.L.S. degree, Rhonda Hunnicutt is working in the reference section of a suburban library. She started at this library in a part-time job in the children's section. Previously, she had worked as a schoolteacher. Like most reference librarians, some of her time on the job is spent reading reviews so that she can select new materials for an assigned area. Rhonda also reads articles in the vertical files to see which ones are out of date and should be discarded. She also has the responsibilities of keeping the college catalogs in order, working on the music section of the vertical file, and checking that the phone books are cataloged. Ninety percent of Rhonda's time is spent behind the desk helping patrons.

Director of Library at a Think Tank

Joan Kolias performs library services and acts as a "junior researcher." She works as an information and resource person for the staff of a think tank—one of those places where experts sit around and think. Then they write papers or speak on different topics. But it is Joan and her staff who find so many of the sources that the experts read.

Joan's job requires thoughtful reading. Each day she reads at least two newspapers trying to find articles that are related to research being done at the think tank. She also looks at news magazines and journals that are related to current research. But most of her time is spent trying to find information on topics currently being researched by the think tank staff.

Joan's job requires creative research skills as she is always looking for hard-to-find information. Not only does Joan have an M.L.S., she has taken many continuing courses in library science and computer science. For her job, she feels that a knowledge of microcomputers is absolutely essential. Joan obtained what she considers an extremely interesting job in an unusual way for this type of position—she answered a newspaper want ad.

Reference Librarian in a Law Library

Steve Ries worked as an assistant in a law firm, went on to get his M.L.S., and went back to the same law firm as a librarian. Today, he has three assistants and a part-time employee. These people do such things as shelving books, filing new materials, and keeping track of circulation. A college education is not required for these positions, but these employees do need to know how a library operates.

Steve's staff does not do as much reading as Steve does. He spends most of his time using books and the computer to search for the case studies that the lawyers in the firm need. For 75 percent of the workday, Steve can be found using the computer to find information.

Positive and Negative Aspects of Being a Librarian

Just like any other career, there are both positive and negative aspects to being a librarian. While this career may not let bookworms read as much as they like, it does allow them to spend time near their fondest possessions—books.

Good Things about Being a Librarian

1. Part of the time in your job you will be paid for doing what you love most—reading.

2. You will be working with people who share your love of books.

3. You will have the opportunity to share your knowledge of books with the library patrons.

4. You will be joining a profession that demands you keep learning about what is happening in the world.

5. You will have a job that lets you use all your creativity and initiative in searching for hard-to-find materials.

6. You can choose to be either a generalist or a specialist concentrating on a particular field of interest.

7. You can choose between working with people or working for the most part by yourself.

8. You can feel the reward of furthering other people's knowledge whether they are esoteric researchers or third graders doing their first report.

Things to Consider Before Becoming a Librarian

1. Considerable preparation is required for this career. Librarians usually need to have a master's degree.

2. Librarian's pay is not equal to other professions that require the same amount of schooling.

3. You will have to cope at times with unreasonable demands and discourteous behavior from library patrons.

4. You will have to be able to stoop, lift, and stretch as you shelve or reach for books.

5. You will have to be willing to use computers in searching for information.

6. You will not always work the typical nine to five day. Libraries are open in the evenings and on weekends.

Getting a Job as a Librarian

If you just want a clerical or a technical job in a library, you can usually find this type of work by contacting a local library or looking at want ads in the newspaper. To get a job as a professional librarian, you will probably use other techniques, although some librarians have obtained jobs in those ways.

PART-TIME JOBS   You can begin paving the way for your first full-time job before you ever finish your education by working part time in a library. Prior experience is always an added bonus on a résumé. Furthermore, getting your foot in the door with a part-time job can lead to a full-time job after graduation.

INTERNSHIPS AND WORK-STUDY PROGRAMS   You should also look into other options for experience like internships and work-study programs. Besides extremely sought-after internships at the Library of Congress and the National Library of Medicine, many research, academic, and special libraries have internships which can lead to future jobs.

HELP ON CAMPUS   College placement services can really be helpful in finding a job. They have job listings, and many help with the writing of résumés and send your credentials to prospective employers. Don't overlook studying college bulletin boards and talking to faculty members, fellow students, and alumni when searching for a job.

HOTLINES   The phone is your friend when seeking a job. There are a fantastic number of hotlines that have the latest job listings. Just dial 1 800-545-2433 to find out the numbers of state, regional, and association hotlines. Or look in the classified section of *American Libraries*.

WANT ADS   Most library journals have classified ad sections that list jobs. You can even advertise your own availability in some of these journals.

CONVENTIONS   Go to the annual conventions of library associations. Many have job placement programs. You can even send your credentials in before some conventions start.

DIRECTORIES AND BROCHURES   The *American Library Directory* lists all kinds of libraries in a two-volume directory. Its only weakness is that some school and special libraries don't return their forms so they aren't listed.

Another great resource with all kinds of hotline numbers and addresses is the *Guide to Library Placement Sources*. For only seventy-five cents you can obtain single copies of this guide by writing to:

Office for Library Personnel Resources
American Library Association
50 East Huron Street
Chicago, IL 60611

FEDERAL GOVERNMENT LIBRARY JOBS   Don't overlook getting a job with the government. To work in many of the federal libraries you will have to establish civil service eligibility and be placed on the Office of Personnel Management (OPM) register in Washington, D.C., which involves meeting certain requirements. Other agencies like the F.B.I., C.I.A., and Library of Congress have their own special procedures for getting a job.

Making a Living as a Librarian

There is good news about the amount of money librarians are earning. In 1989, an ALA survey showed that librarians' salaries increased far more than those in comparable occupations. The table on page 23 shows the mean salaries paid for particular positions in 1988 and 1989.

The ALA survey also showed that in 1989 beginning librarians with master's degrees in library science without any professional experience had mean earnings of $21,997. The range of salaries went from a low of $13,000 to a high of $60,213. Beginning salaries were highest in the West and Southwest and lowest in the Southeast. You can get a better idea of what you might make as a librarian by studying the salaries listed in ads for librarians in professional journals.

Title	1989 Salary	1988 Salary
Director	$43,623	$40,076
Deputy/Associate/Assistant Director	40,054	35,249
Collection Development Librarian/ Subject Bibliographer	32,853	29,392
Department Head/Branch Head	32,780	29,318
Cataloger and/or Classifier	28,577	25,284
Reference/Information Librarian	28,227	25,830
Children's and/or Young Adult Services Librarian	26,008	22,576

Source: Reprinted with permission of the American Library Association, excerpts taken from "ALA Survey of Librarian Salaries, 1989" by Mary Jo Lynch and Margaret Myers; copyright © 1989 by ALA.

What Else Can You Do with a Library Degree?

Just because you graduated from college with a librarian's degree is no reason you have to become a librarian. There are many other careers in which librarians can use their knowledge of books to find satisfying careers. Look at this list of book-related careers many librarians are following:

researcher

bookseller

archivist

editor

information consultant

indexer

storyteller

author

book reviewer

historian

Future Outlook for Librarians

There is definitely an explosion of printed material today. In just one day, according to Herbert S. White, dean of the School of Library and Information Science at Indiana University, there are enough articles written about chemistry to make up seven sets of the *Encyclopaedia Britannica*. This is sets, not volumes. And it is not just in the area of chemistry that volumes of material are being published; it's in every field that you can think of.

With all this information being published each day, the job of librarian is not going to disappear immediately. Even though computers are rapidly becoming a part of almost every library, they are only assisting librarians in handling the information explosion—not replacing them.

For Further Reading

The image of a librarian sitting behind a desk checking books in and out is decidedly not a description of today's librarians. They have become information specialists who use computer technology to search for books in libraries throughout the world. Learn more about what being a librarian is like by reading the following career books:

Anderson, Lynne. *Exploring Careers in Library Science.* New York: The Rosen Publishing Group, Inc., 1985.

Dewey, Barbara. *Library Jobs—How to Fill Them, How to Find Them.* Phoenix, Ariz.: Oryx, 1987.

Garoogian, Rhoda and Andrew Garoogian. *Careers in Other Fields for Librarians.* Chicago: American Library Association, 1985.

Heim, Kathleen and Peggy Sullivan. *Opportunities in Library and Information Science.* Lincolnwood, Ill.: National Textbook Company, 1986.

Sellen, Betty Carol, ed. *What Else You Can Do With a Library Degree.* Syracuse, N.Y.: Gaylord Professional Publications, 1980.

CHAPTER THREE

Book Publishing
The People Behind the Books

O nce upon a time authors did it all. They needed no one else to put out a book. An author wrote a book by picking up a stylus to etch the book onto clay tablets. Then the author shared the book with interested readers. No longer do books come directly from the author to you; things have changed. Authors still write books, but hordes of editors, proofreaders, designers, and printers work on books before they ever reach readers' hands. Should you decide to work in the book publishing industry, you could be one of these people.

In the United States there are more than 2,000 book publishers. Together, they publish more than 50,000 hardcover and paperback books every year. A career in this industry can be just right for a confirmed bookworm as so many jobs in book publishing involve considerable reading.

Did you realize that there are jobs that would let you:

- read manuscripts all day and decide whether they will be published,

- change an author's presentation to make it more powerful,

- sell books to bookstores and schools,

- find typographical errors that a printer has made,

- and even write your opinion of books?

A Glimpse into the Book Publishing Industry

Browse through a bookstore, and you will find children's books, travel books, religious books, handyman books, cookbooks, romances, and an amazing number of other kinds of books. Most of these books are called trade books, and they make up about one-third of all the books sold. Believe it or not, more textbooks for use by students from kindergarten through college are sold than trade books. There is also a market for reference books like dictionaries, encyclopedias, and atlases as well as for scholarly books put out by university presses. Some publishing companies will put out a wide variety of books while others will only fill a particular niche.

Just as books come in all sizes so do publishing companies. The largest ones may employ thousands of people while the smallest may only have two employees—the publisher and an assistant. You are more likely to have a specific job like copyeditor or proofreader at a larger firm while at a smaller firm you could wear several hats at once.

You may find it helpful to know what the usual organization chart looks like in a large publishing company.

Editor-in-Chief

Editor—Managing or Acquisitions

Associate Editor

Assistant Editor

Editorial Assistant

Naturally, this chart will look slightly different at each publishing house. Assistant editor, instead of editorial assistant, is often the entry-level position. Copyeditors can be part of the above hierarchy as assistant or associate editors; however, in large houses they are usually found in a separate department.

Getting Your Feet Wet

Starting as an Editorial Assistant

You'll never get bored starting in the publishing industry as an editorial assistant because of the large variety of tasks that you will be required to do. There will be plenty of tedious jobs like typing, filing, verifying facts, retyping manuscripts, and returning unacceptable manuscripts. The good news is that you will probably be able to do quite a bit of reading on the job as soon as you know how the publishing house works.

Much of your reading will center on going through the "slush" pile which is the accumulation of unsolicited manuscripts that drown most publishers. You will be evaluating the potential of each manuscript. It will be painful to read some of these efforts. On the other hand, you may be the one to discover a new Hemingway. You won't be able to select manuscripts for consideration just because you like them; they will have to fit in with what the publishing house prints. A Christian publishing house will not be looking for steamy romance stories.

Starting as a Clerk

Janet Peterson entered the publishing industry as a clerk, moved up to become a secretary, and is now an administrative assistant/permissions editor. Janet was definitely not a bookworm while she was in school. Today, however, she finds that she is reading at least one-third of the time on her job. Janet feels that reading is essential if you plan to grow in a job. She has to keep up with what is happening in the publishing industry and know where to find resources.

As a permissions editor, Janet reviews requests and grants permission to teachers and authors to use information from any publication put out by her publisher. Janet also has to negotiate with authors and publishers to get permission for her company to use their materials.

Starting at a Children's Publishing House

Sometimes getting an entry-level job can be based upon who you know. A burned-out schoolteacher found a job as a junior editor at a children's publishing house because she knew someone who worked there. Today, this former teacher is a children's book editor. As an editorial assistant, called junior editor at her company, her work was not glamorous as she typed, filed, researched, and learned to edit with the help of an editor. Gradually, she was given books to edit.

Climbing the Editorial Ladder

After one or two years as an editorial assistant, you will probably begin to move up the editorial ladder. The irony is that the higher you climb, the less time you will be able to devote to reading because so many administrative tasks intervene. Very senior editors find that their job-related reading has become their homework. They do it while they commute, in the evening, on weekends, and on holidays.

Assistant Editor—A Reader's Job

Up one notch from an editorial assistant, the assistant editor at most publishing houses will be doing primarily copyediting and proofreading. At this level, bookworms should be in heaven because there is so much reading to do. Be warned, though, that some assistant editors will be weaned away from their reading to become involved with the editorial production of books. This can mean working with the art department or designers on page layout and illustrations.

Copyediting

Copyeditors usually get manuscripts from editors or assistant editors who have worked on the content and organization. They fix what is still wrong. No two copyeditors have exactly the same job. At some houses, they may do considerable rewriting while at others they are only marking typographical errors. In either case, copyeditors are responsible for checking spelling, grammar, and punctuation. They look for inconsistencies in copy, such as first boarding a plane and later disembarking from a ship (rather than the plane). They also have to find and eliminate repetitions. They read an entire manuscript paragraph-by-paragraph, line-by-line, and finally word-by-word. Some copyeditors use computers, but many prefer to do their job by using good old-fashioned pencils directly on manuscripts.

A manuscript is always read more than once since copyediting also involves keeping track of the plot and making sure that events fall into the correct slots on a time line. Often the first reading is quick to get the overall idea of the manuscript. Then corrections are make. After a final rereading, the manuscript goes back to the author who may make changes which are also copyedited. The manuscript is checked again when it comes back from the typesetter, and every time any changes are made in the copy.

Proofreading

Do you have the eyes of an eagle? Are you good at finding typographical errors on the printed page? Do you have the ability to scrutinize manuscript closely? Are you a good speller? Even if you answer "yes" to the above questions, you will need to be able to prove your proofreading skills by taking a test which includes a spelling section before you will be hired.

Proofreading involves checking that copy from the printer exactly matches the manuscript. To proofreaders, finding inconsistencies is almost like a game. Training is required for this job. Many proofreaders have gone to schools; more have probably learned on the job. Although all copyeditors do some proofreading, much of it is done by free-lancers.

An Assistant Editor

Karen Zack Ingebretsen started working as a proofreader at Time-Life Books ten days after her graduation from college. She willingly skipped the ceremony in order to get a jump on the June crowd of job seekers by interviewing on her commencement day. Karen was required to take a typical proofreading test. After getting the job, Karen, who truly enjoys reading, found out that her job consisted entirely of reading. For forty hours a week, Karen read manuscripts for everything from recipe books to opera librettos in foreign languages which she couldn't speak. In two years, her job disappeared due to a layoff.

Karen then became a production/copyeditor at Prentice-Hall. As a production editor, she worked with the art department on concepts for illustrations and covers. She was also responsible for designing interiors, trafficking schedules and monitoring the flow of manuscript and proof between the typesetter and author. This part of the job only took 25 percent of her time. She spent the rest of the time reading as she edited copy. Once again Karen lost her job to a layoff.

Karen began to believe that she would never last long enough on a job to get the seniority that was needed to survive a layoff. She considered many alternatives, including teaching English in a foreign country and joining the Peace Corps. However, before she could implement a career change, she acquired a new job at Editing, Design and Production as a project editor. This job still required Karen to read for 75 percent of her workday. The company took over the production of books for publishing houses that had small staffs. At this job, she was doing the same work as at her previous job, with the added dimension of keeping the publisher, who was now a client, informed of the progress on a book that she was working on. Subsequently, marriage brought a move to Chicago where Karen now works as a senior editor at an educational publishing firm.

Assistant Editor—Romances

At Harlequin Books, which publishes fifty-six paperback romance books each month, the entry-level position on the editorial side is assistant editor. To obtain this position you have to demonstrate the ability to read a book and know if it meets the company's standards, fix a story so it flows, critique a plot, line edit, and write cover copy. Most successful applicants have degrees in English.

Assistant editors at Harlequin begin working under senior editors, who supervise their training. One thing they have to learn is how to write revision letters, which explain changes editors think would improve an author's manuscript. Assistant editors will read senior editors' revision letters as part of acquiring this skill. They will also read submissions from the "slush" pile to find possible acquisitions.

Each assistant editor is assigned a stable of authors who regularly write Harlequin books. He or she will edit these books, and also begin to find their own repeat authors from the "slush" pile.

Associate Editor—A Varied Position

After working for a few years as an assistant editor, the next step at many companies is associate editor. It's a good promotion for a reader because it means less clerical work, and you will still be doing considerable reading. Of course, at the same time, your responsibilities are going to increase. This usually means more contact with authors, especially since you are going to have the authority to make more changes in manuscripts. You will be making rewrite suggestions for cuts and additions and will have far more leverage in how a book is edited. And you will also begin to become involved in the acquisition of new books.

Editor—Managing or Acquisitions

What an editor does varies greatly from company to company. Some publishing houses have both managing and acquisitions editors. At other houses, an editor will be both a managing and an acquisitions editor. How much editors read truly depends on what their responsibilities are. Some will still do quite a lot of reading at their offices while others will spend most of their time working on the business side of publishing.

Managing Editor

These editors are in charge of day-to-day operations. They see that schedules are maintained and supervise junior editors. Managing editors typically oversee the work of the copyeditors, proofreaders, and in many cases, the designers and illustrators, who are responsible for the way books will look.

Acquisitions Editor

At times being an acquisitions editor can be quite a glamorous job. These are the editors who have long chats and lunches with famous authors, go to autograph parties, and attend book fairs all over the world. They have the task of bringing in and signing up new books and authors and working with literary agents. They are also supposed to come up with new book ideas.

Editor at a Trade Book Company

The editorial assistant who was described earlier worked her way up the ladder until today she is an editor of children's books. At the company where she works, she wears the hats of both a managing and acquisitions editor.

Every fourth week she becomes an acquisitions editor and goes through as many as seventy-five books in a week. Not all of the seventy-five books are read cover-to-cover. However, after careful scanning and skimming, each book is thrown in a pile indicating its future. This editor clearly knows what she likes and what her company is looking for. She discusses her acquisition choices with other editors. If the majority approve a book, it is sent to the marketing department for a "yes" or "no" vote.

While wearing the hat of managing editor, this editor oversees the production of as many as twenty books in a year. Not only does she decide on text changes, she also acts as a copyeditor, which is something not all editors do.

In describing the pluses and minuses of her job, this editor points out that the job is not dull or routine. Because the subject matter varies greatly, the opportunity to learn something new is always there. The one negative to her job is the tension you feel when you fall behind on your schedule.

Editor-in-Chief

At the top of the editorial ladder is the editor-in-chief who has almost always climbed the ladder rung by rung to reach this position. This job requires great involvement in the business side of publishing books. The editor-in-chief makes major decisions on budgeting, scheduling, acquisitions, and marketing strategies. Time is also spent on developing ideas for new books and monitoring the progress of projects. Only a very limited amount of time is spent reading and editing manuscripts.

Editor-in-Chief at World Book

Bob Zeleny has been in the publishing industry for 32 years. As editor-in-chief, he spends 30 to 40 percent of his day reading memos and studying budgets, outlines, and proposals. He also spends a portion of his day doing background reading in the *New York Times*, *Wall Street Journal*, *Publishers Weekly*, American Library Association publications, and other materials related to the creative and business side of publishing. Since World Book is an international company, Bob also reads such publications as *International Economist* and foreign newspapers to keep up with overseas developments.

Publisher or President

At many publishing houses, there is a publisher or president at the top directing the entire operation. This is not a hands-on manuscript job. It involves supervising every department of the company. Of course, there is a lot of reading on this job, but it is reading memos, financial statements, and professional journals.

President of Modern Curriculum Press

Today, after fifteen years in the publishing business, Tom Hatch is doing considerably less manuscript reading than he did earlier in his career. As president of a publishing company, he doesn't have time. Tom is now involved with all aspects of Modern Curriculum Press from the installation of a new roof to overseeing the computerization of the editorial department. Tom, who has always been an avid reader, takes material home so he can keep up with product development and curriculum planning.

Tom received his undergraduate degree in literature/English and started teaching in New York City which he soon found was a very expensive place to live. Through a blind ad in the *New York Times*, he obtained a free-lancing job in the math department of Holt Rinehart and Winston to supplement his teaching salary. He advises people wanting to do free-lance work to look for jobs in major newspapers and *Publishers Weekly*. His free-lance job quickly led to many other free-lance opportunities, and Tom decided to leave teaching and enter the publishing world.

Tom became an assistant editor at Random House. Four years later he became managing editor at Modern Curriculum Press. When he first started with the company, 50 percent of his workday was spent reading manuscripts. As the company grew, Tom's responsibilities increased. He became vice-president of product development and then president.

Publisher at Free Spirit Publishing Inc.

Not all publishing companies are large. At Free Spirit there is a publisher who is also president, a full-time sales and marketing person, and a full-time office manager. There are also three part-time employees—a shipping clerk, an assistant to the publisher, and a customer service representative. Editors and graphic designers are all hired free-lance.

Not all publishers make their way through the editorial ranks to achieve their positions. Judy Galbraith started Free Spirit after purchasing the publishing rights to her first book which had been published by another publisher. The company has steadily grown and has published eighteen books and a newsletter for young people since its inception in 1983.

Indexing—Another Publishing
Job for Bookworms

If you like the idea of doing free-lance work in the publishing industry, indexing is an excellent job possibility as few companies have full-time indexers on their staff. Furthermore, some publishing houses leave indexing up to authors who are usually looking for free-lance indexers to do this work.

In creating an index, an indexer makes an alphabetical list of a book's contents and lists page numbers where each item is discussed. Here is a job where a bookworm is being paid to read a book. Although books on every subject from podiatry to forestry are indexed, you will need some experience in a subject to index a book. Most indexers have advanced degrees and specialize in certain subjects. The job also requires organizational skills and the ability to determine what is important in a book. Plus, you almost have to be able to handle a computer as indexing has gone high tech. Doing indexes on 3 x 5 cards is a thing of the past for most indexers. In addition, indexers must be able to function well under pressure. Indexing is always a rush job because indexers are the last in line to get copy.

Acquiring Indexing Skills

You need some training to become an indexer. A publisher is going to expect you to know certain things. Unfortunately, there are few indexing classes. Some can be found at colleges that have schools of library science. The United States Department of Agriculture (USDA) offers two correspondence courses. For information about these courses, write to:

Graduate School, USDA
Correspondence Study Program
South Agriculture Bldg., Room 1114
14th & Independence, SW
Washington, DC 20250

The National Federation of Abstracting and Information Services (NFAIS) offers seminars in indexing which can help both beginning and experienced indexers. This organization also offers a number of pamphlets on indexing. Contact this organization at:

NFAIS
1429 Walnut Street
Philadelphia, PA 19102

The indexing field is a small one. Many indexers belong to The American Society of Indexers. Through membership in this organization, indexers get newsletters, other publications at a discount, a subscription to *The Indexer,* a discount on conference fees, plus the opportunity to talk with other indexers at local organizations of the society. Information about this organization can be obtained by writing to:

The American Society of Indexers
1700 18th Street, NW
Washington, DC 20009

Working as an Indexer

You can make a living as a free-lance indexer. Although what you are paid will vary from area to area, an experienced indexer could gross thirty dollars an hour. You get a job as an indexer through contacts with editors and other indexers and by sending résumés to publishing companies.

An Indexer at World Book

Claire Bolton feels very lucky to work at a company as an indexer. There are not many of these jobs. Claire did her first index while she was still a student majoring in English. A public health professor and his partner were writing a book that needed an index, and she needed money. Claire had never indexed a book, but she just sat down and did it.

Claire has been indexing at World Book ever since she left school. The job has become far more mechanized in the past ten years. Indexers no longer have to worry so much about clerical details and are now freer to concentrate on the quality of what they are producing. The advent of the computer has also cut the number of indexers required on her company's staff.

Claire enjoys her job because she likes to read and especially likes reading a variety of materials and learning so much about different areas.

However, there are negatives to the job. She spends her entire day looking at a terminal, and some consider her job clerical although it is getting far more professional. She also works under pressure to get jobs done.

Literary Agents Get Books to Editors

Just because an author writes a book doesn't mean you'll ever be able to find it on a library shelf. It isn't easy for an author to get a book published, especially since many publishing companies won't even look at a manuscript unless it is submitted by a literary agent. In this country, there are over three hundred literary agencies. Whether an agency is run by one person or has hundreds of employees, the dream is to find the next bestseller.

Literary agents represent authors to publishers, and they also act as negotiators between the two. Today, due to time restraints, more publishers are relying on literary agents to produce new authors and materials.

Literary agents' days are never routine. They always buzz with activity. A typical day may include working with authors, editors, lawyers, and accountants. Agents may suggest changes to an author that will make a book marketable, mediate a conflict between an author and an editor, as well as boost the flagging spirits of yet another author. They may try to convince an editor that an author in their stable has just written a novel that will become an American classic or at least sell more than 10,000 copies. The agents may wheel and deal with lawyers to get the best contract for a first-time author. They may check recent sales figures with an accountant. More than likely they will also suffer rejection. Some books that they absolutely love will never be sold to a publisher. Others may take years to sell. Rejection, even frequent rejection, is an accepted part of a literary agent's job.

Between all the paperwork and the neverending phone calls, literary agents do not have a lot of time for reading during office hours. Yet reading is such an important part of a literary agent's work, for it is the only way to discover books to sell to editors. So reading time must be snatched whenever possible at the office, but most will be done after hours.

You don't just set up shop as a literary agent. Most literary agents are former editors who have an eye for manuscripts that will sell. They can read the first thirty pages of a manuscript or the proposal for a book and know right away whether or not it has possibilities. Besides having the ability to recognize a saleable manuscript, a literary agent is really a jack-of-all-trades who has the ability to—

- handle people effectively,
- shape an author's career,
- know where different manuscripts can be sold,
- negotiate contracts, and
- help authors edit their work.

Bookworms will even enjoy an entry-level position as an assistant in a literary agency. The job involves many of the same duties as an editorial assistant. However, since many of the agencies are small, an assistant at an agency will be doing more reading than in a large publishing house. The job could include reading manuscripts and writing reviews along with typing and filing correspondence to authors and publishers as well as scheduling meetings between authors, agents, and publishers. Some assistants become full-fledged agents or editors at publishing firms while a few start their own agencies.

Book Reviewers Are Paid for Their Opinions

Imagine getting a free copy of a book, and also getting paid to read it. That's what happens if you are a book reviewer. Because the job is so appealing, there are a great number of book reviewers. Unfortunately, only a few of them are able to make their living at this job. For that reason, book reviewing is usually done by free-lancers.

Book reviewers are normally paid for each review. How much you receive for a review depends on the size of the newspaper or magazine, the length and complexity of the review, and occasionally on your reputation as a reviewer. You could receive nothing except a brand new book or as much as five hundred dollars. By selling the same review to different markets in geographically separated areas, it is possible to increase your income.

To become a book reviewer you will need to be far more than an avid reader; you also have to have writing ability. You can learn how to be an expert book reviewer by studying book reviews that others have written and by taking courses. Just working in the publishing industry will also give you some of the experience you need.

Reading a book is the easiest part of being a book reviewer. The hardest is finding someone who wants you to write a review. Dave Wood, the book editor of the *Minneapolis Star Tribune,* has the names of 250 book reviewers in his file. During a typical year, less than half of these reviewers will actually write reviews for the newspaper. And only twenty-five to thirty-five will be used frequently to write reviews.

The road to being one of the lucky people chosen to write a review is a rough one. What you have to do is send a résumé and samples of your work to newspapers and magazines. This frequently accomplishes nothing more than getting your name in a rolodex file. You can also send unsolicited reviews. If an editor is looking for the book you reviewed, you may be on your way to becoming paid for reviewing books.

Book reviewers with some experience, even if it is for a small newspaper or magazine, can join the National Book Critics Circle. Members' names, along with their specialties, are put into a directory which book editors use to find reviewers. The organization also has a newsletter as well as regional and national seminars which provide information that is helpful to book reviewers. You can find out about joining the National Book Critics Circle by writing to:

Dave Wood, Membership Vice President
National Book Critics Circle
Star Tribune
425 Portland
Minneapolis, MN 55488

Reviewing Books for a Magazine

One of the first places in which books are reviewed is *Publishers Weekly*. Valiska Gregory reviews four to six children's books each month for this magazine. At times, the books are so new that she is reading from color proofs which are not even bound together.

When she reviews a children's book, Valiska tries to assess the author's purpose from the text and illustrations. She always reads a book more than once. She doesn't follow any particular format in writing her reviews, but she does try to give an indication of what the book is about as well as an assessment of the book's literary and artistic merit. She often compares a book to similar ones.

Valiska, who is an author and a poet as well as a free-lance book reviewer, obtained her job through personal contacts. While attending a publishing course, she met a woman who became an editor of the magazine which uses her reviews.

Reviewing Books for a Newspaper

Working in the library at a newspaper gave Betsy Caulfield the opportunity to meet the book editor and led to her becoming a free-lance book reviewer. Being a dedicated bookworm, Betsy always read book reviews. She got the idea of becoming a reviewer because she frequently disagreed with reviewers of books that she had read and wanted to share her opinion with others. She now reviews about one book each month after reading the entire book to get its essence.

Selecting Books for the Book Clubs

Every few weeks, millions of homes, especially the homes of bookworms, receive selection magazines from book clubs. Besides the well-known Book-of-the-Month Club and Literary Guild, there are specific clubs that cater to interests ranging from cooking, astronomy, and religion to photography, farming, and ecology. Children's books are offered through many of these clubs as well as separate children's clubs. Each club will typically offer the opportunity to purchase new selections along with backlist titles.

Like the climber who reaches the top of Mount Everest, a bookworm who becomes a selector for a book club has reached the summit of his or her dreams. This job involves reading books and then deciding which ones should be offered to members of the clubs. At some clubs, all the selectors are in-house editors reading literally from nine to five. At other houses, the editors do most of their reading at home while attending to marketing and administrative chores on the job. Most houses will also use some free-lance selectors.

Bookworms who become selectors usually have bachelor's degrees behind their names. Their degrees certainly don't have to be in English but usually are in some area of liberal arts. It is possible to get a job as a selector right after graduating from college. But many get this job after working as administrative assistants, copyeditors, or at some other job in publishing. Don't bother applying for this job unless you are a speed reader. You should be able to read a thousand pages in twelve to fifteen hours.

Working as a Book Selector

"Sometimes, the pages just turn themselves," according to Jaye Isler, an editorial assistant at a major book club. At other times, she doesn't even complete a book as it isn't right for the book club's members. Jaye, like other selectors, is a confirmed booklover. She confesses that she would far rather meet an author than a Hollywood star.

Jaye's job is a busy one with long hours. She doesn't usually read manuscripts at the office but is involved in such things there as making sure that books which will be listened in the club's magazine are in stock, and there are pictures of these books. She also checks that the copy describing the books is accurate. At any one time, she is working on book information that will go in any one of eight selection magazines. And then, of course, she spends considerable time in meetings and also negotiating with publishers to attain the rights to a book.

Outside of the office, Jaye reads for approximately ten hours a week. During that time, she will read two or three books to determine if the club should offer them to its members. When selectors begin working at Jaye's book club, they learn how to do their job by reading book evaluations that experienced selectors have made. At first, their evaluations are checked to make sure they understand what the club is looking for. "The longer one selects books for a club," Jaye says, "the easier it becomes to tell which books will satisfy the club members."

Owning Your Own Bookstore

To a bookworm, owning a bookstore must seem like the best of all possible worlds. You can choose the books that you want for the store and look at new books before they are even bound. Before Shirley Mullin became a bookstore owner, she was a teacher. Now she owns two children's bookstores, called Kids Ink.

Bookstore owners do get to do a lot of job-related reading. Shirley sees most new children's book from six to nine months before they are published. When she first sees a book, she is usually not looking at the finished copy but at galleys for the book. She reads all the children's picture books herself but doesn't have time to read all the other books so she farms some of them out to her staff. Shirley often reads reviews which usually come out after she has read the galleys for new books. By reading the reviews, she can see if she has missed seeing any promising new books or if she wishes to reexamine any books that she has read. Shirley is helped in her selection process by knowledgeable publishing company representatives and her own staff.

Working at a Bookstore

Along with libraries, bookstores seem the perfect habitat for bookworms. In a bookstore, surrounded by books, a bookworm may not have too much opportunity to read on the job. However, bookstore employees are encouraged to read book reviews and books so that they can help customers find the books they want. At many stores, the owners and managers also want employee input on what books should be added to a store's stock. An added dividend for bookstore employees can be purchasing books for a discounted price.

More Jobs Associated with Books

The more you learn about all the steps involved in bringing a book from author to reader, the more you'll know about the great variety of jobs that will actually let you read books. Taking an entry-level job or an internship are two ways many bookworms have become acquainted with interesting jobs like the following ones:

Working on Designing a Book

Someone has to decide just what a finished book is going to look like so it will appeal to readers. All the artwork, the headings, and the arrangement of the material on the pages have to be related to what is said on the pages. Each book needs to have a design theme. A job working in this area can tie your interest in books with an artistic background.

Working on Illustrating a Book

Illustrations are an important part of many books and must tie closely to the text. In order to do this successfully, the illustrator needs to carefully read the manuscript. Children's books and textbooks are usually full of illustrations. At times, illustrating is done in-house, but more often it is done by free-lance illustrators.

Working on Selling a Book

For a bookworm, it's a lot more enjoyable to sell books than to sell aluminum siding or automobiles. Working as a sales representative for a publisher not only gives you the chance to read many of the books that you are trying to sell, you also get to talk about them to bookstore owners, buyers for chains, and librarians. If you are selling textbooks, you will talk to both teachers and selection committees. No matter where you are selling books, your commission will be based on how well you know the product—books. Being a sales representative is a great career for a bookworm as the more you read, the more you earn, and you will also get the added benefit of traveling.

In this position everyone is a beginner. The better you sell, the better your territory will be. Success in sales can also lead to management job offers in the home office. Some sales representatives even branch off on their own and become independent representatives.

More Career Possibilities

Even more career opportunities exist for bookworms. Besides the many careers that have been mentioned, you may want to investigate some of the following career areas:

marketing

promotion

publicity

corporate staff

advertising

production

public relations

publisher

You won't just find jobs with publishers. Book jobbers and distributors, direct and subscription mail sales organizations, and book chains are other areas where bookworms can find jobs that let them be close to books in some way.

Earning Your Living in the Book Business

The book publishing industry is definitely not a get-rich-quick place to work. Entry-level employees are poorly paid, frequently making less than $20,000 a year. Even an editor with seven years experience is only averaging $33,000 a year according to a 1989 survey in *Publishers Weekly*.

Furthermore, since most of the book publishing industry is centered in New York and Chicago, your climb up the ladder will involve paying a premium price for your living quarters. Remembering that your salary should increase a little with each rung of the ladder and the fact that you are working with books should help bookworms overcome the negatives involved in working in book publishing.

Preparing Yourself for a Career in Book Publishing

Working in book publishing may not be well-paid, but it is an exciting field that many college graduates want to enter. There is strong competition for entry-level jobs, especially at major publishing houses. You will need a college degree. You will also need to excel in your usage of the English language. It will be a definite plus if you can type and use a computer.

Getting experience by working with books in some capacity will make you a stronger candidate for a job. Working part-time in a bookstore or library can be helpful. Finding a part-time job with a publishing house is even better as you can then show actual work experience in the industry. Working as an intern at a publishing company will also strengthen your résumé. Both part-time jobs and internships can lead to job offers because they let publishing companies become acquainted with your work. You can find out what internships are available by looking at directories listing internships. You will find these directories in the reference section of the library.

Attending book publishing courses, conferences, workshops, and seminars will increase your insight into what the industry is like. Reading *Publisher's Weekly*, will let you know what is happening in publishing. There is a calendar which gives current information on courses, workshops, and seminars; and there is even a jobs section in the magazine. It is also smart to become acquainted with *Literary Market Place* (LMP). This directory has the names, addresses, and phone numbers of book publishers in the United States. The publishers are even classified by subject matter. You will also find information about book courses, conferences, and events. There are also lists of literary agents, book clubs, and foreign publishers as well as information about acquisitions and mergers in the industry.

For Further Reading

Isn't it ironic that one of the best ways to prepare for a career in book publishing is by reading to learn all you can about the industry? As Lord Chesterfield wrote in a letter to Lord Huntington, "The best companions are the best books." The following books should become your companions if you are serious about learning more about a career in book publishing.

Carter, Robert A. *Book Publishing Careers.* Lincolnwood, Ill.: VGM Career Horizons, 1987.
Coser, Lewis A. and Charles Kadushin and Walter W. Powell. *Books—The Culture and Commerce of Publishing.* New York: Basic Books, Inc., Publishers, 1982.
Dessauer, John P. *Book Publishing: What It Is, What It Does.* New York: R.R. Bowker Company, 1981.
Gross, Gerald, ed. *Editors on Editing: An Inside View of What Editors Really Do.* New York: Harper and Row, 1985.
Jobst, Katherine, ed. *Directory of Internships.* Cincinnati, Ohio: Writer's Digest Books, 1988.
Larsen, Michael. *Literary Agents—How to Get and Work with the Right One for You.* Cincinnati, Ohio: Writer's Digest Books, 1986.
Literary Market Place—The Directory of American Book Publishing. New York: R.R. Bowker Company. (annual)
Renetzky, Alvin, ed. *Directory of Internships, Work Experience Programs, and on the Job Training Opportunities.* Santa Monica, Calif.: Ready Reference Press, 1986.

CHAPTER FOUR

Magazines and Newspapers
A Big Industry

F irst there were newspapers. Then magazines developed from newspapers. The reason for having magazines was to review books while newspapers concentrated more on news. Both early magazines and newspapers looked much the same and were held together by folds. The difference was that newspapers had numerous folds while magazines only had one. Because magazines fell apart easily, they were soon bound. Then most magazines and newspapers no longer looked alike.

While today some magazines and newspapers still may look the same, most magazines differ from newspapers in these obvious ways:

higher grade of paper

distinctive cover

more varied typeface

more color illustrations

different writing style

more white space

Both newspapers and magazines have many jobs that require considerable reading. By finding out more about what jobs are available at each of these publications, bookworms can decide which one is a better career fit for their personalities.

Becoming Better Acquainted
with Magazines

Publications bound in paper covers that appear regularly and contain stories, articles, and illustrations by various contributors are usually called magazines. Magazines are also called periodicals, publications, journals, reviews, newsletters, and even books. So whenever you see one of those words in a want ad, you are looking at an advertisement for a job on a magazine.

Join the staff of a magazine, and you are joining a long list of literary greats. Throughout the history of magazines, many well-known authors have worked on magazine staffs, contributed articles to magazines, and even started magazines. You may be surprised to learn that Charles Dickens, Washington Irving, Oliver Wendell Holmes, Ralph Waldo Emerson, and Henry Adams were all involved in some way with magazines.

The Other Media Have Not
Vanquished Magazines

Neither movies, television, or VCRs have grabbed such a giant share of people's attention that magazines are no longer being read. In fact, today, more than 11,000 different magazines are being published in the United States. Furthermore, each year about 300 new magazines are started. Admittedly, it is a tough market to crack since only a handful last. Benjamin Franklin couldn't make it with his *General Magazine*. But in spite of all the competition, some new magazines, like *People*, for example, do succeed quite sensationally.

Magazine sales are now at an all-time high. According to the *United States Industrial Outlook, 1989*, total magazine sales in 1988 topped eighteen billion dollars. With over 120,000 people employed in magazine publishing, this is a good place for bookworms to look for jobs that involve reading.

Finding the Right Magazine for a Job

Just walk into any drugstore, bookstore, or even the grocery store and check out the magazine racks. It won't take you longer than a few minutes to discover that there are magazines on almost any subject that you can think of from coin collecting to family health. Most of these magazines fall into the category of consumer magazines. The other large category is business magazines. There are jobs for bookworms in both categories.

Consumer Magazines

Over 2,000 different consumer magazines are sold in the United States. Their circulation and revenue far exceed that of the greater number of business magazines. Approximately 146 of these magazines deal with general interests; the rest are devoted to specialized interests. Jobseekers desiring to work on magazines appealing to general interests usually have degrees in journalism or English. Obtaining a job on magazines with very large circulation can be quite competitive. Experience will count in getting one of these jobs.

On the other hand, if you want to work for a specialized consumer magazine like one dealing with computers, needlework, motorcycles, crafts, dancing, or antiques, you definitely need some knowledge of that area. You are not going to get a job at a specialized computer magazine—an area that has over fifty magazines—unless you know what bytes, bits, crashing, and control keys are. Nor will you be a good candidate for a job with a motorcycle magazine if you have never put on a helmet and ridden on a motorcycle. Being a bookworm can help you get a job with a specialized magazine if you have done in-depth reading in the area it covers. You can find lists of all consumer magazines that are currently being published by looking at *Industrial Magazine Marketplace* or *SRDS (Standard Rate and Data Service) Consumer Magazine Directory.*

Business Magazines

You won't usually find business or trade magazines, as they are also called, on magazine racks. You might find one in a doctor's, lawyer's, or accountant's office as many of these publications deal with professions. Just think of any profession; there is probably one or more magazines dealing with that profession. The medical profession has a very impressive list of almost five hundred magazines.

What do you think *Bank News, Boating Industry, Modern Tire Dealer,* and *Nuclear News* have in common? They bring information to people who are interested in what is happening in these industries. There is scarcely an industry in the United States that does not have a magazine. Advertising, tobacco, welding, railroads, textiles, travel, sewage disposal, coal mining, bicycles, and luggage all have magazines, to name just a few industries. If you are interested in a career in business magazines, make sure you look at the *SRDS (Standard Rate and Data Service) Business Magazine Directory* for a list of all the business magazines that are published. You also should know that several large companies publish more than one magazine. Some publish as many as forty business magazines.

To work on certain business magazines you are going to need academic training in a specific area. People working on medical magazines do need to have a scientific background. In other areas, it certainly helps to be knowledgeable about a particular profession or industry, but it is not always essential. You can learn about a profession or industry through on-the-job training. Fortunately, bookworms are employees who are willing to learn through reading.

Jobs on the Editorial Side at Magazines

Magazines are definitely good places for bookworms to look for work. Employees on the editorial side do a lot of reading. Perhaps, the better workplace for a bookworm is a consumer magazine or a business magazine for a particular profession. More reading will occur at these magazines because most of the material is being written by outside authors or people within a profession. This means that articles and stories will have to be considered for acquisition and copyedited—both jobs that require considerable reading. If you work for a business magazine that publishes information about an industry, it is likely that you will be doing more writing than reading as many of these magazines are mainly written in-house.

When you think about working for a magazine, the size of the magazine really determines the kind of job that you are going to have. If you work for one of the giants in the magazine industry, your job will simply be in one specific area. Work for a magazine with a staff of thirty or forty people, and your job description will be considerably broader. If you really want to be a jack-of-all-trades, get a job on a magazine that has an editorial staff of only one or two people.

The Pecking Order at Magazines

There really is not much difference between the organization charts of book publishing companies and most magazine publishers. The size of the magazine dictates just how many different slots there will be on an editorial ladder, and what an employee will do at any job varies from one magazine to another.

Editor-in-Chief or Editor

Standing on the top rung of the ladder is the editor-in-chief who is responsible for the editorial content of the magazine. A person in this position must delegate many responsibilities to other members of the staff.

Managing Editor

Reporting directly to the editor-in-chief, there is usually a managing editor or a group of associate or senior editors doing this job, which is to supervise the daily activities at the magazine. The managing editor's job also entails handling the staff and free-lance writers as well as writing and editing personal projects. The larger the magazine, the greater the number of assistant editors reporting to the managing editor. Most managing editors come up through the editorial ranks.

The Other Editors

Depending on the size and organization of a magazine, you will find senior editors, associate editors, copyeditors, and assistant editors. Many of these editors are specialists in a certain field like fashion, travel, or cooking, and may be called fashion editor, travel editor, cooking editor, or editor of whatever their specialty is. All of these editors do some reading; however, out of this group the copyeditor is the one doing the most reading.

Editorial Assistant

Editorial assistant is an entry-level position in which you not only learn about how a magazine is put out but also learn how to handle a variety of tasks from copyediting to acquisition.

Starting at the Bottom of the Ladder

Leigh Davis, with a recent degree in journalism, is working as an editorial assistant at the *Saturday Evening Post*. She regards her job as a great beginning for an eager bookworm. Leigh feels that it is difficult to get a job in magazine publishing, and that more than a degree is needed. She has found that experience counts and thinks that her work on the college newspaper really helped her get this job. Even having worked on a high school newspaper staff would be helpful experience on a job seeker's résumé.

Leigh's job on the editorial side of the magazine requires a lot of reading. First of all, she spends a brief period of time every day reading through other general magazines to see what trends these magazines are following, especially in their travel sections.

Approximately one-third of Leigh's day is spent reading and researching as a fact checker. After checking the facts on a travel story on South Padre Island, she researched for general information on barrier islands like South Padre Island. Then she added some of these facts to the travel story.

Another job that takes a considerable portion of Leigh's time is reading unsolicited manuscripts. A select few are forwarded to editors as possibilities for later publication.

Copyediting, however, is what takes up most of Leigh's time on the job. Not only does she have to read and proofread entire articles, she even has to do quite a bit of rewriting on them. What is left of Leigh's day is spent doing clerical tasks like sending manuscript guidelines to free-lance authors and responding to author's questions about where their manuscripts are. Because the staff at the *Saturday Evening Post* is quite small, Leigh feels that she is learning more than she would in the same position at a larger magazine since she has the opportunity to work in more areas.

Letters Editor

There are other jobs on magazine staffs that require considerable reading. Ted Slate, Letters Editor at *Newsweek* magazine, has one of those jobs. You first read about Ted in the chapter on librarians because he is Library Director at *Newsweek*. In this chapter, you will learn about his other job at *Newsweek*—as Letters Editor.

More than a thousand letters arrive at *Newsweek* magazine each week. Ted and his staff have the responsibility of handling this mail. After the letters are opened, a clerk determines where they will be routed. Some will be forwarded to other departments. The remaining letters are distributed to the staff of the letters department for reply. Six staff members—many with master's degrees in journalism—answer all these letters.

A great number of the letters are routine and can be answered by form letters or slightly adapted form letters. Others require original replies, often necessitating some research. These letters must be accurate as they reflect the views of *Newsweek*'s editors. The letters correspondents often find it necessary to consult with the author of an article for help in drafting a reply.

Each week one of the staff members sorts through all the letters and divides them into groups reflecting the stories they are commenting on and the viewpoints of the letter writers. Then Ted and one of his staff select the letters that will be used in the letters column of the magazine. Many letters have to be edited for reasons of clarity and space. Ted also adds editor's comments when necessary.

Ted believes that reading letters is an excellent way to start at *Newsweek*. Not only does this job allow for a letters correspondent to be noticed; it also provides valuable experience in editing, researching, and writing. Before getting this job, it is necessary to pass a test demonstrating one's ability to write well and properly answer letters.

The Magazine Pay Scale

Starting out on the editorial side of the magazine industry will give you much the same income as starting in the book publishing industry. Most entry-level positions pay less than twenty thousand dollars a year. At all levels you will make more working for business magazines than at consumer magazines. You will also make more money at the same position at magazines with larger circulations. If you are working on a magazine in the Northeast, you will earn more than in any other region. It is also quite likely that you will be working in the area around New York City since that is the hub of the magazine industry. Unfortunately, it also costs more to live in this region.

Getting Your Foot in the Door

There is no one perfect route guaranteeing a job with a magazine. Certainly, a liberal arts degree seems to be a starting point for most people working on the editorial side of magazine publishing. Experience with a publication from high school newspaper to college literary magazine is also helpful. Even a little experience lets a prospective magazine employee write down something in the spaces asking for experience on application forms.

Having an internship on a magazine is an excellent way to get the experience job hunters need. Some internships are part-time jobs during the school year in which students receive academic credit and no money. There are also summer programs that offer some pay. You will find that most publishers have intern programs. These jobs are both for undergraduates and recent graduates. The reference section of the library has many directories listing internships. Before you sign up for an internship program, make sure that it is project-oriented and that you know exactly what you will be doing. Twelve weeks of meaningless clerical work could seem like an eternity. It can also be helpful to select an internship at a firm where you would like to work later on.

Another avenue in preparing for a job in magazine publishing is attending a writing course during the summer. The oldest course is the Radcliffe/Harvard publishing program. Stanford University also has a program; however, it requires participants to have worked in the publishing industry for at least three years.

The Future of the Magazine Industry

Wall Street is bullish on the magazine industry and sees its continuing growth through the 1990s. Continued growth means more jobs. On the downside, new magazines continue to fail at high rates, and some specialized fields have too many magazines. The market will only absorb so many magazines on computers, raising children, and fishing. On the upside, publishers believe that demand exceeds supply for talented applicants seeking entry-level positions.

Becoming Better Acquainted with Newspapers

The first printed newspaper, the *Dibao*, was published during the eighth century in China. Even earlier newspapers were handwritten and posted in public places. One of these was the *Acta Diurna*, meaning Daily Events, which actually started in Rome in 59 B.C.

Benjamin Harris of Boston founded the first newspaper in the United States in 1690. It was called the *Publick Occurrences Both Forreign and Domestick* and had an extraordinarily brief history as the government stopped it after the first issue. The 1800s were the heyday for the development of newspapers. The largest number of newspapers ever in the United States was about 2,600 dailies in 1909. Today, the number of newspapers is less than 1,700. Although overall circulation is increasing, it's a mixed picture. Morning circulation is increasing, and evening circulation is dropping. Furthermore, some major metropolitan newspapers are losing circulation to suburban newspapers.

See if you can identify the three newspapers with the largest circulation today from the following list:

Wall Street Journal

New York Times

Detroit Free Press

New York Daily News

Los Angeles Times

Miami Herald

U.S.A. Today

Minneapolis Star Tribune

Your first choice should have been the *Wall Street Journal* followed by *U.S.A. Today* and the *New York Daily News*.

The *U.S.A. Today* Story

In the few years since it first hit the newsstands on September 16, 1982, *U.S.A. Today* has become the second largest newspaper in terms of circulation and the largest in terms of readership. More than six million people read *U.S.A. Today* five days a week. In 1989, the newspaper employed 18,000 people at thirty-three print sites. This paper is the first and only national daily general-interest newspaper in the United States.

The money that you put in a newspaper box or pay the carrier does not cover the cost of the labor and materials involved in producing the paper. Just like the magazine industry, the money to run newspapers comes from advertising sales. The high operating cost, especially the price of newsprint, has driven many newspapers out of business.

The good news for bookworms is that the newspaper industry employs over 500,000 people, which is almost five times the number of people employed by the magazine industry. Of course, not every employee reads for eight hours a day, but most employees do some reading. Furthermore, positions like copyeditor and wire editor offer almost eight hours a day of reading.

Climbing to the Top

The climb to the top in the newspaper publishing industry is very similar to the book and magazine industries. Dennis Hetzel is a bookworm who has gone from writing for a local paper in high school to being the managing editor of the *Capital Times* in Madison, Wisconsin.

Starting out in Newspaper Publishing

Dennis began his newspaper career in high school. Not being able to excel in sports, Dennis coupled his love of sports with his writing ability to write about sports for the local weekly. He majored in political science and minored in journalism in college and had plans to become a high school teacher—even doing his student teaching. However, an opportunity to become the sports editor for two weekly papers changed his career path. He believes that it was his high school experience that got him this job. Working in sports, according to Dennis, requires a tremendous amount of reading each day just to keep track of what is happening in sports.

After a year, Dennis went to another paper in Galesburg, Illinois, as a reporter. On this paper, one of his beats was the courts. This job required an ability to read fast and to read for understanding. Dennis had to look at lengthy, complicated documents and figure out what the important points were.

Starting to Climb the Editorial Ladder

After going to another paper in Racine, Wisconsin, as a reporter, within a few years Dennis became special projects editor at that paper. He did a lot of research on this job as he read and edited others' work and researched special projects. Continuing his upward climb, Dennis became an associate editor. This job required him to supervise the copy desk and do the front page. He had to read stories coming in from outside news services and pick out the ones to use in the paper. Several hundred stories might be available while there was only room for a few dozen.

Managing Editor

Since 1986, Dennis has been managing editor of the *Capital Times*. Half or more of his time must be spent on managerial tasks. He is reading and writing a lot of memos, but he is also reading newspapers and articles in trade magazines like *Editor and Publisher*. Besides reading his own newspaper, he reads two or three other newspapers every morning and an afternoon newspaper. Dennis believes that it is absolutely essential to read in order to succeed in the newspaper industry. This should be good news for bookworms.

Copyediting Means Reading All Day

For many bookworms, copyediting may seem like the perfect job. It requires on-the-job reading—not for just part of the day, but all day each and every workday. Copyediting is the process of reviewing and editing the work of reporters so it is ready to be set in type. It involves finding and correcting spelling, grammar, and punctuation errors. Copyediting on a magazine or a book may involve fact checking, but copy is generally considered to be correct on newspapers. There just isn't time on a newspaper for fact checking beyond looking for obvious errors or inconsistencies. Bookworms have to realize that copyeditors do not sit in soft easy chairs leisurely doing their editing. At most newspapers, they sit in front of computers staring for hours at stories on monitors. Furthermore, the pace is quite fast as they hurry to get copy ready to be printed. Perhaps, one of the best ways to determine if copyediting is the job for you is to read about what a copyediting job on a large metropolitan newspaper with a circulation of over 100,000 involves.

The Copyeditor's Job

L. T. Brown is one of twelve copyeditors at the *Indianapolis News*. At the start of the day, thirty or forty stories may be stored in the newspaper's computer system waiting to be edited. Reporters have written the stories and given them to their editors who may have made some changes. The editors also have placed instructions on the stories detailing what kind of headlines are to be used and what the size of the story should be (column length and width). These stories are then sent to the slot man—the editor who parcels out assignments and makes sure that the copyeditors are working on what is needed. All this is done by computer on most newspapers.

L. T. tries to choose stories that interest him and to avoid those written by sloppy reporters. He pulls a story up on his computer monitor, and the copyediting process begins. Now according to journalism textbooks, stories should be read through completely before copyediting begins. With the time restraints of newspaper deadlines, this just doesn't happen too much of the time. As L. T. reads through the copy, he edits. For an experienced copyeditor, like L. T., the errors usually jump out. He knows what words are always misspelled and even what mistakes individual reporters make. At times, he must do considerable rewriting to meet space specifications which are so tight that he may substitute the word "try" for "attempt." By the press of a button on his computer, L. T. can tell whether the story is the correct length or not. When a story is the correct size, L. T. writes the headline according to the instructions. The story is then sent to the slot man who glances through it and sends it to typesetting.

When the first edition of the paper comes out, L. T. and the other copyeditors read through it, and note any needed corrections on the paper. New stories in subsequent editions are also checked for errors. All corrections are given to the slot man.

Personal Qualifications of Copyeditors

You must have a love affair with words. You should enjoy playing with words. Most copyeditors are confirmed punsters. They also work crosswords, as L. T. does, to learn smaller words for larger words. Above all, you need to be a bookworm who enjoys reading a wide variety of material both on and off the job. Your academic background will probably consist of a bachelor's degree in journalism or English.

Two Satisfying Careers for Bookworms

What do people working on magazines and newspapers have in common? They almost always love their work. They thrive on the excitement of deadlines, whether they are the deadlines for different editions of a newspaper or the weekly, monthly, or quarterly deadlines of magazines. They universally complain about low pay. They garner satisfaction from providing information so that people can know what is going on around them. But most of all, they savour working with words in some way. For undeniably, jobs on both magazines and newspapers offer considerable opportunity to read.

For Further Reading

Because so many opportunities exist for employment in magazine and newspaper publishing, it is a good idea to look at directories which list the large number of companies in this field. All kinds of interesting job possibilities exist. You might find it possible to combine your interest in birds or clothing with working on a consumer specialty magazine. Perhaps, your addiction to reading about current events would be satisfied through working on a newspaper. You should find information in the following books to be helpful:

Directories

Boyden, Donald P., ed. *Gale Directory of Publications.* Detroit: Gale Research Inc. (newspapers, magazines, journals, and related publications)

Magazines Career Directory. Hawthorne, N. J.: The Career Press Inc., 1988. (magazine career information)

The National Directory of Magazines. New York: Oxbridge Communications. (magazines plus newsprint tabloids)

The National Directory of Magazines. New York: Oxbridge Communications, Inc. (periodicals)

Newspapers Career Directory. Hawthorne, N. J.: The Career Press Inc., 1988. (newspaper career information)

Career Books

Career Associates. *Career Choice for Students of Communications and Journalism.* New York: Walker and Company, 1985.

Mann, Jim. *Magazine Editing: Its Art and Practice.* Stamford, Conn.: Hanson Publishing Group, Inc., 1985.

Mogel, Leonard. *Making it in the Media Professions.* Chester, Conn.: The Globe Pequot Press, 1988.

Noble, John H. *Mass Media.* Cambridge, Mass.: President and Fellows of Harvard College, 1987.

Pawlick, Thomas. *Exploring Careers in Journalism.* New York: Richards Rosen Press, Inc., 1981.

Tebbel, John. *Opportunities in Newspaper Publishing Careers.* Lincolnwood, Ill.: National Textbook Company, 1989.

CHAPTER FIVE

Glamour Industries
Reading in the Limelight

Wh y would anyone ever want to work at a job that requires long and hard hours, offers low pay for years, and does not have a great deal of job security? The answer is simple—the job is a glamorous one. It probably involves working in radio, television, movies, or public relations. The lure of working in these areas is so great that college graduates are fiercely competing for entry-level positions. After all, even jobs starting at the bottom offer the chance to answer a superstar's mail, critique a script that goes on to become a television or movie blockbuster, or to do research for a talk show host. And many of the entry-level jobs like the ones just mentioned involve considerable reading. What's more, there are jobs further up the glamour career ladder that are perfect for bookworms.

Preparation for entering a glamour industry job is just up a bookworm's alley. You simply have to read as much as you can to get an idea of the basics of how radio and television shows are produced, movies are made, and public relations campaigns are handled.

Radio—The Vocal Medium

Many people don't realize that before television became so popular families sat around their radios every evening. They listened to "Great Gildersleeve," "The Jack Benny Program," and "Inner Sanctum Mysteries" for entertainment. They found out about what was happening in the world by listening to Lowell Thomas, Edward R. Murrow, and other famous news commentators. Some danced to the music of the big bands or top forty tunes. But this golden age of radio ended as television took over these roles.

Radio did not roll over and play dead. Instead, radio changed its format. All talk, all news, and all music stations emerged as well as stations with formats designed to attract a particular audience. Soon radio had captured more listeners than ever before. In fact, homes today have a far greater number of radios than television sets. Perhaps, part of this can be traced to the convenience of radio. You can drive a car and listen to the radio. You can jog down the street listening to a radio. You can listen to radios on buses, trains, and ferris wheels. The current popularity of radio means more jobs for people wanting to work in this medium. Many of these jobs are designed for people who love to talk and read.

Radio Deejays Read

Jeff Pigeon is a radio deejay on an adult contemporary program at WIBC in Indianapolis. Jeff is an early morning bookworm—not a twenty-four-hour-a-day bookworm. Arriving at the station every morning at 4:15 A.M. for his 5:30 A.M. show, he begins reading immediately. He reads the local morning paper plus two other newspapers so he will know what has been happening locally and around the world when he goes on the air. His producer is also busily reading and giving Jeff highlighted articles to take into the studio.

While Jeff enjoys reading, he is definitely not a speed reader. Since he likes to take his time with the printed word and slowly absorb what he is reading, he does a lot of his reading at home. He always reads the evening paper along with a whole list of popular magazines, and even the tabloids. Jeff is also kept busy trying to keep up with all the new books which publishers send to him. He has to resort to skimming many of these books.

Jeff is constantly preparing for his show. Everything that happens to him during the day as well as anything he reads could be a good topic of conversation on one of his shows. He feels that those who want to succeed in the radio industry will read as much material as they can get their hands on.

Movies—A Glamorous
Environment for Readers

The movie industry is a rather small one with fewer than 250,000 people working in it. If your dream is to work in this industry, you should pack your bags and head for southern California as it's still the center of moviemaking. Most of the movie jobs which are ideal for bookworms center on handling scripts. There are jobs that will put you in touch with the stars—from handling their fan mail to reading scripts for them. Some jobs also exist in doing research to determine that everything shown in a film is as authentic as possible. Whatever your job in this industry, there is always the possibility of meeting famous stars and directors.

The movie industry is a close-knit one. Getting a job seems to be tied to knowing someone who has a job or knows about a job. The secret in finding the job you want lies in taking an entry-level job which will let you make contacts in the industry and will also acquaint you with the different types of jobs available. Reading also helps. Through reading *Variety* and *The Hollywood Reporter,* two dailies on the movie industry, you can find out what is happening in every phase of the industry from new film stars to movies currently in production.

A Possible Starting Point

There is a rumor that Woody Allen started as a script typist. Whether this is true or not, the job is one that gives you a look at a lot of scripts. Being a script typist is excellent preparation for becoming a story analyst or a screenwriter. After you have handled hundreds of scripts, you will learn what is good and thoroughly understand the format in which scripts are written.

According to Valerie Koutnik, who was a script typist in Hollywood and is now a screenwriter, the job involves taking a script and putting it into the correct format. There are many complex rules for the layout of dialogue and descriptive passages, with different styles for film and television.

There are two basic requirements for getting a job as a script typist. One: you must be an excellent typist. Two: you must be a person who will safeguard the confidentiality of the scripts you type. Just think of how important script confidentiality was when J.R. was shot on "Dallas."

Valerie believes that a significant advantage of script typing work is that it is one of the easier ways to get inside the film industry. Script typists can find work with independent production companies, studios, artists' agencies, free-lance writers, and professional script typing companies. You can find script typing companies listed in the Los Angeles yellow pages. Although the pay is hourly and the work can sometimes be tedious, she feels it is invaluable experience in seeing how scripts are put together.

Working as a Story Analyst

Working as a story analyst or as a reader, which is another name for the same job, is ideal for a bookworm. The job involves reading movie scripts, books, and plays to find one that will make a movie that will earn money. The whole industry is searching for these movies so there are jobs at agencies, studios, production companies, and with individual stars. To work at most studios you have to belong to a union for story analysts. There are many places where you can read without belonging to this union as well as many opportunities to be a free-lancer. A free-lancer can earn from ten to fifteen dollars at the low end of the scale to forty or fifty dollars at the high end for reading each script. The pay range is from sixty to two hundred dollars for books and longer-than-usual scripts.

THE JOB DESCRIPTION   Story analysts read movie scripts, books, and plays and write coverages. Each studio, production company, or agency will use a different form for coverages which involve the following three things:

1. A *synopsis* is written which retells the story as clearly as possible. The length and detail of the synopsis vary with the story analyst's employer.

2. The story analyst's *opinion* is given explaining whether or not the story has commercial value, is castable, and is similar to other movies or well-known books.

3. A *rating scale* is usually filled in which rates such things as production value, structure, characterization, and dialogue on a scale from poor to excellent.

JOB QUALIFICATIONS NEEDED   No degree is required for the job of story analyst. However, the analyst should have developed a literary sense from reading and have seen a lot of movies to develop a visual sense as well. Story analysts also need to know how to write.

Getting a Job as a Story Analyst

With a degree in film, radio, and television in hand, Randy Kornfield entered the job market with the desire to become a screenwriter. A friend got him a part-time job duplicating scripts at a studio. Then he was promoted to the mailroom. During this time he was meeting people and deciding where he wanted to work as well as trying to write screenplays. A move to another studio brought Randy a job as a secretary and assistant in personnel. At this job, he met a story editor who let him read some scripts and write coverages. This gave him the chance to see what good and bad scripts were like as well as what kind of scripts were being bought. When this job folded, Randy became a free-lance story analyst. Then he found a job at another studio as an assistant to an executive who was looking for scripts. At this job, which was primarily secretarial, he was able to read some scripts but didn't have to write coverages. After management changes at the studio, Randy was out of a job again. He next found a job as story analyst at a nonunion studio. Then he was able to get a story analyst job at MGM/UA, a union studio, because the story editor whom he met earlier was now working at this studio. The advantage of working at a union studio is better pay plus benefits.

During all this time, Randy was busy writing and actually sold a screenplay and had a low-budget movie made from one of his scripts. Reading scripts has been helpful in his writing.

Story Analyst at MGM/UA

Like Randy, Anne Brand works at MGM/UA as a story analyst. She works in an office building across from the studio lot so she doesn't see many stars. Many analysts in her office work at home and only come into the office once or twice a week. At the major studios like MGM the story analysts must be members of the story analysts' union. During a typical day Anne will read one and one-half to two scripts. The average script has 100 to 125 pages. When she finishes reading a script, she writes a coverage for it. She will also read and write coverages for books and stage plays.

Anne finds her work is sometimes glamorous. She read the proposal for *Rainman* and has seen several other scripts she liked become movies. She also enjoys being able to do so much reading on her job. One of the negatives to her job is not being able to sit through a movie without wondering if she would have recommended the script.

Story Analyst for a Movie Star

Would you like to talk to a movie star on the phone or perhaps have him or her come to your office several times a week? All of this is part of Sandy Erickson's job as a story analyst who reads scripts and books looking for the right properties for Matt Dillon. This is a glamour job that lets Sandy read 70 percent of the time. You can find jobs like hers in the offices of managers and agents of movie stars.

Reading Fan Mail

Movie stars gets loads of letters from their fans. Almost all of this mail is handled by a fan club service provided by a star's manager, agent, or studio. Most of the letters are from people simply requesting pictures. The rest of the letters can usually be answered by form letters. Only a few letters require a personal reply.

Television—Almost Everyone's Favorite Medium

In the United States television sets are found in over 95 percent of the homes, and these sets are on for an average of over six hours a day. From the crack of dawn until late at night, there are many households where the television set is rarely off. People can be totally entertained right in their own homes just by turning on their television sets. They can find whatever interests them whether it is movies, quiz shows, soap operas, cartoons, educational programs, situation comedies, action-packed dramas, variety shows, news shows, or sports events. What is significant to the jobseeker is that each show requires more people behind the scenes than the ones seen on the television screen. And many of these jobs both on-camera and off-camera are good choices for bookworms who want jobs that require considerable reading.

Network Story Editor

DeNece Gilbert knew that she wanted to work for a large television network even before she graduated from college with a communications degree. So after graduation she headed west—straight for Hollywood. Not knowing anyone and without any experience, she couldn't get a job in television. She did get a job in the publishing division of Motown which required her to place songs with the appropriate Motown artist.

After gaining experience at Motown, DeNece became a secretary at a major network. Several promotions later, she was the assistant to the director of comedy and drama. This job was a bookworm's delight. DeNece's job was to read scripts and treatments and to write a one-page synopsis of each work for the director. She worked on the weekly episodes of such popular shows as "Magnum, P.I." "Dallas," "Dukes of Hazard," and "All in the Family."

Today, DeNece is working for a major network in New York City as a story editor covering books. It is her job to find books that would make good television movies or miniseries. She works with thirty large publishing houses in New York and thirty other smaller publishing houses throughout the country. Her only job is to look for a good story. DeNece does not do any writing or rewriting. The network hires writers or uses in-house writers for any changes or adaptations that are needed.

On the job, most of DeNece's reading time is spent going through publishing catalogs. She usually orders ten or eleven books from each catalog. DeNece also looks through the *Kirkus Review*, which lists upcoming books, and *Publishers Weekly*. She reads popular consumer magazines as well as newspapers to discover future trends. She usually

takes manuscripts and books home to read so that she can read them
without any interruptions.

DeNece can't read everything so she has ten free-lance readers who
keep busy reading for her. Readers receive approximately seventy-five
dollars for a book and thirty-five dollars for a screenplay. They write a
two-and-one-half page summary of the material and a one-page personal
comment sheet. If a free-lancer suggests a second reading or praises the
work, DeNece will read the material.

It takes over one year from the time material goes into development
until it is seen on the air. DeNece looks for fresh work and often goes for
first-time authors like Chris Bohjalian who wrote A *Killing in the Real
World*. His book was adapted into a television play called *Deadly Reunion*.

Glamour does enter into this ideal job for a bookworm. The casting
office is right next to DeNece's office. Then there are trips to the large
book fairs and the Louisville Playwriter's Festival. At this festival, she is
not only looking at the plays but is also on the lookout for good new
writers.

According to DeNece, there are many other jobs that bookworms
would like at a network. Script readers are needed for every division in
a network. For the children's afterschool specials, the readers even read
children's books to find new program ideas. There are also jobs for
research librarians.

Segment Producers and
Producers of Talk Shows

All those talk shows you see on television have producers. Some even
have producers for each segment of the show. These producers are
responsible for what happens on a show—a job usually requiring considerable reading.

A talk show producer may read the books of authors who are going to
be on the program and then frame questions for the talk show host. Then
there are all the books that land on the talk show producer's desk which
must be looked at to see which authors should be selected to appear on
the program. Research may also be done on each guest on the program
to acquaint the host with the day's guest or guests. Furthermore, there
is the task of keeping up with what is happening in the world so

provocative guests and subjects can be chosen. A daily talk show consumes material so the search for new ideas is neverending. Most of these ideas will evolve from the reading done by the show's producer or producers.

Jobs as producers and segment producers are not usually entry-level jobs except at smaller television stations. To be a producer of a major network show requires previous experience. A producer might start at a station as an assistant, advance to associate producer, and then be a coordinating producer before becoming a producer.

Talk Show Host

If Steve Allen is coming on a talk show, the host needs some background information. It's the same story if the guests are football players or nutritionists. Someone has to get this information. Dick Wolfsie, who hosts "AM America" in Indianapolis, Indiana, does most of his own research. This means doing a lot of reading—at least two or three books a week. Some talk show hosts are avid readers while others depend upon producers or segment producers to do the research and frame questions for them.

For Dick, reading is rather like jogging. It is not always enjoyable while you are doing it, but the results are worthwhile. Most of his on-the-job reading is either books written by guests or background material on issues which will be discussed on the program. Typically, Dick will read a book and then write down the first ten questions that come to his mind. After asking a guest the first question, the program may go off on an unexpected track which precludes asking the other questions. This happens because a talk show host must also be a good listener.

A Producer in the News Department

It is not just producers of talk shows who read. Producers of news shows also must read. Ben Strout produces the "More You Know Show" which is a prime time hour special on education that is aired every three months. Ben also is producer for the probe team at an NBC affiliate which does investigative reporting on topics like street gangs. In addition, he writes some voice-overs for the news anchors at his station.

Producers, like Ben, do considerable reading. During his workday, he reads journals for at least three hours and frequently longer. He also takes books and heavier reading material home. Ben reads to gather information for his programs. He is always clipping and saving material and putting it into his file. The entire news team at his station uses his resources.

Ben is a true bookworm. His love for the printed word is so great that in the first grade his ambition was to read every book in the library. To achieve this goal, he would check out and read six books each week. Ben also loves to write. However, he has found that writing for television is quite different from writing for other media. The language must be simple and so must the sentences.

News Reporters Need to Read

If you write the scripts for your news reports on television, then you will need to read for information. You simply can't do an in-depth treatment of a topic without having background information on it. To keep abreast of what is going on in the world for his job as a television news reporter for an NBC affiliate, David MacAnally reads daily papers including the *New York Times* plus news feature magazines.

News Anchor on a Midwest Station

Maybe some anchors are just performers. However, Tom Cochrun, evening news anchor at an NBC station in Indianapolis, is not one of them. Tom is a true bookworm who as a child stayed up many evenings with a flashlight trying to finish sports adventure books that got him hooked on reading.

In his job as news anchor, Tom reads for 60 to 80 percent of his workday. He reads newspapers, research reports, background reports, and magazines. Tom feels that in order to write news copy that his viewers will understand he has to have a strong grasp of the information. He says he cannot get this understanding from just reading wire service information. David Brinkley, Tom Brokaw, and Ted Koppel are other anchors who do a great deal of reading to prepare for their shows.

Public Relations

Companies, institutions, unions, activist groups, and all kinds of organizations want to win public approval. The people who do this job for them are in the public relations field which is commonly called PR. Some organizations have their own public relations departments while others use public relations firms. In either case, the task is to communicate with a specific audience. Airlines may want to stress how safe it is to fly after several crashes have shaken the public's confidence in air travel. An asbestos company may want to reassure its workers on the safety of the workplace. A food company may want to communicate to its stockholders the reasons why the price of its stock is steadily rising.

People employed in public relations work have two main activities: research and communication. Most of the glamour lies in the communication side as PR people arrange for media publicity. It is the research side that allows bookworms to read. In order to handle an account, it is essential to be well-versed in what a client does. This may mean not only reading about a company but also an entire industry. The majority of reading is probably done to find out what newspapers and magazines are writing about clients. It is also important to gather information that may affect a client. Today's public relations employees are voracious readers who must read everything in order to service their clients effectively.

Travel Agents

The type of reading that travel agents do is frequently investigative. Cynthia Kroos, the managing director of a travel agency, finds it essential to learn about new tourist spots, resorts, and tours. She is constantly reading trade publications to do this. Obviously, a lot of reading also has to be done to keep up with all the packages that are offered by airlines and tour companies. According to Cynthia, travel agents have so much reading to do that it can almost bury them. Since so much of the workday is devoted to dealing with clients, considerable reading must be done at home. The glamorous bonus to all of this reading is the frequent trips that Cynthia takes to learn more about places her clients may wish to visit.

Reading Can Be Glamorous

While a glamour career may be appealing to many people, including bookworms, it is not a field that is easy to break into. Even college graduates are usually required to begin in low-level positions because experience is needed for the positions they seek. Few have that experience so graduates are often forced to begin as secretaries, typists, or gofers to gain experience. There is always room for good people in glamour industries. However, getting the job of your dreams involves hard work as well as some luck and good timing.

Glamour careers at all levels can be pressure-filled and tension-packed as people struggle to meet deadlines for such things as television shows, advertising promotions, and the production of movies. There is no guarantee of a nine-to-five job. Like all careers, there is considerable drudgery involved. However, glamour careers do offer involvement in exciting industries like radio, television, the movies, travel, advertising, and public relations, which makes these careers so sought after.

For Further Reading

The more you know about the glamour industries, the easier it will be for you to discover the job you want. A surprising number of jobs in this industry are filled by people who read for a substantial period of time each day. While most bookworms are working behind the scenes in these industries, a few are also in the public eye. The following books should give you a better idea of what careers are available in the glamour industries:

Blanksteen, Jane and Avi Odeni. *TV Careers Behind the Screen*. New York: John Wiley and Sons, 1987.

Bone, Jan. *Opportunities in Telecommunications.* Lincolnwood, Ill.: National Textbook Company, 1985.

Grant, Edgar. *Exploring Careers in the Travel Industry.* New York: The Rosen Publishing Group Inc., 1984.

Hallstead, William F. *Broadcasting Careers for You.* New York: Lodestar Books, 1983.

Kirkham, James D. *Television Production Today!* Lincolnwood, Ill.: National Textbook Company, 1989.

Mogel, Leonard. *Making it in the Media Professions.* Chester, Conn.: The Globe Pequot Press, 1988.

Nobel, John H. *The Harvard Guide to Careers in Mass Media.* Cambridge, Mass.: Office of Career Services, Harvard University, 1987.

Noronha, Shonan F.R. *Opportunities in Television and Video Careers.* Lincolnwood, Ill.: National Textbook Company, 1988.

Reed, Maxine K. and Robert M. Reed. *Career Opportunities in Television, Cable and Video.* New York: Facts on File Publications, 1986.

Rotman, Morris. *Opportunities in Public Relations.* Lincolnwood, Ill.: National Textbook Company, 1985.

Smith, Carol Cox. *Glamor Careers—How to Break Into.* New York: Monarch Press, 1985.

Weinstein, Bob. *Your Career in Public Relations.* New York: Arco Publishing, 1983.

CHAPTER SIX

The Education World
Reading for Knowledge

Books are the quietest and most constant of friends; they are the most accessible and wisest of counsellors, and the most patient of teachers. CHARLES W. ELIOT

Teaching is a profession for bookworms. As the quote by Eliot, president of Harvard University from 1869 to 1909 and a pioneer in teacher education, clearly states, books themselves are teachers. In order to teach, teachers from elementary school through college must love books, read books, and understand them. Books are an integral part of teaching. However, being a bookworm is not enough to make someone a good teacher. Good teachers must also be able to pass the knowledge, skills, and information that they have acquired from books on to their students.

Preparing Yourself to Teach

Teaching is not a new profession. Scholars like Aristotle, Plato, and Socrates were teachers. But it was not until the 1800s that teaching schools began to develop. Today, anyone planning to teach, whether in a kindergarten or at the college level, will need a college degree. Many elementary, junior high, and high school teachers will also need to get master's degrees to advance in the profession and to increase their earnings. Bookworms who want to teach at the college level will find it is very helpful to have a doctorate degree.

Prospective elementary, junior high, and senior high school teachers will study similar courses during their first two years of college. These courses are basic liberal arts courses and will include the study of history, language arts, mathematics, and science. During their college years, they will also take teaching methods courses and do actual practice teaching in a classroom under the guidance of an experienced teacher. In addition, future high school teachers will also specialize in the particular subject area or areas in which they plan to teach.

Before most bookworms can start teaching, they will need to meet state requirements for teacher certification. These requirements deal with the college courses which teachers must complete satisfactorily to become certified elementary, junior, and senior high school teachers. Each state has different requirements. In some states teachers at nursery schools, private schools, and junior colleges also have to be certified. However, teachers at four-year colleges and universities do not need state certification.

Generic Teaching Duties

All teachers, no matter what level they are teaching, have a number of duties that must be performed from taking attendance to filling out report cards.

Getting Ready

Bookworms will find preparation for classroom work enjoyable as it involves so much reading. Teachers read textbooks, teacher's manuals, course related materials, professional journals, and curriculum guides to prepare for their daily stint in the classroom. However, preparation goes beyond reading to making sure everything is completely ready for each lesson. Materials have to be duplicated. Supplementary books and materials as well as supplies have to be obtained and laid out in readiness for each class.

Leading the Way

Teachers are the classroom leaders. Through a variety of different teaching methods, they have to motivate their students to learn, show them how to learn, and instill intellectual curiosity in them. Books will help them in this task, so will all kinds of audiovisual materials like records, tapes, filmstrips, movies, and television programs plus computers.

Checking Progress

All teachers need to make sure that their students have learned the material. Mastery is important whether it is the alphabet, the multiplication tables, or French grammar. Teachers check their students' progress through analyzing written and oral work and quizzes and tests. Records need to be kept so that teachers know how each individual student is doing. And this information must be placed on report cards and discussed at conferences.

Being a Role Model

Students do notice how their teachers behave. Younger students, especially, often want to be just like their teachers. Teachers set a very powerful example for their students through their own sincerity, patience, kindness, understanding, honesty, and objectivity.

Doing the Extra Tasks

Teachers have other obligations besides routine classroom tasks. They are also expected to do their share of duties such as supervising the lunchroom and bus loading, and hall and playground duty. They chaperone after-school events, attend faculty meetings, and sponsor clubs. Don't consider teaching as a profession if you expect to be home by three o'clock each day.

A Closer Look at the Teaching Profession

Today, education is both America's largest business and profession. There are over 2,622,000 teachers in the United States, and over one billion dollars is spent on education every school day in this country. The good news for people interested in this profession is that the number of students attending school will increase which raises the demand for teachers. By 1997, 171,000 new teachers will have to be hired to meet the educational needs in the United States.

Teaching at the Lower Elementary Level

For bookworms, teaching children in the lower elementary grades can be very satisfying. These teachers have the opportunity to actually teach young children how to read and to help each child develop an appreciation for books. It is a chance for bookworms to instill their love of books in others.

According to Fran Hageboeck, a first grade teacher for many years, half of her teaching day is devoted to some aspect of teaching reading. During that time, she will read outloud to the class for thirty minutes. Time is also spent having children read to her and listening to them read to each other. Away from the classroom, she spends time in the library searching for books to read to the children and for them to read.

Of course, first grade teachers also teach other subjects beside reading. In addition, they spend time tying shoes, buttoning coats, putting on boots, and handing out tissues. But reading is the main focus of all the learning activities in first grade.

Teaching at the Upper Elementary Level

If you were turned off by the need to tie shoes and button coats at the lower elementary level but still like children, you might find it more enjoyable to teach in one of the upper elementary grades. In fourth, fifth, and sixth grades students can handle all their own personal needs and have also mastered the basic reading skills. Teachers at these grade levels are helping students become independent learners. Besides classes in reading and mathematics, students are now beginning to learn in the content areas of history, science, health, and English. For bookworms, it is an opportunity to help children expand their horizons through a broad reading program.

Teaching at the Junior High Level

Sue Engledow, a true bookworm, made a career change from being a bank manager to being a junior high school science teacher. Sue decided that she wanted to spend more time with books than with numbers. She went back to college and took the required education courses. Due to the influence of an elementary science teacher, Sue decided to become a science teacher. Sue has been teaching science to seventh graders in a suburban junior high school for four years.

Sue finds that science teachers do considerable reading. She usually has one concentrated preparation period each week. During this time, she will read from three to four hours. Besides reading the teacher's manual, she reads the actual students' book. Then she takes notes and makes outlines for herself and her students. Arriving an hour early every morning gives Sue the time to read over all her notes and outlines for the day along with reading and preparing for the laboratory work her students will be doing.

Sue's reading time is not just devoted to preparing for her classes. She makes all her own tests so she has to spend more hours rereading all the material to develop these tests. If she gives an essay test, she has to spend additional hours reading the students' papers. Sue reads another two to three hours every evening so that she will be able to enhance what her students are reading in their textbooks. A bookworm since her childhood when she always received a book for Christmas, Sue has found a career that lets her read.

Teaching at the High School Level

Giving students objectives before each reading assignment is Felice Knarr's way of developing critical readers in her twelfth grade English literature classes. Felice has been teaching English at a private high school for five years.

In August, before school starts, Felice charts out her course of study for the entire school year. She reads every book that the students will be reading so that she knows how long each reading assignment should take. This is not the only time Felice reads the material that will be assigned to her students. Before each reading assignment is made, she rereads the material to develop the objectives for her lesson plans. Beyond all the reading that Felice does in her preparation, she also spends six to eight hours a week grading the essays and compositions of her one hundred students. This does not include the reading that she must do in grading vocabulary, spelling, and short writing assignments.

Felice is a true bookworm who seems to always be reading. She spends several hours each day reading academic journals. It is not uncommon for her to spend eight to twelve hours on weekends keeping up with her academic reading as she is taking courses to complete her master's degree in English. For relaxation, Felice likes to read magazines.

Teaching at the College Level

The usual entry teaching position at college is as an assistant professor. Then the battle commences to get tenure, which is permanent status as a faculty member. During the trial years before tenure is granted, which range from seven to ten years, assistant professors struggle valiantly to make names for themselves. The usual route to doing this at universities is by publishing papers for journals and books. This is the reason for the expression "publish or perish."

During this probationary period, reading fills every spare minute of assistant professors' time as research is done to produce the needed publications. The reading at this stage must necessarily be quite narrow within the teaching field. Once the desired tenure is granted, reading can become much broader so that a fuller understanding of a field of study is achieved.

Assistant professors eventually become professors, and some even become department chairpersons. Reading is an absolute necessity throughout an academic career. Teachers at the college level must keep up with what is happening in their individual fields and must also read to develop new courses. Indeed, this career seems to be a perfect one for bookworms.

All Kinds of Teachers

There are many other teachers besides classroom teachers. Today, most elementary schools have reading teachers, speech teachers, music teachers, and physical education teachers on their teaching staffs. These teachers have specialized in a particular subject area just like teachers in junior and senior high schools do. There are also teachers who work in gifted and talented programs and in special education. Some teachers become counselors, curriculum directors, and principals.

Other Positions in the Field of Education

Bookworms who are interested in education but don't want to work in the classroom can find satisfying jobs outside of the classroom that involve reading.

College Admissions Counselor

According to Steve Bushouse, former Dean of Admissions at Butler University in Indianapolis, you need strong basic reading skills to work as an admissions counselor at a college. However, he points out, you need to have other skills too in order to be successful at this job. People in the admissions office also need to be very people-oriented. Not only do admissions counselors interview students, they also give speeches at schools and work in booths at college fairs.

College admissions counselors read and evaluate high school records. Then as part of a committee they decide which students will be admitted to a college. In this job, entire days—far into the night—are spent reading. Furthermore, this is not a five-day-a-week job, especially when applications are being read. Quite frequently, this job is held by recent college graduates.

State Department of Education

Within the Department of Education in each state, there are advisory positions that would appeal to bookworms. One position that involves reading is working as a reading consultant. These consultants need to read widely so that they can advise teachers on the wide variety of materials that can be used in the classroom. Jobs in curriculum planning should also interest bookworms.

Education Associations and Organizations

In the United States, there are many professional organizations for teachers. The National Education Association (NEA) has the largest membership. The American Federation of Teachers (AFT) is a teaching union that works to improve teaching conditions. There are also professional associations like the National Association of Secondary School Principals. All of the education organizations and associations offer jobs for educators in different capacities from counseling to copyediting.

Travel Opportunities for Teachers

If you are a bookworm who likes to travel, there are many teaching jobs in all parts of the world. The pay is not always as good as it is in the United States, but the opportunities for travel and adventure are often an added pull for bookworms looking for excitement. If you are interested in working abroad as a teacher, you may want to write to some of the organizations listed below:

Fullbright Teacher Exchange Branch
United States Information Agency
Washington, DC 20547

Office of Overseas Schools
Room 234, SA-6
U.S. Department of State
Washington, DC 20520

United Nations Educational, Scientific, and Cultural Organization
   (UNESCO)
U.S. Department of Education
Washington, DC 20202

Action Peace Corps
Washington, DC 20202

U.S. Department of Defense
Overseas Dependent Schools
2461 Eisenhower Avenue
Alexandria, VA 22331

Teachers' Salaries

Teachers' salaries are constantly increasing, although they vary greatly between states. Can you guess which state has the highest salary for beginning teachers? Is it California, New York, Alaska, Pennsylvania, Hawaii, or New Jersey? If you picked Alaska, you are correct. In 1989, beginning teachers in Alaska were paid $40,905. This figure includes an adjustment for cost-of-living in Alaska. If you are interested in knowing what the starting salaries for schools in your area are, you can get this information from your State Department of Education or your local school district.

Teachers' salaries usually increase each year based on merit, years of experience, and educational degrees. In some states, secondary school-teachers receive higher pay than elementary schoolteachers. The average pay for college professors is approximately $45,000 a year.

For Further Reading

Teaching is a bookworm's career today more than ever. The responsibilities and work loads of teachers have increased along with the volume of reading that must be done in order to keep pace with the rapid accumulation of knowledge. The following books will give you a good look at what the teaching profession is like:

Dunham, Jack. *Stress in Teaching.* New York: Nicholas publishing, 1984.
Edelfelt, Roy A. *Careers in Education.* Lincolnwood, Ill.: National Textbook Company, 1988.
Fine, Janet. *Opportunities in Teaching Careers.* Lincolnwood, Ill.: National Textbook Company, 1989.

Milgram, Gail Gleason. *Your Future in Education*. New York: Richards Rosen Press, Inc., 1979.

National Council for Accreditation of Teacher Education. *Annual List*. Washington, D.C.

National Education Association. *Teaching Career Fact Book*. Washington, D.C. (annual)

Ramsey, Patricia. *Teaching Multi-Cultural Education*. New York: Teachers College Press, 1987.

Teaching in America: The Common Ground. New York: Yale University Press, 1985.

CHAPTER SEVEN

Research Jobs
Sorting and Seeking Information

W hat kind of material do you like to read? Is it history, astronomy, religion, or medical science? Perhaps, you prefer space science, ecology, government relations, or education. No matter what you like to read, just as long as it's primarily nonfiction, there is probably a job somewhere in research that will let you read material that really interests you.

Research jobs involve seeking information so that papers and books can be written by university and research center scholars and historians. They also involve reading material so that it can be sorted into some kind of order as archivists do. Much research is also done for local, state, and federal governments; museums; and businesses.

More than any other country in the world, the United States has recognized the importance of research both in the public and private sector. Just the number of research organizations is mind-boggling. There are over 11,700 university and nonprofit research organizations. This doesn't necessarily mean that there is an unlimited number of jobs in these organizations as many will have very small staffs.

Research Jobs at Universities

Universities are true research centers. At a large university numerous research projects are going on all the time. Jobs become available whenever a new project is started. Many university projects are headed by resident faculty members; others will be led by accomplished scholars from other universities who have come to the university to work on a research project. To head a project, you must have outstanding credentials. A doctorate degree is just a basic requirement. Then you have to demonstrate that you are an expert in your field.

Fortunately for those who want to be researchers at a university, research projects need to have more staff than the one person heading the project who may only work at it part-time. Although people seeking research staff positions don't have to have the same professional status as the project heads, they do have to have top-notch qualifications to land these desirable jobs. In 1989, the competition for two jobs as entry-level research assistants was so intense at a prestigious university that there were seventy applicants.

The Research Assistant Job

There are different levels of research assistants. To climb each rung on the ladder, or to start beyond an entry-level position, you will need more than a bachelor's degree, plus experience. You will also have to demonstrate that you have a working knowledge of scientific theory and can evaluate and analyze what you read. As you move to higher levels, your responsibilities will increase. You may become responsible for a phase of a project or for an entire project.

You can find out about entry-level jobs in research through university employment offices or bulletins. These jobs will not require as much reading as bookworms would probably like. Usually, you can expect to spend about half of your time extracting information from a library—that's the reading portion of the job—and the other half doing clerical work. In fact, having some clerical experience or at least knowing how to type and file is almost a prerequisite for getting entry-level jobs.

As a research assistant, you usually only work on one project at a time for a scholar. This does give you the opportunity to become a miniexpert on a subject through your reading. Some projects have a time limit while others go on as more funding becomes available. After one project is finished, you will typically go on to work on another project.

Research Jobs at Think Tanks

If you are constantly reading newspapers and news magazines to keep up with what is going on in the world and would like doing this for a living, then a job at a think tank could be ideal for you. Think tanks are strictly American. No other country has private institutions which are dedicated to public-policy research.

When you hear the words, "think tank," you may conjure up visions of intellectuals concentrating on heady problems. It is decidedly true that considerable thinking goes on at think tanks, but much of that thinking is based upon reading.

When the first think tanks emerged in the early decades of this century, research resulted in books and papers that influenced public decisions. Today's think tanks are more activist. While still producing books and papers (the Heritage Foundation produces over two hundred policy papers a year), think tanks also actively lobby legislators and court the press to influence the government. So besides researching and writing, the think tank employee's job description has to be rewritten to include public relations work.

The first generation of think tanks was slightly to the left or right of center in their political thinking. However, their research tended to show both viewpoints. A new generation of think tanks that had strong conservative roots emerged during the mid-1970s and is flourishing today. People thinking of applying for a job at a think tank should probably consider their own political biases when deciding where to look for a job. Note the political leanings of these prominent think tanks.

Conservative

American Enterprise Institute

Heritage Foundation

Hoover Institution

Hudson Institute

Manhattan Institute

Liberal

Center for Defense Information

Center for National Policy

Council on Economic Priorities

Institute for Policy Studies

World Policy Institute

If you want to work in North Dakota or Florida, you will have trouble finding a job with a think tank. Traditionally, most think tanks are located close to Washington, D.C. or New York City, although there are exceptions. One of the earliest conservative think tanks, the Hoover Institution, which was founded in 1919, is located in California. The Hudson Institute really overturned the East Coast location emphasis by moving from a location forty-five miles from New York City to Indianapolis, Indiana, in 1984.

Working at a Think Tank

You may bump into people like Gerald Ford, Henry Kissinger, Alexander Haig, Zbigniew Brzezinski, or James Schlesinger if you work at a think tank. Many of the high-level jobs are held by people who have been in the public limelight. Of course, most of the people working at think tanks don't have names that you see every day in the newspaper. But many are quite well-known scholars in their field of expertise or show promise of being future academic superstars.

At the older think tanks, you are more likely to work with well-known scholars and people who have made their names in government. Charles Schultz, who was the chairman of the Council of Economic Advisers under Carter, is now at Brookings while former UN Ambassador Jeane Kirkpatrick is at the American Enterprise Institute. The stars at the newer think tanks tend to be political activists instead of former government officials.

First-level Researcher

If your vision of the perfect job is one where your desk is inundated with reading materials, an entry-level job at a think tank may be the right one for you. To get this type of job, impressive credentials are needed. For most jobs, some type of graduate degree—usually a master's degree—is essential. You also should have some experience in doing research, even if it is only writing your own research papers. When seeking a job it can be helpful to know someone involved in a project at a think tank in order to discover what jobs are available; however, sending out résumés is also a good way to get a job.

THE ACTUAL JOB   If you have a job as a first-level researcher, you can work on researching just one topic for a think tank scholar or on a number of topics for different people. When a project starts up, you will read to get a basic understanding of an issue. Then you may be asked to develop a bibliography for the head of the project. At times you will summarize what you read. You may even be given a particular issue to focus on. You will have considerable autonomy in deciding how your job will be performed. Ultimately, scholars at the think tank write papers or books on the topics which have been researched.

To advance up the ladder from a first-level researcher, a doctorate is usually required. To get a feel for what a job is like at a think tank, you should consider taking an internship at one of these institutions.

Archivists Are Researchers and Readers

Not too many people are acquainted with what archives are or what archivists do. First of all, archives are records of individuals, groups, institutions, and governments at all levels which are preserved because they have information of lasting value. Such historic documents as the Declaration of Independence, the United States Constitution, and the Bill of Rights are preserved in the National Archives Building in Washington, D.C. All the valuable documents from each president's term of office are preserved in presidential libraries which are archives. You can also find the records which must be kept by law for local and state government in archives. Archival records are not just government documents. Businesses have archives; so do universities, hospitals, labor unions, and even small historical societies.

Before the age of computers, microfilm, and recordings, archives were chiefly made up of unpublished manuscripts. Now archives contain records in such additional formats as computer tapes, photographs, films, and sound recordings.

The Job of an Archivist

The primary job of an archivist is to establish control over records. This involves organizing records so that they can easily be accessed. A collection must have a title, and all of the contents must be organized in a logical sequence and described so that they can be used. The job also requires a judgment of what records have historical value; for example, the federal government only saves 3 percent of its records. Much of the work of the archivist, therefore, is going through documents to decide which should be kept permanently. All of these tasks require reading. Not only must the documents be read, the archivist needs to read to have an understanding of the historical period in which they were created to understand their value.

Another job of the archivist is overseeing the preservation of documents. Since original newsprint will not last, they must supervise the reproduction of newspaper clippings onto acid-free paper. Archivists must also determine whether to restore or conserve an original document by microfilming or some other technique or to both restore and reproduce the original. The preservation is done by scientific and technical specialists.

The archivist's job also includes gathering information that is requested. Archivists are becoming more involved, too, in the publication of materials and in their exhibition. In addition, some archivists have the task of soliciting funds to preserve or establish a collection. And, of course, archivists who are in charge of collections have administrative responsibilities involved in supervising a staff.

Requirements for Becoming an Archivist

Once a person decides to be an archivist, it is usually a lifetime career. At first archivists may move from one archive to another, but most eventually stay in one place. And that place may well be a governmental unit as the majority of archivists have civil service standing. Those who work at universities may also be faculty members.

The one personal characteristic that archivists have in common, no matter where they work, is an interest in preserving the past. There is also a need for organizational ability, good judgment, an interest in research, and self-reliance.

While there may be some entry-level jobs that only require a bachelor's degree, almost always a master's degree is required. Undergraduate majors can vary, but master's degrees are usually in either American history or library science. Increasingly, job candidates have master's degrees in both areas with course work in the theory and practice of archives. Only two schools offer master's degree programs in archival studies. For senior staff positions, especially at universities, a doctoral degree may be required.

The archival profession is a growing one. One way to learn more about this profession is by contacting The Society of American Archivists (SAA), 600 South Federal, Suite 504, Chicago, Illinois 60605.

Curators Are Researchers and Readers

Like archivists, curators are concerned with keeping records of the past. The difference is that archivists are primarily concerned with written material and curators are primarily concerned with man-made objects and specimens. You will find curators at museums, zoos, aquariums, botanic gardens, and historic sites. Curators who work for the federal government are found at the Smithsonian Institute, military museums, and in archeological and other museums run by the Department of Interior.

The Curator's Job

A curator's job will vary depending on the size of the place where the curator works. In a small institution, the curator must not only acquire, identify, catalog, and store objects but also restore objects, arrange for exhibitions, and conduct educational programs. This job description can be further expanded to include hammering and nailing and doing all the research when it comes to setting up an exhibition. At a large institution, a curator's job would be more specific. A curator might specialize in a particular area like toys, anthropology, science, or technology or be assigned a function like cataloging, acquisition, or restoring the collection.

Whether a curator has a specific responsibility or is responsible for everything at an institution, considerable reading is essential in this job. When an institution acquires new objects or specimens, curators must read to identify them accurately. When a new exhibit is being set up, the curator researches to see what belongs in the exhibit and that everything is properly displayed. Curators must also read to find out about the newest and best ways to preserve and display objects and specimens. There is also reading to answer questions posed by the public. And of course considerable reading of professional journals is essential to keep up with what is happening in the profession.

Requirements for Becoming a Curator

While some curators have obtained bachelor's or master's degrees in museum studies (museology), many institutions are looking for curators with degrees in specific areas like art, anthropology, biology, or history. The minimum requirements for obtaining a curator's job are a bachelor's degree and experience. Most museums, however, want curators to have a master's degree in a specific field plus experience. Curators working in smaller institutions may also need some business courses to handle administrative responsibilities.

There are fewer than 10,000 jobs available as archivists and curators. Because of the current interest in art, history, technology, and culture, the number of curators is growing. It should be pointed out, however, that there will never be a great number of openings for jobs as curators. Furthermore, the job is appealing to many qualified applicants so there is considerable competition. Those who have had experience as interns or volunteers often have the best chance to get these coveted jobs. The pay for beginning archivists and curators usually starts in the low 20s. Pay will generally be higher at large well-funded museum and government jobs than at smaller organizations or museums.

Historians Read About the Past

Why did Winston Churchill lose his post as prime minister after successfully leading Britain through World War II? How successful was the first

Five-Year Plan in China in terms of stimulating agricultural production? Historians formulate questions like these to direct their study of the past. They are imaginative researchers who read all kinds of documents to determine what happened in the past, why it happened, and how it has affected the present and may affect the future. After collecting data by reading vast amounts of material, historians analyze it and then present it in the form of textbooks, lectures, studies, reports, and articles.

Most historians, over 70 percent of them, are college teachers who research and write as well as carry out their teaching duties. The remaining historians work at jobs where their historical skills and knowledge are required. This may mean writing histories for companies and governmental units. It can mean researching historical records for businesses, law firms, television or movie companies, and public agencies. It can also mean analyzing past trends for banks, insurance companies, investment services, manufacturers, utilities, and public relations firms. No matter where a historian works, the job is ideal for bookworms as it always allows them to bury their noses in books and read while they are doing their jobs.

Education and Job Opportunities

Since most historians work as college teachers, a doctorate degree in history is almost essential to obtain employment. Teaching jobs open up when faculty members retire or enrollment in history courses increases.

Opportunity to obtain a position as a historian is very limited. Overall, less than 1,000 job openings for historians occur each year. There is keen competition for these openings whether they are at colleges, museums, archives, historical societies, businesses, or with the government. Only a few historians are self-employed as writers, consultants, or researchers.

A Historian in Women's Studies

Until a few years ago, the role of women was overlooked in history. There was a dearth of material written on this subject. Sara Evans, a University of Minnesota professor, is a historian who recognized that the history of women was undervalued. Hired by the university to teach women's history, Sara combined this job with the writing of scholarly works on women. Her approach is not to romanticize the role of women by telling of heroines but to prove that women whose names aren't household words have helped to shape the United States.

Sara's research has taken her to libraries, museums, and archives to answer questions about the past. An important part of her research has been figuring out what type of material to study. For example, to find out about the diet and work load of slaves, her students have studied plantation records.

Both Sara's teaching duties and research in women's studies have entailed considerable reading. Obviously, historians are readers; however, the time Sara spends reading varies enormously. When she is on leave, she will read as much as forty hours a week. The pluses to her work are that she feels she is doing something new all the time and that her work is making a difference in the way people see the past.

Researchers for Publishers

When you read an article in an encyclopedia, the *New Yorker*, *National Geographic*, *Newsweek*, or *Time*, you expect the facts to be accurate. There is a small brigade of workers at these organizations who research to make sure that what you read is accurate. They are seekers of the truth whether their job titles are fact checkers, junior researchers, or senior researchers. These researchers spend their days reading and phoning as they go over articles word-by-word to make them reliable. The backgrounds of these researchers vary. However, a knowledge of research techniques and an insatiable desire to find the true facts are essential. It is also necessary to be able to write clearly as changes and explanations of proposed changes must be written by these researchers.

Researching for an Encyclopedia

Like the famed Sergeant Joe Friday of "Dragnet," Richard Bready seeks just the facts. Richard is a senior researcher for *World Book Encyclopedia*. In one year, he may check or question 20,000 bits of information. Many of the revisions are small, but all are essential. Eagle-eyed readers carefully check the contents of articles. They expect things that have happened six months ago to be in the encyclopedia. They expect the latest models of the M-1 tank and the army's M-16 rifle to be shown in illustrations. If an encyclopedia is not kept up-to-date, its sales will falter.

Richard begins his day as a researcher by thoroughly reading the Chicago newspapers. He skims through five other newspapers for book reviews on topics that are part of his job. Then he starts on his research pile which will have from five to twenty-five articles to be checked. Richard and the other researchers try to get the information they need without leaving the building by using the World Book library and making phone calls. Richard believes that someone out there knows the answer for every question. However, he admits for practical purposes you need to know when to stop researching, based on the importance of the information you might find.

Richard is a bookworm as most researchers are. He learned to read at the age of three and grew up in a home with 20,000 books. Although Richard prepared to teach and actually taught, he grew tired of correcting grammatical errors and showing students how to say what they wanted to say. After free-lancing as a book reviewer, he became a dictionary editor, which was a lot of fun. Then in 1984, he came to World Book. He finds his job to be intellectually stimulating and appreciates the opportunity to work independently and schedule his own time.

For Further Reading

So much of research involves reading. Here is a job that truly allows bookworms to combine avocation with vocation. The following books will give you more information on careers in research:

Barzun, Jacques and Henry F. Graff. *The Modern Researcher*. Orlando, Fla.: Harcourt Brace Jovanovich, Publishers, 1985.

Berner, Richard C. *Archival Theory and Practice in the United States: A Historical Analysis*. Seattle, Wash.: University of Washington Press, 1983.

Hexter, J.H. *On Historians*. Cambridge, Mass.: Harvard University Press, 1979.

Tuchman, Barbara W. *Practicing History*. New York: Alfred A. Knopf, 1981.

Walsh, Timothy, ed. *Guardian of Heritage*. Washington, D.C.: National Archives and Records Administration, 1985.

CHAPTER EIGHT

The Public Sector
Reading for the Government

T here is no shortage of jobs in the public sector. In fact, the government is the single largest employer in the United States. If you add the jobs of all the federal, state, and local governmental units together, you will find over sixteen million jobs in executive branch agencies. Add in all the positions at all levels for the legislative and judicial branches plus the armed forces, and the total number of government jobs approaches eighteen million. Within this great number of jobs, there are many that will appeal to bookworms. Some are identical to jobs in the private sector while others are unique to the public sector.

Jobs in the public sector offer certain advantages. First of all, there is usually more long-term job security than in the private sector. Most jobs will pay salaries comparable to those earned in the private sector. The benefits, however, may be more generous in the public sector, especially vacation and sick leave benefits. In addition, employees can count on annual raises.

Working for the Federal Government

Over three million civilian employees work for agencies of the executive branch of the federal government. They work in more than nine hundred different occupations for over a hundred different agencies. They don't just work in Washington, D.C. In fact, close to 90 percent work in other geographical areas including more than 100,000 people who work abroad. What's more, you can often keep the same job and move from state to state or even city to city.

Sixty percent of the federal workers are involved in just two jobs—delivering the mail and providing for the national defense. The rest of the workers are almost evenly divided among these activities: management of natural resources and transportation, administration of benefit payment to states and assistance to states and localities, provision of health care to war veterans, tax collection and other general government management, and research and information activities. It is within this last category that most bookworms will find their job niche in the government.

Although people tend to think that the number of people working for the federal government is growing rapidly, this is certainly not true. The period of rapid growth was the 1960s and 1970s. In the past decade, federal employment has grown by about 7 percent while nonfederal employment has expanded approximately 25 percent. Most of the employment growth has occurred in the Department of Defense and the Postal Service; otherwise, employment has generally fallen. Still there are many jobs available, especially as replacements. Frequently, as many as twenty thousand people are hired by the federal government in a month.

How to Find Out about Jobs

Perhaps one of the hardest things to do is to find out where the jobs in government are that would appeal to you as a bookworm. In general, the category where you will find these jobs is the GS-100 group which is social science, psychology, and welfare; and the GS-1000 group which is information and arts. You can learn more about these jobs by reading *The Guide to Federal Jobs* which provides job descriptions.

Once you have an idea of what kind of job you are looking for, you have the difficult task of finding out where vacancies for those jobs exist. The federal government is quite decentralized so you can't just go to one spot and find out about all the jobs that are available. Some job vacancies are advertised in newspapers. You can also find listings in professional journals. A college placement office is another place to find out about positions. In addition, state employment offices will have lists of job vacancies. You can also visit, write, or phone federal job information centers. The federal government has divided the country into ten regions, and you will find at least one job information center in each region. One of the best places to find job information is at a regional office of a government agency because agencies must post all their vacancies. You can find the addresses and phone numbers of job information centers and regional offices of government agencies at a public library.

Although the federal government does not publish a complete list of all job openings, several private companies publish lists of jobs currently available. You should be able to find this information in *Federal Career Opportunities* and *Federal Jobs Digest* which are available in public libraries.

How to Get a Job

Whenever you find out about a job opening, you should get a copy of the vacancy announcement as it will give you all the details that you must have to apply successfully for the job. It provides the exact identifying number of the job which you must have because the same job could be found in more than one agency. It will give the deadlines for submitting an application. It also provides helpful information on salary, job title, number of positions available, the location of the job, the description of the job, and the qualifications required for the job. This announcement can be obtained from the agency that has the vacancy.

To apply for most jobs in the federal government you have to complete an application form—formally called Standard Form 171 or more usually known as SF-171. This is your résumé, and it will play a large role in determining whether you will even get an interview for a position. Rather than just completing this application once, it should be revised to suit each job you apply for. This is because applications are evaluated for each job on the basis of the job's duties and your qualifications. Besides formally submitting an application for a job, it is also helpful to contact individuals who hire at agencies that interest you for advice, information, and possible interviews.

Jobs That Pay You to Read

Jobs that involve doing studies and research—and there are many in these categories within the federal government—are the ones that are literally going to pay you to read. One such job is as a social science analyst. There are approximately 15,000 jobs in this category located in different government units throughout the country. Because this position is very desirable, there is keen competition for entry-level positions. Many jobseekers will have master's degrees when only a bachelor's degree is required.

Another area in which bookworms may find jobs is within the intelligence community. This includes the Central Intelligence Agency, the Federal Bureau of Investigation, the Drug Enforcement Agency, and other related agencies. The National Archives, presidential libraries, the Smithsonian Institute, and the National Trust for Historic Preservation are additional places where bookworms should look for jobs.

Jobs in the Legislative and Judicial Branches

Although the lion's share of jobs in the federal government is found in agencies of the executive branch, there are also jobs in the legislative and judicial branches. You can find out about these jobs in some of the same ways that you find out about jobs in the executive branch. However, you will have to contact each legislative agency to find out about specific job vacancies and hiring procedures. Many of the agencies will have job hotline numbers. On the legislative side, bookworms are most likely to find jobs at the General Accounting Office, the Library of Congress, the Government Printing Office, and the Congressional Budget Office.

Jobs at the Library of Congress

An excellent place for bookworms to find jobs is in the Congressional Research Service of the Library of Congress. Hundreds of social science analysts are employed here to give members of congress and congressional committees information and to make impartial analyses of pending policy issues. Analysts might be assigned to find out what the alternatives are to the current structure of congressional committees or the ways in which affordable housing can best be provided. The analysts will do research, compile materials, and gather the pros and cons on an issue. A senior researcher may put together his or her own data. Entire days can be spent doing nothing but on-the-job reading.

Jobs on Capitol Hill

Senators and representatives have offices both in Washington, D.C. and in their home districts. The Washington, D.C. staffs are larger and are better job bets for bookworms as they have staff members who will do some research. If you want a job with a senator or representative, it doesn't hurt to go to the congressperson's office. There is an unbelievable amount of competition for staff vacancies, and it can be helpful to have made contact with those who are doing the hiring.

Bookworms can also find jobs on legislative committees and subcommittees that require people who are experts in certain policy areas. Both the House and Senate have referral services where you can fill out applications which will be circulated to congressional offices, committees, and subcommittees. Their addresses and phone numbers are:

House Placement Office
House Annex #2, Room 219
(202) 226-6732

Senate Placement Office
Hart Senate Office Building
(202) 224-9167

Working for State Governments

There are actually more jobs at the state level than at the federal level. Many of these jobs are in higher education and libraries which are favorite places for bookworms to work. Jobs at the state level in the executive, legislative, and judicial branches are similar to those in the federal government except that they obviously do not deal with international relations, nor do they usually pay as well.

You will find announcements of jobs in state government in many of the same ways that you find announcements of federal jobs. In addition, you will find job announcements in such places as bulletin boards in government buildings, public libraries, and community organizations. Once you have found the announcement of a job that appeals to you, follow the instructions on the announcement to submit your application. It is also a good idea to contact people at agencies who are doing the hiring for job information.

Some Jobs for Bookworms

Look for jobs for social science analysts because these jobs will require considerable reading on the state level just as they do on the federal level. In most states, you will find some of these jobs in legislative auditor's offices. As an analyst, you would determine how well state programs like welfare or highway maintenance are working. Then reports would be written to give this information to the legislature. Job requirements for this position usually are a master's degree in an area like public affairs, economics, political science, or one of the social sciences plus some research experience. You can sometimes get a temporary position on a project which will lead to full-time employment.

Another state job that requires reading is the job of legislative analyst for a house or senate research department. These analysts draft bills and amendments, summarize bills, and do research studies. They are trying to apply academic research to public policy. Holders of these jobs have master's degrees or are lawyers. It is also essential to be able to use a computer.

Working for Local Governments

The largest number of people are employed in local governments—the cities, towns, counties, townships, and school districts. It is at this level that you can work closest to the people. The greatest number of employees in this group are teachers. Finding and getting a job at this level is often a very informal process especially in very small governmental units. Larger units will have personnel departments that have vacancy announcements.

Working as an Elected Official

Some elected officials find themselves absolutely drowning in materials to be read. Most legislators, at all government levels, can never get all their job related reading done. The president, governors, and mayors of large cities all have so much reading to do that they frequently ask assistants to limit reports to one page summaries. Judges also must necessarily spend much of their time reading.

For Further Reading

Because the federal government has so many jobs and hiring practices vary so much, bookworms who want to find jobs that let them read are going to have to do a lot of reading to find those jobs. It is absolutely essential to have an understanding of how the government works. In addition, you need to read books like the following ones which explain about the government and governmental jobs:

Acheson, Patricia C. *Our Federal Government: How It Works: An Introduction to the United States Government.* New York: Dodd, Mead & Company, 1984.
Baxter, Neale. *Opportunities in State and Local Government.* Lincolnwood, Ill.: National Textbook Company, 1985.
Dumbaugh, Kerry and Gary Serota. *Capitol Jobs: An Insider's Guide to Finding a Job in Congress.* Washington, D.C.: Tilden Press, 1986.
Krannich, Ronald L. and Caryl Rae Krannich. *The Complete Guide to Public Employment.* Manassas, Va.: Impact Publications, 1986.
Kraus, Krandall. *How to Get a Federal Job.* New York: Facts on File Publications, 1986.
Waelde, David E. *How to Get a Federal Job.* Washington, D.C.: Fedhelp Publications, 1989.
Washington Information Directory. Washington, D.C.: Congressional Quarterly Inc., 1989.

CHAPTER NINE

The Private Sector
Reading for the Profit Makers

A lthough the government is the largest single employer in the United States, approximately nine out of ten people work in the private sector. Obviously, this is where bookworms will find most of the jobs that involve reading. You have already read about the jobs in publishing, glamour industries, and research in this sector. Now you will find out about all the professional and business jobs that should be filled by people who love to read.

With the constant explosion of new technology and knowledge in almost every field, few employees can afford not to read to keep up with what is happening in their area of employment. The secret is to find the jobs that require more than routine reading. Quite often these jobs will be found in areas where research is done.

If a bookworm has a specific field of interest, it may be possible to turn this interest into a job asset. The reader who has developed an in-depth knowledge of an industry, a country, or a product is a more attractive candidate for a job than someone who will have to learn vital background information on the job.

Reading Jobs in Traditional Professions

Occupations that require advanced education and training and also involve intellectual skills, such as medicine, law, engineering, theology, and teaching are regarded as professions. If you have an intense interest in one of these professions, it is possible to find a job within it that lets you read. First of all, you can become a teacher of future doctors, lawyers, engineers, teachers, or other professionals at a college. Second, you can look for a job in the profession that emphasizes research. Third, because many professions allow one to be self-employed, you can tailor your job to fit your love of reading.

Doctors Read

Doctors who teach and those who work at research institutions spend much of their time reading—not only to increase their understanding but also in order to write papers. Even a doctor who primarily treats patients will find it essential to do at least four or five hours a week of solid professional reading beyond the routine reading of charts.

Lawyers Read

The younger lawyers are, the more they will read as they will need to do more research. It would not be unusual for a junior attorney in a law firm to spend three or four hours a day reading briefs and cases. In addition, law clerks for judges, especially appellate judges, do a lot of reading. As lawyers become more senior, their reading time decreases. Still, most will be reading from one and one-half to two hours a day, and it is not unusual for them to read three hours. Nowadays, more and more of this reading is done on computers rather than in law books as information can be accessed faster in this way.

Lawyers do not just practice law. One job that requires a legal background as well as very intense reading is putting head notes on cases for publishers of law books. Another job is as teacher in a law school.

Members of the Clergy Read

Reading for members of the clergy can be for contemplation, getting information for sermons, learning more about one's faith, and increasing knowledge in an area like counseling.

The Money-People Read

When people buy stocks and bonds (securities), they usually deal with stockbrokers. Since things are always changing so fast in these markets, brokers have to snatch every moment they can to keep up with what is happening. Unfortunately, not too much of this time can take place during the day as the market is open and they are busy dealing with clients. Also because they receive absolutely reams of material to digest, much of their reading must just be skimming.

If you are fascinated by what is happening in the securities market, there are research jobs in the investment area which are just made for bookworms. On the sell side the jobs are with brokerage firms and investment banks that sell securities to investors while on the buy side the jobs are with bank trust departments, insurance companies, and fund management firms.

On the sell side, researchers look at securities to determine the most attractive investments for their firm's clients. On the buy side, researchers spend their time figuring out what should be bought and sold for their firm's portfolio. On either side knowledge increases the probability that a decision will be a correct one. Researchers read constantly to stay up-to-date with what is happening as things are changing every day. Stocks and bonds that appear to be an excellent investment at the start of a week may be a poor choice by the end of the week.

Most researchers are assigned a specific industry. Within that area they will read all the information that they can get their hands on about the industry, firms in the industry, related government regulations, and world events that will affect the industry. Weather, revolutions, and governmental policy changes are just a few of the things that can change the value of securities. Besides reading, much time is spent talking to people to find out what is happening. Once information is gathered, reports must be written to share that information.

If you decide to work as a researcher in the securities industry, you are likely to be working in New York City which is the financial headquarters for more firms than any other place. It is important for you to know that employment in these firms is very cyclical. When times are good, employment is up. After contractions in the market, the number of employees is quickly reduced.

There is a very high level of competition for positions as researchers in the securities industry. It is possible for recent college graduates to enter this field and learn on the job. However, senior researchers will usually have master's degrees in business. More and more also have attained the professional designation chartered financial analyst (CFA) which is obtained after passing a series of three tests and showing experience in the field.

Bank Economists Read

The management team at a bank needs to know what is happening around the world in the economy. At banks that have ten billion dollars or more in deposits, there are economists. The chief economist is likely to have a doctorate in economics. Assistants will probably also have advanced degrees. However, there are entry-level jobs for college graduates with majors in economics. At all levels, reading is done so reports can be written on the economy for the bank and its clients.

Information Givers Are Readers

Repeatedly, you have read about the explosion of information. It is becoming more and more difficult for people in the public and private sectors to keep on top of everything that they should know in order to do their jobs effectively. For that reason, there are firms that are designed to just provide information. Usually, this information will be given in the form of reports, newsletters, speeches, and seminars. The people who supply this information must spend much of their time reading, sorting, and analyzing information. It is another excellent job for bookworms.

A Political Analyst

Julie Sedky reads from 40 to 50 percent of the time on her job as a political analyst. She tries to anticipate and analyze changes in governmental policy that will affect her clients who invest other people's money and don't want to be surprised by what happens in Washington, D.C. She regularly reads such material as the *Washington Post, Wall Street Journal, Bureau of National Affairs Daily Report,* the *Congressional Quarterly,* the *Economist,* as well as excerpts from the *Congressional Record,* materials put out by the Congressional Budget Office and congressional leaders, and a number of private newsletters that tell what's going on in Washington, D.C. Julie's expertise in finding information is such that she sometimes finds her own words in references.

Consultants Are Readers

Consultants act as problem solvers in both the public and private sectors. They are also hired to do work similar to that done in "think tanks." Being a consultant means doing research and analysis for a client. It could involve determining how a scarcity of labor would affect a firm. It might be a question of determining what the major trends in an industry are. No matter what the task, the major tool for accomplishing it is always reading.

While consulting firms vary in size from one-person operations to large international corporations, it is at the larger firms that most entry-level positions are found. It is possible for recent college graduates to get jobs as assistants on projects. You can find out the names of consulting firms by looking at the *National Directory of Consulting Firms.*

Corporate America Needs Readers

The companies that make soap, frozen dinners, paper, and automobiles, as well as the companies that drill for oil or build airplanes, have jobs for bookworms. No matter what a company produces—if it is large enough—there will be jobs that require reading. When you look for a job in corporate America, be sure to investigate areas like human resources, consumer relations, and marketing research.

Human Resources Departments Deal with People

All the hiring and firing of employees, the negotiating of labor agreements, and the determining of benefits and salaries are done in the human resources department at a large company. This is the department that deals with all the people who work at a company. Because the federal government as well as state governments have many laws that spell out exactly how employees are to be treated, employees in this department must do a lot of reading just to keep up with statutory requirements. Then they have to make sure that the people in operations know what these laws are and follow them.

Terri Nelson works for a Fortune 500 food company as a placement specialist. This is not a job that you can just step into because so many companies want college graduates who have experience, and there are few training positions. Many placement specialists begin as clerical workers to get basic business experience. Terri, who has a college degree, worked as a secretary in human resources, a bookkeeper, and a customer service representative before becoming a placement specialist.

During a typical week, Terri may read as many as 500 résumés of people seeking employment with her company. She is looking for people who meet the qualifications for positions that are available. She will review the résumés of all the qualified candidates for a position and then write down questions to ask each of these applicants. Besides reading résumés, she also interviews applicants, conducts an orientation program for new employees, and is currently working on developing a career counseling program.

Terri estimates that she reads 70 to 80 percent of the time on the job. Besides reading résumés, she keeps up with the literature in her field and reads government rulings.

Consumer Relations Departments Deal with Customers

When consumers are unhappy, they write to companies to voice their complaints. Companies receive mail asking why a prize was not included in a cereal box as promised or complaining that a new car has needed numerous adjustments. Companies also receive mail asking for information about such things as products or company activities. Letters may ask why a product isn't biodegradable or why a company is doing business with a certain country.

To keep their customer's goodwill, these letters are answered by employees in customer relations departments. Some employees read and answer mail all day while others alternate between handling mail and telephone calls. Many letters can be answered by form letters which are personalized. Answering some letters requires research. Companies try to answer every letter as accurately as possible.

To get a job answering mail or the telephone, it is not always necessary to have a college degree. Employees do have to demonstrate an ability to write. In addition, here is a job where experience is not required.

Marketing Research

Some companies use information services to find out about marketing trends or how consumers like a product. Other companies have their own marketing research departments and may also use information services. Jobs in marketing research involve keeping in touch with what consumers want through test marketing and product testing. This includes the collection of data through research and reading. The background needed for this job varies from company to company. Many market researchers have a bachelor's degree in business and an advanced degree in marketing, finance, or accounting.

For Further Reading

Since the private sector is where most of the jobs are, this is the area where bookworms should do the most reading. Investigate what careers in different professions offer as well as what jobs with financial institutions and information services are like. Finally, read to find out about what jobs are available in corporate America. Reading the following books is just a starting point for learning about jobs in the private sector:

Alperin, Melvin and Stanley Alperin. *120 Careers in the Health Care Field.* Cambridge, Mass.: Ballinger Publishing Company, 1981.

Bard, Ray and Fran Moody. *Breaking In—The Guide to over 500 Top Corporate Training Programs.* New York: Stonesong Press, Inc.

Billy, Christopher, ed. *Business and Management Jobs 1989.* Princeton, N. J.: Peterson's Guides, 1988.

Birnbach, Lisa. *Going to Work—A Unique Guided Tour Through Coporate America.* New York: Villard Books, 1988.

Cohen, William A. *The Student's Guide to Finding a Superior Job.* San Diego, Calif.: Slawson Communications, Inc., 1987.

Herrup, Steven J. *Exploring Careers in Research and Information Retrieval.* New York: The Rosen Publishing Group, Inc., 1986.

Johnson, Kathleen M., ed. *Investment Banking 1989.* Cambridge, Mass.: President and Fellows of Harvard College, 1988.

Stair, Lila B. and Dorothy Domkowski. *Careers in Business.* Lincolnwood, Ill.: National Textbook Company, 1986.

CHAPTER TEN

More Jobs for Readers
Unlimited Opportunities

S ome people are obsessed with sports; others are addicted to watching television. But true happiness for a bookworm is being paid to read. The purpose of this book is to give bookworms career ideas so that they could realize their dream of reading from 9 to 5. There are still more careers than have been mentioned in this book that are good choices for bookworms. You have to be creative to find some of them. Try browsing through an occupational handbook while thinking of your fondness for reading, and you will discover some of them. You can further expand your list of jobs that require reading by looking at want ads, visiting placement offices in schools, looking at job listings at state and federal employment information offices, and by visiting private employment agencies. Furthermore, here are a few other careers that would be quite satisfying to bookworms.

Translator

A good translator needs to be able to change the written or printed word from one language to another. In order to do this, a translator really needs to be a bookworm in two languages. Translators are especially in demand in businesses, government agencies, and research organizations. Many also work for translation services or free-lance. This is a job that offers both full-time and part-time employment. Bookworms in this field need to be prepared to read all kinds of scientific, technical, commercial, and legal material.

Braille Transcriber

You will not get rich being a braille transcriber, but you will be providing a very important service to blind people who read braille. Braille transcribers turn the printed word in all kinds of material into braille. This can be done by using the function keys on a computer or by using a device called a braille writer. To become proficient in these techniques could take almost two years. Braille transcribing also can be done by just typing exact copy and using special computer programs. The drawbacks to the computer programs are that they can't handle music and mathematics nor can they convey certain formats easily. You can find jobs as a braille transcriber within some school districts and at braille book publishers.

A Books-on-Tape Reader

If you have an excellent reading voice, you may be able to find a job that pays you for reading aloud. As you have probably noticed, more and more books are now available on audio cassettes. People who make these recordings can earn hundreds of dollars a day. The problem is that obtaining one of these jobs is extremely difficult. Many of these readers are professional actors and broadcasters. Furthermore, recording studios are generally located only in metropolitan areas.

Recorder for the Blind

Although you will not get paid to make recordings for the blind, it can be a very satisfying activity for bookworms of all ages. Several organizations can give you information about making these recordings. One organization is Recording for the Blind which will send you a packet of information for volunteer readers if you write to: Recording for the Blind, 20 Roszel Road, Princeton, New Jersey 08540. The only thing that you need to do is to pass the vocal test; then you are ready to read in one of their 31 studios. Volunteers are required to read at least two hours a week and can usually read what interests them. For example, a person with a doctorate in computer science will not be reading a fifth grade reader. And it does take a special volunteer to read a high school or college chemistry book so that blind students can understand the illustrations.

Genealogist

People want to know where their great-grandmother was born and what their great-great-grandfather did for a living. Genealogists help people learn about their ancestors. They research for clues in libraries, church records, court houses, old letters, diaries, newspaper clippings, census records, and government archives. This job requires the keeping of careful records. It also requires people who like to work alone as most genealogists are self-employed. There are no formal educational requirements for becoming a genealogist. Although there are some courses in genealogy which can be helpful, most people acquire their job knowledge through other genealogists and reading material on genealogy.

Abstractor

If you enjoy independent research and doing very exacting work, you might like to be an abstractor for an abstract or title insurance company. This work involves finding all the records on a piece of property so a clear title can be issued when it is sold. Abstractors search through dusty volumes in the basements of court houses and also use computers to find this information. They never stop reading all day long. Although you don't have to have a college education to be an abstractor, some courses in law, real estate, and business can be helpful. It takes from four to six years of on-the-job training to learn how to do all kinds of abstracts. Most abstractors work in metropolitan areas where there are usually job openings for this position.

Wire Editor

If you are curious about what is happening in Australia, South Dakota, and every corner of the world, the job of editor for a news agency that distributes news and photographs to newspapers, radio and television stations, and news magazines is a good job for you. These editors sit in front of a computer screen and read news. They pull copy and edit it and also route copy to clients. It is a job that lets one read for almost eight hours and also puts news of the world at your fingertips.

Author

Without authors, there would not be books, magazines, textbooks, newsletters, pamphlets, bulletins, or newspapers for bookworms to read. Authors aren't just writers; many are bookworms, too. Think of all the research that has to be done by authors. Imagine how much reading James Michener had to do in order to write *Hawaii* or *Centennial.* Consider how much reading was done to write this book. And don't forget the tremendous amount of reading that authors of textbooks do. Indeed, being an author is a superb career for bookworms and other literary types.

Still More Careers

The more you think about the different kinds of material that people read, the longer your list of careers for bookworms will become. There are people who make crossword puzzles and people who make all kinds of tests from achievement tests to intelligence tests. Then there are people who clip what others have written for clipping services.

The Future for Bookworms

The future is bright for bookworms seeking jobs that allow them to be paid for reading. The fastest growing job market is in areas that require education, and as a group bookworms tend to be well-educated. Bookworms will find even more jobs in the future in banking, education, law, research, and management consulting. As far as the public sector goes, most of the growth in government jobs will be at the state and local levels.

Since the number of jobs that require reading is closely tied to the amount of written material, the years ahead should offer bookworms more and more opportunities to combine avocation and vocation as the world is deluged with an ever-increasing volume of written information. It does look like bookworms can look forward to having their best companions, books, with them on their jobs in a great variety of careers.

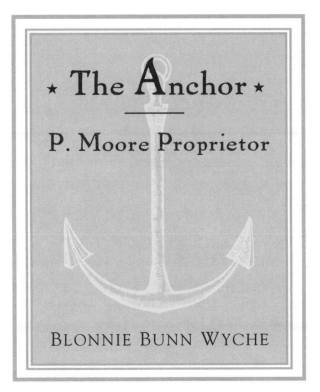

★ The Anchor ★

P. Moore Proprietor

BLONNIE BUNN WYCHE

BANKS CHANNEL BOOKS
Wilmington, NC

For my sister, Frances,
who helps hold the memories

ISBN 1-889199-05-2

Library of Congress Control Number: 2003103305

Cover and book design: Carol Tornatore

Cover illustration: Margaret James

First Edition, 2003

10 9 8 7 6 5 4 3 2 1

Acknowledgments

My sons, David and Graham, have read my stories since they learned to peruse a page of print. Their faith in my work has been a bulwark through many years. Thank you, boys, for always believing in me.

My daughters-in-law, Tracy and Teresa, support my ridiculous schedules and love me anyway. Thank you, girls, for your tremendous comfort and warm hugs.

The Lower Cape Fear Historical Society maintains a wonderful collection of archival material on the Lower Cape Fear region. Archivists Merle Chamberlain and Dr. J. Rush Beeler found a multitude of material for study on the colonial period in the area and pointed me toward other information that I needed. My sincere thanks to Merle and Rush for their loving help.

Thanks to Beverly Tetterton, director of the Local History Room, New Hanover County Public Library, Wilmington, who enjoys sharing information about the Lower Cape Fear area.

On the grounds of the Brunswick Town/Fort Anderson Historic Site in Brunswick County stand the ruins of the original St. Philip's Church and foundations of buildings from the colonial period. The Visitor's Center at the site is open to the public and welcomes researchers and visitors.

The writing group to which I belong began in 1984. For each member, past and present, who has read my material, critiqued my work and extended a helping hand during these years together, my heartfelt appreciation.

Chapter 1

"**P**olly, I can't pin my apron." Six-year-old Cecilia's cry carried down the stairs.

"I can't find my gloves," eleven-year-old Charlotte yelled from their bed chamber. "My gloves are supposed to be with my shawl. Polly, where did you put my gloves?"

Polly sighed at her sisters' complaints as she gave a final stir to the stew simmering on the hearth. She swung the crane away from the fire and wondered again if she had cooked enough food for the crowds that would be in Brunswick today.

"Go on up to your sisters, Miss Polly," said Leah. "I'll see 'bout this." Leah wiped her face with an edge of her petticoat and reached to turn the ham roasting on the spit. "Best look in on Miss Henrietta while you up there."

"Yes, I'll check on her," Polly said. She looked about the tavern room. The table cloths were spread, napkins stacked neatly at each place, candles in holders on the long table and in the wall sconces. A large pewter platter of grapes and apples stood on the counter beside the washed breakfast bowls. Papa, sitting on a stool behind the counter, was silent. He hadn't moved all morning, except to refill his tankard.

"The food ready, Miss Polly," Leah said. "You and the girls best hurry up if you wants to see the new Lieutenant Governor and his wife get off the ship. A heap of folk be going by here for the last while."

"Polly," came Cecilia's plaintive cry.

"I'm coming, sweet Cee," Polly called. "I'm coming."

At the top of the stairs she stopped and looked into her mother's bed chamber. "Good morning, Mama. How are you feeling?"

"Oh, Pauline, I'm so tired." Henrietta tugged at the pillows propped behind her. Black curls spilled from under her night cap and she brushed at them impatiently. "I tried to fix my hair and it must look a fright. It just seems to go every which way this morning."

Polly fluffed the pillows and rearranged them. She quickly brushed her mother's hair and reset her cap. She pulled the bed covers straight and made sure that the quilts were not too tight. "There. Is that better, Mama?"

"Oh, yes, Pauline."

Cecilia came in and handed her sister two brass pins. Quickly Polly fastened the apron in place on Cecilia's bodice. She tucked a stray strand of brown wispy hair under her cap. Looking at her younger sister was almost like looking in a mirror, she thought. They both had the same fine hair that hung limp on a hot day, the same cornflower blue eyes that looked out from under high brows, the same strong frame that came from the Moores. And Cecilia was so smart. She'd finished her first primer and was adding numbers.

The little girl grinned, showing one missing front tooth. She held up her corn husk doll for inspection. Polly took the doll and admired the freshly starched petticoat with embroidery that Cecilia had worked about the hem.

And Charlotte looked just like Mama, Polly thought, with her black curls and dark eyes that made the men in the tavern turn to take a second glance as she passed the serving bowls about the tables. Her beauty, and the same discontent that filled Mama, came from the Dupree side of the family.

"I finally found them," Charlotte said, as she came into their mother's room, waving her crocheted gloves. "Polly, I do wish you'd put my things where they belong."

"Charlotte, I do wish you'd take care of your own things," Polly said.

"Mama, she can't talk to me like that!"

"Hush, girls," Henrietta said.

"The Tryons have a little girl just about my age," Cecilia chattered as they went down the stairs and through the large tavern room. "Did I tell you that before? Do you think we'll see her get off the snow? Do you, Polly?"

The street outside The Anchor was filled with people. Polly saw their cousin, Maurice Moore, ride his roan toward the barn, and knew that meant he would be staying for a visit. A pair of oxen pulled a wagon up the incline from the Cape Fear River and made its slow way through the crowd.

"Where did they all come from?" Cecilia asked, as they walked toward the docks.

"From everywhere, silly goose," Charlotte answered. "They want to see the new Lieutenant Governor as much as we do."

Polly stretched on her toes. It was no use. She could see only the tall masts of the dozen or so ships anchored in the river. It seemed that everyone who lived in Brunswick, Wilmington, and everywhere in-between, had come to greet the new Lieutenant Governor arriving on the *Friendship*. The snow was much larger than the two-masted square-rigged brigs which brought in their cargoes of molasses and Madeira wine, cloth and fine hats, cones of sugar, fruits and nuts, from around the world. Two brigs rode at anchor near the great ship, and men had been unloading cargo all morning. Several sloops, bobbing with the current, seemed to welcome the *Friendship* to the Brunswick port.

Charlotte tugged on Polly's hand. "I can't see," she complained. "You said we would see Mister Tryon."

"I can't see either, Charlotte," she said.

Cecilia pulled on her from the other side and whispered, "Polly, people are pushing me. I feel sick."

Polly scooped up her little sister and held her tight. "Don't you dare be sick, Cee. Don't you dare."

A gust of wind whipped at Polly's petticoats and lifted Charlotte's hat from her head. Before she could reach for it, the hat went sailing over the crowd toward the water.

A crutch appeared from the crowd at the edge of the pier and caught the ribbon on the hat. Quickly the stick twisted around the ribbon and pulled it, hat and all, from sight.

"Polly!" Charlotte shrieked.

"Moze caught it," Polly said. "If we can push over to those hogsheads, we can get your hat and maybe climb up on the barrels to see better."

A roar went up from the people on the dock as the Lieutenant Governor stepped on the deck of the *Friendship*. Mister Tryon waved toward shore and turned to speak to the ship's captain.

Holding Cecilia by one arm and pushing with the hand that still gripped Charlotte's, Polly made a way for the three of them to reach the edge of the dock. Moze, his grin stretching across his wrinkled face, held out his crutch to Charlotte to give her balance while she climbed on a hogshead. Polly lifted Cecilia to stand next to Charlotte and clambered up to join them.

"Might want your bonnet back, Miss Charlotte, ma'am," he said, handing it to her.

Charlotte snatched the hat from his hand, settled it on her head, and tied the blue ribbon firmly under her chin.

"Thank you, Moze," Polly said. "That was a good rescue."

"Miss Charlotte gave me a thank you I'd plumb fall

over," the old man said. "But now you, Miss Polly, say the thank yous for all your family."

A flatboat, filled with containers and crated furniture, pulled up to the pier. Sailors reached out to catch the lines and hitch them to posts on the dock. With directions shouted up from the boat, the men began to lift the lighter boxes up to the waiting hands of workers ready to receive them.

"See Mister Harnett coming," Moze said to Polly. "I wondered when some of those Wilmington dignitaries would show up." He nodded. " 'Course, Judge Maurice been here for a while."

"I know," Polly said. "I saw Cousin Maurice at the barn. I figured he would visit with Papa before he came down here."

"Leaving Judge Maurice Moore and Mister Phillip Moore at the tavern might not of been the best thing, Miss Polly. They be scrapping together since they both in swaddling clothes."

Polly frowned. She couldn't tell her papa what to do. She just had to clean up behind him and keep her mouth shut. She did know that she would be working at the tavern today and that as many coins as possible would go into her own pocket. That was the only thing she could do to keep Papa from gambling it all away. Papa would gamble on anything with anybody.

Another ox-drawn wagon, loaded with containers from the ships, maneuvered its way through the crowd. The wagon driver cracked his whip and the team pulled onto the sand and oyster shell covered street.

Cecilia pulled at Polly's petticoat. "There's a little girl," she said.

"A little girl? Where?"

"On the ship. See?" Cecilia pointed toward the snow.

"And that is Lieutenant Governor Tryon, standing with her," said Polly. "He is a most dignified looking man."

A woman, clasping her flowered hat with one hand and the other clutching the shoulder of the small child, was beside him.

"Oh, Polly, that must be Mistress Tryon! Look at her gown," exclaimed Charlotte. "Isn't that the most beautiful camisole waist you've ever seen! And she must have on ten petticoats to make the top one flare out like that. Now that's the way I want to dress."

"And when you card the wool, and spin the thread, and weave the cloth, and sew the fine seam, dear sister, you can."

"Oh, Polly, you higgle over everything. It takes away all the fun." Charlotte's voice changed to sullen.

"I am a higgler, Charlotte. And you are right. Mistress Tryon is indeed wearing a beautiful gown. And I'm sure she didn't sew a stitch of it." Polly caught her sister's hand and held it for a moment. When would she learn how to handle this difficult sister? They had to stick together—she and Charlotte and Cecilia. They had to.

A man with the Tryons leaned over the rail and passed a case to waiting hands lifted up from the flatboat beside the ship. Then he stepped over the rail and began the slow descent down the side toward the flatboat that would bring him ashore. As soon as he was in the boat, Mister Tryon helped his wife to begin her move down the ladder.

"And now I guess you're going to tell me that ten petticoats would drown her if she fell in the water," Charlotte said. Polly hid a grin. Seeing Mistress Tryon falling in the water, with that many petticoats tied about her waist, was exactly what she was thinking. She couldn't say it to Charlotte. She said, instead, "We will need to go visit in the next few days. Mama has a lovely embroidered waist that I think I can cut down for you to wear."

"Could you, Polly? Oh, look."

They watched as the little girl was carried down the side of the ship in the arms of an officer. As soon as they were all settled, the captain waved the flatboat off, and the sailors began rowing toward the dock.

"Polly?" said a man's voice.

She turned to see Daniel Cooper standing beside her. Her stomach fluttered, just as it did every time he came close. It didn't matter that Daniel was indentured. It didn't matter that sometimes he was at The Anchor and sometimes he was across the river at Cousin Maurice's plantation. Daniel tugged at the shock of yellow hair falling across his forehead and looked at her, his blue eyes somber. Even as she clutched her hands to her middle to make the flutters stop, she knew that he would not be here if something hadn't happened at the tavern.

"Your father's getting full drunk, Polly. He and Judge Moore had a fight," Daniel said quietly.

"He's been gloomy all day," she said. "Can he tend the tavern?"

"No, he can't. That's why I came to get you."

Polly sighed and turned to Charlotte.

"I heard, Polly. I heard. We have to go."

"Yes, we do. You and Cecilia are going to have to help me serve."

Charlotte tugged at her bonnet ribbon. "I know. Serve and wash up and wipe tables and dodge around those stinking men with their pipes and drinks and then serve some more." She climbed down from the hogshead and made her way through the crowd. Polly followed, holding tightly to Cecilia's hand. She looked for Daniel, but he had disappeared.

She didn't know Moze had followed her until she was

up on the street. The old man planted his crutch and swung his one leg, planted the crutch and swung his leg. By the time they reached the tavern he was out of breath, but he had kept up with her the full distance. He settled on a bench under the overhang outside the door. Several men loitered about the tavern yard, talking.

Polly stepped inside The Anchor. She blinked, adjusting her eyes to the dimness of the room. Papa slumped at a table next to the counter. He gave a little snore, reached out toward the wooden cup on the table, and then just let his hand rest there. Broken crockery lay scattered everywhere. Leah was sprawled on the floor, her back propped against the ballast stone wall of the fireplace, her face covered in blood.

Chapter 2

Polly felt a nudge at her back as Charlotte pushed her way past her into the tavern room. "What happened? Oh, what a mess this will be to clean up."

Cecilia clung to Charlotte's skirt. "Poor Papa," she whispered.

Polly took a deep breath. "Charlotte, turn the spit. We have to have that meat for the men eating here today. Cecilia, get the broom and start cleaning the floor. Be careful not to cut yourself. Leah, can you get up?"

Leah pulled herself from the floor and stood gripping the tall mantel. She swayed as if her legs could not hold her. Polly quickly pushed a short bench over to her and helped her sit. Then she ran to the door.

"Moze, see if you can find Daniel." Polly caught her breath. "Now, Moze, please."

The old man nodded to her and pulled on his crutch to help him stand. Polly watched his slow progress as he moved across the dirt street before she went back inside the tavern.

Cecilia finished sweeping up the crockery and put the brush broom behind the door. Charlotte worked at the fireplace turning the huge ham and stirring the pot of stew simmering over the low flames. She added a piece of wood to the side of the fire and poked it into place to keep the heat as even as possible under the smaller pots, filled with pumpkin and simmering apples, hanging from chains attached to the iron lug-pole.

Polly turned her attention to Leah. She wiped the drying blood from Leah's face and looked at the gash that ran from the woman's hair line to her chin. The cut had just missed her eye.

"What happened, Leah?"

"Judge Moore and Mister Phillip was in a big argument 'bout money, from what I could hear." Leah pressed a cloth against her forehead where the cut was beginning to bleed again. "It's 'bout money Mister Phillip owes to somebody and Judge Moore talked about family honor and paying up."

"Then what happened?"

"Well, the judge got through his sermon to Mister Phillip. Leastwise, it sounded like preaching. Then he left to go down to see the ships and the governor man. That's when Mister Philip's drinking really got strong and he was throwing plates and tankards all over the place."

"And you got in the way of a plate," Polly said.

"Yes, Miss Polly."

Two men came in the door and called for ale. Charlotte filled their wooden tankards and slipped the pennies in her pocket before she glanced toward her big sister.

Polly nodded her approval. Charlotte smiled at her and went back to work.

Several men entered calling for drinks. A farmer and his wife, with their three children, came in to eat before traveling to their home several miles out in the country. A group of junior officers from one of the ships asked for ham and wine. As Polly moved from hearth to counter she watched Cecilia carry platters of food, never spilling a drop. She watched Charlotte carve portions from the ham and ladle out stew and vegetables. Her sisters were such good girls. Charlotte would pout about things, but when she was needed, she was always there. Oh, if only and if only and if only—and then she did not even know how to complete the thought.

Polly helped Leah to a stool behind the counter where she could sit out of the way. She could tell that the woman was badly hurt. When Daniel came into the tavern room she hurried to him.

"Please help Leah down to her cabin. She can't stay here bleeding like she is. She really should be in bed. And then can you get Papa out of here? I need that table."

"Thoughts of where I should take him?" Daniel asked.

"I don't care." She could see people milling about in the yard, talking in groups, waiting for seating. She looked at the crowded room and threw up her hands. "Just do something."

Daniel nodded. He talked to Leah for a moment and then watched as she wandered slowly out of the tavern. Then he pulled Phillip from his chair and walked him out the door.

When she realized how many men were coming up to the tavern to eat, Polly climbed on a bench to take down a pork shoulder from a hook in the ceiling and started it roasting over the fire. Into the pan of drippings, below the meat, she diced potatoes and carrots and onions, letting them cook as she turn the spit. The fragrance of ham and stew, baked apples and yeast bread, filled the room. The three girls cooked and served, washed dishes and served some more.

Coins filled Polly's pockets. Twice she went behind the counter to place pennies and shillings in a pewter bowl.

When she had a minute, as the sun was setting, Polly slipped out the front door. A light breeze, blowing from the river, gave a nip to the fall air and she hugged her arms about herself.

There had been a good crowd today. She felt the coins in her pocket. And a good collection, too. If Charlotte and Cecilia had as much as she, then they had a very good collection indeed. If Papa had been behind the counter there would have been rounds of free drinks and great servings of food given away. Every piece of money she couldn't hide from him would have been gambled away. Papa's gambling must have been what Cousin Maurice had come to see him about.

"What are we going to do? What are we going to do about Papa's drinking and gambling?" Polly said softly.

"People been asking what to do with Mister Phillip for a long time."

Polly whirled about to face the voice.

" 'Scuse me, please. Didn't mean to startle you, Miss Polly," Moze said. "But you do seem to have unmuzzled thoughts tonight. You talking to that old oak tree? Or maybe you talking to some haint that you think might wander up and give you answers?"

She shivered and wrapped her arms closely to her chest.

"Miss Polly, you need a shawl if you going to stand in the night air."

She rubbed her arms. "Yes, it is cool tonight. Moze, have you been sitting there since we came from the docks?"

" 'Cept when I went to find young Mister Daniel, I be here. I be thinking I too old to raise another generation of Moores."

Polly smiled. "And just how many of us have you raised?"

"Well, now." Moze shifted his weight on the bench. "There was Mister James Moore, when he come into South Carolina. He bought me so young he raised me like a son in his big plantation house. He was the governor there, you know."

Moze held up a finger. "And along come his young'uns for me to teach like Mister James taught me. There was the one that was Colonel Maurice Moore and his brother Roger. Mister Roger built that big place over at Orton. They didn't call him King Roger for nothing, Miss Polly. He always did think he was suppose to be in charge of things. They had a brother named Nathaniel, too. He done pretty well."

Moze held up another finger. "Then Colonel Maurice had a bunch of girls. But when he had a boy he sent for me to help him. Folks call him Judge Maurice Moore now, but he was just a tree-climbing little boy when I first got hold of him. And your papa, Mister Phillip, was born to one of their relations and the Colonel took him in to bring up."

Through the stillness of the night the sounds of a guitar faintly echoed from deep in the woods. Polly tilted her head to listen to the sad lament.

The old man shook his head. "And when your papa, Mister Phillip, married Mistress Henrietta, the Colonel gave me to this family. Guess he thought I might still help out. But it's hard to help Mister Phillip."

"All boys. Are we your first girls to raise?" Polly thought of the two little graves under the oaks at the back of the house. She didn't remember much about her first brother. She had been young then and the baby had only lived a few weeks. She did remember the second one. He was so little, so cold and still, as she helped Mama bathe and dress him for his tiny casket. She remembered what she'd said about Charlotte when she held her for the first time. "She's warm, Mama. She's squirmy and warm."

"Who's warm? Miss Polly, you talking strange tonight."

"I was just thinking out loud, Moze. It didn't mean anything, really." She shook her head. "I'd best get back inside and start closing down."

Cecilia was asleep on a bench by one of the tables. Charlotte sat slumped next to her. Four men were finishing a card game, and she knew they would soon leave.

She banked down the fire, so there would be hot coals in the morning to start the breakfast meal. She bolted the door behind the four men who made their quiet way out into the night. Carrying a candle she guided the sleepy Cecilia and tired Charlotte up the stairs toward their bed chambers.

At the top of the steps she heard her mother's call. "Pauline? Is that you, Pauline?"

"Charlotte, get Cecilia tucked in." Polly gave her sister's shoulder a little pat before she turned to go into the other chamber.

"Yes, Mama. I'm here," she said.

"It's so late."

Polly sat on the edge of the bed. "We were in the tavern, Mama. Charlotte and Cecilia are good help with the serving. There are so many ships in the river right now that we had a big crowd. We all had a lot to do."

"Are the little ones in bed?"

"Oh, yes, Mama." Polly took her mother's hand. "Are you feeling better?"

Henrietta shook her head.

"Mama, you'll be better when the baby comes." Polly stood and moved toward the door. "Good night, Mama. Sleep well."

As she tugged off her camisole and petticoats to slip her night dress over her head, Polly heard her mother call her again. "Pauline, I wanted to hear about the new Lieutenant Governor and his wife. You didn't tell me anything about them. Pauline, you're not asleep, are you?"

"No more today. I can't look after anybody else today," Polly whispered. She pulled the quilt up to her chin and closed her eyes.

Chapter 3

An early morning cardinal, bursting with exuberance, whistled "sweet girl, sweet girl" from just outside her window. Polly lay still for a minute, listening to its song as first light slowly made a path into the room. Then she groped with the covers that had twisted about her in the night and turned to see her sisters still deep in sleep. She used the chamber pot in the corner of the room. The water pitcher was almost empty. She poured a little of the cold water on a cloth and scrubbed her face and neck. From a peg on the wall she took down two old petticoats and tied them about her middle. She shrugged her arms into a chemise and then covered her shoulders with a large kerchief. She pinned her old work apron over everything. She pushed her long brown hair under a mobcap and turned to look out the window.

The bird had flown away. She could see that a brigantine was beginning to move slowly out with the tide. There were several men working on the docks, loading a wagon. Men would be arriving soon wanting breakfast.

She covered the chamber pot and carried it with her as she went down to the kitchen. Unbolting the door in the lower room she stepped out in time to see Daniel coming from the barn. Quickly she made her way through the dew-damp grass to the necessary house to dump the chamber pot and leave it there.

Daniel had set the milk pail on the counter. He knelt

and blew gently on the coals at the hearth. Polly handed
him a handful of lightwood splinters and watched as the
first tiny flames began to grow. While Daniel tended the
fire, she measured out meal and water, and stirred them
together in a iron kettle to make the morning mush. As
soon as the fire began to burn brightly, Daniel lifted the
kettle to hang it from a hook over the fire and stirred the
mixture with strong strokes.

She loved to watch him work. She loved to see the
muscles stretch across his back when he moved. Whether
he was doing tasks here in the tavern or taking care of the
horses at the barn or just striding down the street, it was a
joy to treasure the sight of him. She would never, ever let
him know how she felt. "A fine help you were last night,"
she said.

"More help than you can know," he answered.

"What did you do with Papa?"

"Tied him up in the barn," Daniel said. "You need
more water in the kettle."

Polly took down the water bucket from its hook on the
wall and went out to get water from the well. Back inside
she added a gourd full of water to the kettle as Daniel continued to stir the mixture. She added a spoonful of salt and
then poured in a measure of molasses.

Daniel nodded. "Honey's good in mush, but I do like
molasses."

"I know," Polly said. She washed a dozen hen eggs and
put them in water in a small pot, which she hung from the
lug-bar. She took the leftover ham that she had covered
with cloth the night before and began to pick the remains
of the meat from the bone. When she had a small heap of
ham on a platter she put the bone in another kettle and
hung it, too, over the fire. She saw Daniel add water to the
mush and then pour in another gourd of molasses.

She hid her smile. "Tell me about Papa," she said.

"I told you. He was fighting when he came to, so I gave him more rum. When he passed out again I tied his feet to a post."

"You really did tie him up?"

"Well, when he wakes up he can get loose. I just tied his feet."

Polly giggled. She could picture her tall, strong papa fighting a barn support post and trying to get his feet free. After all he'd drunk yesterday he would be in a sorry shape.

"With Mister Phillip taken care of, I went over to Governor Dobbs's house at Russellborough. I knew they would need help with the horses. That was some fine party there last night for the Tryons. Judge Moore brought his wife. William Moore had his family from Orton. Mister Howe came over from Wilmington. Mister William Dry left the custom's office to attend. He brought his wife, too."

Daniel stooped to add a log to the fire and picked up the spoon to give another stir to the mush. "There was some woman there visiting from Wilmington. She strutted around putting on airs." Daniel did a wiggly step that swayed his hips and then tossed his head back. His hand fluttered the wooden spoon like a fan.

Polly laughed. "Did you see the Tryons? What are they like?"

"Seem to be nice. Or at least as nice as near-royalty gets. He just might make an acceptable governor. Mistress Tryon was gracious. She played the spinet and sang for the company. Mighty pretty music it was, too."

"Justina? Oh, Daniel, did you see Justina?" Polly put a stack of crockery plates down on the counter. "How did she look? What was she wearing?"

"Polly, I know she's your friend, but I didn't notice

what she was wearing or how she looked." He put the spoon on the mantel and started out the door. "We need wood."

Justina was the only real friend she had ever had. Two winters ago, when Mama wasn't having a baby and Papa hadn't lost all of their money, they sent her to school in Wilmington. Several families had hired a tutor, and Cousin Maurice made arrangements for her to room at the Davis home. Justina Davis was a year older than she was, but because Mama had taught her so well at home, they studied some of the same subjects. It was wonderful for ten whole months, until Papa almost lost the tavern on a gamble, Cecilia got sick with measles, and Mama needed her to come home. She and Justina had exchanged letters, but it wasn't the same.

And then old Governor Dobbs, at the age of seventy-five, decided that Justina Davis should be his new wife. The thing Polly couldn't understand was that Justina's mother thought it was a grand idea for her fifteen-year-old daughter to marry the old man.

Justina had invited her to the governor's house at Russellborough twice. She and the girls had walked over both afternoons they were invited, but Governor Dobbs had been there each time, and they hadn't had a chance to talk at all. The governor grumbled about his gout. He lisped around his false teeth when he talked about the weather that made his arthritis worse. He patted Justina's hand and asked her to write a letter for him. On that second visit Justina didn't even have time to serve them tea.

Cecilia wandered into the tavern room. She had dressed herself and her petticoats were bunched every-which-way. Her apron was tied in front and hung down her back. "The chamber pot was gone, Polly," she said.

"Good morning, sweet Cee. The pot is in the necessary. When you've finished out there please rinse out the pot and take it back up to our room."

The little girl nodded at her and went out.

Leah should have been here by now, Polly thought. She should be the one emptying the chamber pots and taking the water up for the pitchers. She should be upstairs helping Mama bathe and sit up in bed.

When Cecilia came back in, Polly asked, "Did you see Leah?"

The child shook her head.

"Well, take the chamber pot up and tell Charlotte it's time to come down."

"She fusses at me," Cecilia said.

Polly gave the little girl a hug and began to straighten her petticoats. There was something hard knotted at her waist that bunched up the fabric. "What's this?" she asked.

"Shhh," Cecilia whispered. "You told me to keep the money hidden."

"Oh, Cee," Polly said, and hugged her again. "I think you can put this handkerchief under the pillows in your feather bed. Papa isn't going to look there. And even if Charlotte fusses, you tell her it's time to get up."

A drover called from the open door. "Er ye serving a morning meal?"

"That we are," Polly answered. "Come in and have a seat."

The drover and his wife from Cross Creek settled near the fire while Polly filled tankards of cider for them. Papa had bought apples and wheat from them in the past. She ladled up a bowl of mush and put it on the table, with smaller bowls for them to eat from. The man and his wife took their own spoons from their pockets, mixed ham into the mush, and ate without speaking. When they were ready to go, the man put a penny into Polly's hand. The woman reached deep into her pocket and gave Polly two pepper corns.

"Wonderful," Polly said. "Thank you so much. Pepper corns do make such good seasoning."

The woman nodded shyly.

In a few minutes there were several more customers. Charlotte reached to take a plate from her hands before Polly even knew she was there to help with the serving. An hour later the last of the mush had been eaten, the ham and boiled eggs were gone, and Polly fingered the coins in her pocket.

A little girl, not as big as Charlotte, sidled into the room and stood with her hands hanging by her side. "Miss," she said. "Miss Polly."

"What is it?" Polly asked.

"Leah sick this morning. She ain't able to come up here." With the message delivered, the child fled.

"Oh, my," Polly said. "I guess I'd better go see to Mama. Charlotte, can you get vegetables cooking with that ham bone? We have beans and peas and some pumpkin would add to the flavor. And corn. Corn would be good."

Charlotte made a terrible face at her, but she reached for a large pumpkin that stood on the counter and began to carve it.

"Save the seeds," Polly said.

"I don't want to be doing this, you know," Charlotte answered as she worked.

Daniel had come in with the wood and stood by the hearth, eating his breakfast.

She turned to him. "It would be nice to have a duck or goose to roast. Can you hunt this morning? And all this needs to be set to rights." She flung out her arms. "There's no end to it. Never! Never!"

Upstairs she bathed and changed her mother, making

her as comfortable as she knew how. She shook out the bed linens and fluffed the pillows. From the bed covers a paper fluttered to the floor. It was their invitation to the party last night at Russellborough.

"Mama, why didn't you tell me we had been invited to have dinner last night with the new lieutenant governor and his family?"

"You couldn't go without me, Polly. And I couldn't go. I didn't want you to be disappointed or upset."

"Oh, Mama." Polly fled to the hall so her mother would not see her tears. She had been to the parties that the Davises gave in Wilmington. She had listened to the conversations and the music. She had been to one of the dances they gave, where she watched and even danced a few bars of the music with Justina's father. It was all so wonderful.

Well, there was nothing to be done with her disappointment. She dried her eyes with her apron, squared her shoulders, and went back in her mother's room. She walked straight to the cedar chest, in the corner of the room, looking for the bodice she had told Charlotte about. It was there. The beautiful gold and silver embroidery thread pattern was as elegant as she remembered. If she wore it with her green wool petticoat, Charlotte would be dressed as fine as even Mistress Tryon. Polly sat down beside her mother while she ripped out the seams of the bodice and decided how to rework the fabric.

As she sewed Polly told her mother about the *Friendship* and about Charlotte's bonnet sailing off her head. She described the Tryons and how Cecilia had spotted their little daughter at the railing of the ship. She told everything she could remember, except that Daniel had taken a drunk Papa away.

As soon as Mama dozed off, Polly hurried to the tavern room. There was much to be done to prepare for the next group who would come seeking food and news.

After they had served the noon meal to a dozen men, she left Cecilia napping and Charlotte shelling late fall peas while she walked down to Leah's cabin. The little girl who had delivered the message to her that morning was rolling a hoop along the narrow path between two of the cabins. She skidded to a stop and darted on the porch of one of the buildings as if to seek shelter.

Polly called out Leah's name from the steps. A voice answered her in greeting and she went inside. From the light of a small fire that burned at the hearth she could see Leah lying on a cot in the corner of the small room.

"Miss Polly, you didn't have to come down here to the cabins," Leah said.

"Of course I had to come. The message you sent said you were not well. It's not like you to be sick."

"This is Marie, come to help me," Leah said. She gestured toward a woman sitting at a trestle table that dominated the center of the room.

"Sick she be," Marie said.

"And what is wrong?" Polly asked.

"Evil be in she head."

Polly walked over and felt Leah's check. Her skin was hot to the touch. The whole side of her face was swollen. "Oh, Leah, what can I do?" she asked.

Leah took Polly's hands in both of hers. "You just look after my Henrietta. I been with her since she was a little girl growing up in Edenton. And I followed her to Charleston in South Carolina when she married Mister Phillip. And I followed her to Brunswick when you was a tiny baby. My Henrietta ain't strong, Miss Polly. She needs tending."

"I'll look after Mama. Who is this, looking after you?" Polly asked.

Marie stood. Her turban-wrapped head threatened the

rafters of the cabin. Her crimson petticoats swept the floor. Her broad shoulders were wrapped in a dark blue fabric that covered a lighter blue chemise beneath. A thick necklace of shells and nuts and berries hung to her waist.

"I be here." Her voice had a low, sing-song quality to it. She smacked her right fist into the palm of her left hand. "The evil be gone from she head two days more."

Polly's toes curled inside her slippers. She had never before seen anyone like this light-skinned foreign looking woman. "Leah?" she pleaded.

"It be all right, Miss Polly. Marie will look after me and there's nothing for you to be scared of. You go on."

At the door Polly looked back.

"Take care of your mama, Miss Polly," Leah said.

Polly nodded and walked slowly back to the tavern.

Chapter 4

The Moseley boys and a young cabin boy from one of the ships were playing marbles. They had drawn their circle in the dirt at the edge of the street. A marble rolled away and hit the toe of Polly's slipper. She scooped up the clay marble and held it out toward them.

"It's mine," said the Moseley boy, and reached up to take it from her.

Several sailors from ships on the river were playing a game of quoits they'd set up in the tavern yard. The metal ring pinged on the hob as one of the men scored.

Charlotte and her friend Charity were see-sawing on a board Daniel had fixed over a stump. "See-saw, Margery Daw, Jack shall have a new master," Charlotte sang.

"He shall have but a penny a day because he can't work any faster," Charity Moseley sang back to answer her. "Poor Jack."

Cecilia waved to her from under the oak tree where she had set out acorn cups and leaf plates on a board. She was serving tea to her corn husk dolls. Two yellow kittens played under her chair. Polly knew that the next time she saw those kittens they would be in Cecilia's bed.

Moze sat on the bench by the tavern door. As Polly approached he held up a bowl for her to see. She took it and examined the polished surface.

"It's beautiful," she said. "Is it maple?"

He nodded. "I found a good maple tree limb with several bowls in it. There might even be a platter or a plate there. With all the crockery that got broke here last night, I reckoned you might need some new bowls. I started on this one last night. I'll have another one by tomorrow this time."

"Thank you, Moze. How did you get the wood so smooth?"

"White beach sand, Miss Polly. Rubbing and rubbing with fine white beach sand till the wood is ready to speak to you. Then you got a smooth finish."

"I've been down to see about Leah. Moze, do you know anything about a woman named Marie?"

Moze's eyes grew large and his brows almost met his hair line. His lips shaped an O, and he held his breath for so long that Polly wanted to breathe for him. Then whistled air escaped from his mouth. "Did you see her, Miss Polly?"

"Well, yes. I saw her and talked with her. Who is she?"

Moze took a deep breathe. "She is Holy Woman. She is Healer." The old man leaned forward. "She talked to you?"

Polly's toes curled and she squealed, "Moze, is she a witch?"

"No. No, Miss Polly. Marie is not witch." He was silent for a moment. "I will tell you some things 'bout Marie. She part Tuscarora and part Spanish. She part Negro and part white. She live back in the forest. She gather herbs and make medicines and come when she be needed. She be free. She be Healer."

"But why haven't I seen her before?"

Moze didn't answer. He pulled himself up with his crutch and struggled for balance on his one leg before he took a step away from her. Very quietly he said, "Miss Polly, pay heed. If Marie talk to you, then you best listen to her. It must mean you going to need her healing one of these days."

Polly shivered as she watched Moze hobble across the road. She clasped the bowl to her chest with both hands. Her thoughts flew to Mama, for if anyone needed healing it was her mother. Could a Healer help Mama?

Slowly she walked through the door of the tavern. Papa was sitting on a stool behind the counter. His hair was disarrayed, with bits of straw poking out like he'd tangled with a scarecrow in the corn field. His eyes and nose were red and puffy. His linen shirt had a torn sleeve. Her normally properly dressed father seemed like a stranger sitting there. He lifted a tankard and drank deeply. He looked at her, but she wasn't sure he saw her.

The mail pouch was on a table near the hearth. Someone had pawed through the letters and papers, scattered now across the table and spilled on the floor. Polly picked up the strewn letters and began to sort them. There were two copies of the New Bern newspaper, the *North Carolina Magazine*, both dated weeks before. The newspaper from New Bern was the only paper printed in their part of the colony until Mister Steuart began publishing the *North Carolina Gazette* and *Weekly Post Boy* in Wilmington in the fall. She had not yet seen a copy of Mister Steuart's newspapers. She didn't know who had sent for these copies from New Bern, but everyone who came into the tavern would read the news and discuss its importance. She arranged the letters on the mantel so that folks coming in could look to see if anything was addressed for them. Then she sat by the window to read one of the newspapers.

Cousin Maurice came in and tossed his hat toward a peg on the wall by the door.

Papa poured him a measure of beer and stood listening to him. The men were talking so quietly at first that she couldn't hear the words, so she continued reading.

Then Papa yelled, "No, Maurice. That I can not do."

"Why can you not?"

"Henrietta depends on her. And my wife is too ill just now to be upset by anything. There will have to be another way." Papa slammed his tankard on the counter. "Another way, by god. But Leah stays with Henrietta."

Polly's first thought, as she listened to the confrontation, was that Papa, for once, was standing up to his older cousin. Then the full impact of their meaning hit her. Papa's debts must be terrible for the men to even think about selling a valuable woman like Leah.

"Then, Phillip, your other option is the one we discussed previously. A fine offer has been made for Pauline."

Peeping around the edge of the newspaper, Polly saw Cousin Maurice hand Papa his tankard. Papa filled it from the barrel and handed it back.

What option? What offer? Were they going to sell her as an indentured servant to some plantation up the Cape Fear River? Were they going to marry her off to an old man who would pay Papa's debts so he could have her in his bed? And what would happen to her sisters?

Mama had taught her to read and write and cipher. Mama had taught her to sew and spin, to knit and embroider. But Mama was too sick to teach the little girls. She was the one who had taught Charlotte her letters and was teaching Cecilia now.

Leah had taught her to cook and measure the ingredients for cakes, to bank the fire on the hearth and to make candles and soap. Leah had taught her how to starch petticoats and iron the aprons. But Charlotte hadn't learned these skills yet, and she wouldn't listen to Leah.

Moze had taught her to barter with the tradesmen on the docks. He had explained bargaining and trading. He had taught her the value of coins when exchange wasn't enough to get the goods she needed for the tavern. But Moze was getting old.

The men were still talking, their voices low again. She folded the paper and walked over to them.

Cousin Maurice's face turned all shades of red and he sputtered in his beer. Papa looked at her as if he did not know who she was.

She nodded at them both, but addressed the older man. "Cousin Maurice, it is always a pleasure to have you here."

"You heard us," he said. It wasn't a question.

"Cousin Maurice, if you have problems with Papa, then it's none of my business. If you have problems with the tavern, it concerns me greatly." Polly put her hands behind her back so that the men could not see how badly they were shaking. She forced her voice to stay even and tried to remember every word she had ever read in Locke's books.

All that studying she had done in Wilmington had to account for something. Ownership of property was a point that John Locke stressed in his writing. It was the value of property that she needed to argue for these men to understand her position. She was a property they needed here at The Anchor.

"Sir, I have run the tavern since I came back from Wilmington almost two years ago. I have ordered the goods. I have cooked the meals. I have served and cleaned and generally made a welcome trade. The only thing I have not been able to do is to pay the bills. The money is in Papa's hands."

She hoped she was not betraying her father. Right now she had to save herself and her sisters.

Cousin Maurice frowned at her. "Do you have a proposal?"

"Yes, sir. Allow me to have the monies coming in each day. I will pay the bills."

Maurice turned to Papa. "If you don't have the money, you can't gamble it away."

Papa just stood there, not saying a word.

Then Maurice looked at Polly. "How long do you think it would take you to have this place on a paying basis?"

"Sir, if it's just the running of the tavern, six months would have things to rights. If it includes paying off some big debt, then it's a different matter. I would have to have information about the debt and decide how much each day would go toward paying it off."

"Maurice, you're not going to tell her!" Papa yelled.

"No, Phillip, I will not do that to you. But you are going to turn over the running of the tavern to her." He slapped the counter. "By god, if Polly had only been a boy!"

"Maurice, you can't give her the tavern," Papa said.

"Phillip, if I sound like a lawyer and a judge, so be it. You listen to me. Listen carefully." Cousin Maurice leaned against the counter, his face close to Papa's. "I am taking over the guardianship of this property. I have the legal authority, and the duty, to take this action because you have become incapable of managing your affairs or the affairs of your family."

Cousin Maurice turned to her. "Polly, under the guardianship laws, I can appoint an underage person to a special duty. On behalf of a minor orphan, married woman, or other incompetent, the Next of Friend law gives you the right to control this business and the other properties involved." He sat down at a table. "Polly, I declare that you are an incompetent. Get me paper and quill."

Polly wasn't sure just what kind of bargain she had

made, but Cousin Maurice was a judge and he knew the law. If she had to be called an incompetent to do a competent job, then she could put up with the label. She ran upstairs to get paper from her writing folder. She selected the best quill she had and collected the ink bottle from her mantel. She watched as Cousin Maurice wrote out the document that gave her management of The Anchor and all properties belonging to one Phillip Moore. He dated it—October 11, 1764. She signed under his name.

Papa's hands were shaking so badly that his signature was all jogglely and the ink splattered up on his torn shirt.

Cousin Maurice dripped wax from the candle burning on the counter and turned his ring to press his seal under the names. He handed the paper to her. "I suggest you keep this in a safe place, Miss Pauline Moore. A very safe place."

Within the hour Papa had packed his clothes in his traveling portmanteau and was gone, riding his horse— their only horse now that Papa had gambled them all away—behind Maurice's. What had he said to Mama? What had their good-bye been like? Polly only knew, as she watched them leave, that they were taking the ferry at the Haulover. She supposed their destination was Wilmington.

Poor Papa. Would he really have sold Leah? Or pledged her, his oldest daughter, to someone in marriage? Would either of the men have listened to her if she hadn't caught them talking and embarrassed them?

She clutched the legal paper, knowing as sure as she was standing there that it was her life line. Cousin Maurice was a rough man in some things. He cursed and drank and didn't always use his napkin. But when he gave his word, he kept it. And he would see to Papa. They were family.

She ran up to her room and put the paper with her other writing materials. For now that was the safest place for it. She peeped in her mother's chamber and saw that she seemed to be sleeping. The girls were still playing outside. She put on a fresh apron and reset her mobcap to reassure herself. Inside, her stomach was churning and she felt seriously afraid. She was the proprietor of the tavern. She was legally declared an incompetent.

Chapter 5

As she started down the street, Polly thought of how
many times her world had changed. The months she had
spent in Wilmington were so very different from her life
here in Brunswick. Taking over the duties of the tavern
when she got back, especially with Papa drinking so much
more, was backbreaking work at times. Fear was her constant companion—fear of not having enough supplies or
enough food for the days when extra patrons came to the
tavern, fear for her mother's health and the baby that was
coming in the winter, fear that she could not teach her
sisters when they needed guidance. There was the constant
fear that someone would ask for her in marriage, for she had
known for a long time Papa thought that an advantageous
union was a solution to his financial problems. And she had
no one to talk with about how she felt.

She saw neglect everywhere. The woodpile was so low
that she knew they would need firewood within the week.
Who was responsible for cutting the wood? Papa? Mister
Colston? Mister Colston was foreman of the turpentine
gathering and all the maritime products coming from the
forest and the sawmill. He and Papa would huddle over a
tankard of beer or ale and talk so low she never could over-
hear any of their conversations. She would have to find out
about the maritime products.

A slave from the sawmill had brought the last load of firewood. His name was Jeremiah. He was a tall, light-skinned Negro who went about the work of unloading the wood with a whistle on his lips. She would have to check on that today.

Leaves were deep enough that she shuffled clumps of them into her slippers. The yard would have to be swept. Charlotte and Cecilia could do that. Daniel had done most of the hunting for the last year. She would need to talk with him about game for the table.

The tavern sign—The Anchor ~ P. Moore, Proprietor —now meant Pauline Moore, not Phillip. The decisions were hers, no Papa to blame. A rush of fear twisted her stomach and she stood, unable to take a step.

Cecilia called, "Come visit with me, Polly. You will like my tea."

"I'm sure your tea is very good, Cee. Invite me another time. Right now I have to take care of some business."

Charlotte, sitting on the see-saw watching the boys at their game of marbles, called, "What business?"

"Some things I need to see about for the tavern."

"Oh. For the tavern," Charlotte said. "It's always about the tavern."

Polly bit her lip to keep from scolding. Charlotte thought her nothing but a higgler. Well, fussy or not, competent or not, she had to care for her sisters. She stepped into the street and made her way to the blacksmith's forge. Mister Edward was making barrel hoops and she waited for him to finish hammering the hot metal before she spoke. "I need an iron box, Mister Edward. Something about so big." Polly measured a foot square in the air. "And it needs to have a stout lock. Can you make something like that for me?"

"Need it in a hurry?" Mister Edward asked.

"I need it soon."

"It's the lock that will take the most time. I can make it between tasks, I guess. I have the rest of these barrels to finish." He gestured toward a pile of staves stacked at one end of his shop.

"If I decide to make you a box, it should be ready in a week." The blacksmith put the end of a long, narrow piece of iron on the coals and worked the bellows to make the fire hotter. With his hands gripping the tongs that held the metal he glanced at her. "How's Phillip going to pay me, Miss Polly? He lost money on the horse race last week."

She took a shilling from her apron pocket and put it on the work bench. "I will pay you, Mister Edward. I will pay you for any work I request."

The blacksmith nodded and plunged the hot iron in a barrel of water. A hiss exploded from the barrel and streaming vapor filled the air.

"Your box, with a stout lock, will be ready in one week then."

"Thank you, Mister Edward." She walked out of the open shed toward the pier. William Dry should be in his office this time of afternoon. As collector of the Port he would be the one to answer her question about duties to be paid. As kinsman he would not turn her away. They were all cousins and he had known Phillip since he was a boy.

Mister Dry greeted her and motioned to a chair in front of his desk. Polly put her hands under her apron and held them tightly.

"Some dress goods to order, Little Polly?" Mister Dry asked. "Special shoes or lace from Brussels, perhaps?"

She took a deep breath. "Mister Dry, Papa has been called away and I will be making the orders for the tavern for the next few months. I needed to ask if I place my orders through you or if I go directly to the ship's captain. I also need to know if you accept chits or Colonial paper for provisions. If you do not, then what per cent of specie do I have to pay with my order?"

Mister Dry pushed back his chair. He could not have looked more shocked if she had turned into a mongoose, ready to leap across the desk and grab him by the throat.

Polly pressed on. "I understand that the Sugar Act is being very strictly enforced. The duties on molasses are particularly being looked at by the customs inspectors because of the past smuggling. Can you help me with the details of the duties?"

The collector of customs pulled a handkerchief from his pocket and wiped his forehead. He drew his chair back up to the desk and blew his nose. He shuffled several papers around, and still looking at the desk, cleared his throat.

"Well, Polly, you seem to have done some research on the matter of duties and taxes." He shook his head and wiped his forehead again. "The Sugar Act taxes trade on sugar and coffee. On wines and other things. And of course, on molasses. But you know something of that."

Mister Dry picked up some papers from his desk and fanned himself. "Maurice said you should have been the man in the family." He stopped and waved papers in the air. "Confound it, I've never talked to a female about taxes."

Polly waited, trying to give her cousin time to adjust to this new phenomenon. By nightfall the Ashe and Moseley families, who lived up the street, would be shaking their heads over the supper table at the thought of a girl running the tavern. Mister Dry's wife, the former Mary Jane Rhett of Charleston, would be writing the family there that Phillip was gone from Brunswick and had left his eldest daughter in charge of things. Oh, how shocked the Rhetts and Moores would be! By this time the next day Cousin William Moore, just up the road at Orton Plantation, would be telling the news to the folks there. She was making a stir with her incompetence! Her stomach quivered.

William Dry put the papers on his desk and leaned forward. "Polly, since all those products, the wines and coffee and such, are imported, we can accept only specie for duties. And it must be paid in full when your purchase is delivered."

"Paid with my purchase and not with my order?" she asked.

Mister Dry nodded and pushed his handkerchief into the sleeve of his broadcloth coat. "In coin."

"Thank you, Mister Dry." Polly stood.

"So you won't be making out an order today?"

"Not today. I have to take an inventory first and then decide what to do about the money." She paused. "Mister Dry, how can Parliament demand specie when they will not allow us, here in the colonies, to mint money? How can they demand coin when we have trees and lumber, turpentine and pitch, barrels and staves? We send out our maritime products and we receive shoes. We send tobacco and receive lace. How do we pay taxes to England in coin when here we must trade goose feathers for candles?"

Mister Dry pulled out his handkerchief again, but this time he knotted it. "If you were a man, Polly, you could be said to be speaking treason. Parliament has the right to tax the colonies."

"Not everyone agrees with that, sir. I don't consider my questions treason. I think it's more about common sense. Colonies, like children, do grow up. That is not treason but logic."

"Then do be careful where you spread your logic." His voice was grave.

Polly knew it was time to turn on the charm. "Oh, yes, Mister Dry, I will be. I will be careful. Because of our kinship, I felt I could talk openly with you."

The collector of the Brunswick Port tucked away his handkerchief.

"And you have been so very helpful this afternoon, sir. I understand much better now about the duties." Polly moved toward the door.

Mister Dry hurried from behind his desk to hold the door. Polly could feel his eyes on her back as she walked away from the docks.

All the way up the street Polly grinned to herself. She waved to the girls and went in to make sure that the supper meal was cooking. Someone, probably Charlotte between her game with Charity and watching the boys at marbles, had started a goose roasting on the spit. Daniel had done well on his hunt, then.

She took off her good apron and tied on an old one. She mixed flour and butter and began to beat the dough for biscuits. As she pounded the dough against the table she tried to remember every newspaper article she had read on the Sugar Act and custom duties. In her head she ran through every conversation she had heard from the men who conducted their business in the tavern. She tried to remember more of Locke's writing. She had to keep learning.

She pinched off small pieces of the biscuit dough and placed them in a pan. She settled the pan in a cast iron pot, put the top on tightly and set it to the side of the fire. With the tongs she picked up hot coals and heaped them on the top of the lid. Quickly she diced apples into a skillet, added molasses and water, and set them to simmer. She turned the spit, where the sizzling goose was giving off delicious aromas. With rice and stew left from the noon meal there should be enough for supper.

Duties! Taxes! Money for supplies! Could she keep up with it all? Tonight, no matter how tired she was, or how many people needed her, she would find the time to reread John Locke's passage about political equality. She didn't think she would find a word that said she had to be a man to run a tavern.

And then she thought of the gossip that would be whispered about supper tables in their little town of Brunswick. Just as long as people said she was caring for her family, she didn't care what else they talked about. Her stomach, for once, stayed in place.

Chapter 6

The baby was born on the first day of the new year. Their neighbors, Mistress Moseley and Mistress Ashe, were there to help with the birthing. It was Leah who caught the squalling, red-faced infant in her strong black hands and held him up for all of them to see.

"Lawdy, Miss Henrietta, we got us a boy," Leah exclaimed.

Mama turned her face to the wall. "No! No! Not a boy!" She began to cry. "He will not live." She refused to hold the child or to nurse him. When anyone tried to put the baby in her arms, she went rigid and began to moan.

"Henrietta, you must care for this child," Mistress Moseley said. "You must nurse him. There is no one else here at Brunswick with an infant, so we can't get a wet nurse for you. You have to feed him yourself."

"Is there nothing we can do or say to you, Henrietta?" asked Mistress Ashe, when mama shut her eyes and buried her head in the pillow. "You must understand. You have to feed this child. Or he will die."

But Mama refused to take the infant. And she would not speak.

"We've got to name him," Charlotte insisted. She sat in the tavern room, holding the baby.

"What name would you choose?" Polly asked.

"I like Charles."

"I don't," said Cecilia. "I want to name him Timothy."

She put down the kitten she had been petting and reached out for the baby. She sat, rocking the infant in her arms and humming to him.

"Well, I like both names," Polly said. "I know you don't usually give two names, but this is a special boy. What about Timothy Charles Moore? It sounds impressive to me."

"Timothy Charles Moore." Charlotte rolled the words around her tongue. "I like it."

Cecilia begin singing a little made-up song. "Timothy for a good boy. Charles for a stout boy. Moore for a big boy."

"Charlotte, your handwriting is so beautiful. You record his name and date in the Bible," Polly said.

Even Leah leaned over the table to watch Charlotte write the name, Timothy Charles Moore, and the date, January 1, 1765, in the family Bible.

Now, almost two weeks later, the joy was gone. Worried frowns wreathed Leah's face. Cecilia sat close to the cradle, whether she was doing her lessons or sewing on a sampler. Charlotte walked with the baby, rocking him in her arms and singing nonsense rhymes to him.

Daniel had brought in wood yesterday. A great stack of oak and maple logs was piled high in a corner near the hearth. Then Daniel had disappeared. They were supposed to start hog killing this week, if the cold weather held. When Polly went looking for Daniel, to make arrangements for the hog killing, he was nowhere to be found. Moze was gone, too. Not even Leah seemed to know where the old man was.

During the night a nor'easter moved in, bringing winds that swayed the tall pines in a frenzied dance and drove freezing rain to beat against the windows. A bark tossed at anchor in the river. The other vessels that had been loading or unloading were sheltered in creeks or inlets.

Taking advantage of the quiet, Polly worked on her ledger, tallying the items she had ordered for the spring. Her foot moved up and down on the cradle rocker. She shifted the candle closer to the book and rubbed her eyes. Her head and neck ached from bending over the paperwork.

Cecilia sat close beside her, copying her letters on her slate. Charlotte and Leah were cutting dress material, quietly discussing which sleeve pattern to use with the cotton fabric. Sephie, whom she had borrowed from Mistress Ashe, was spinning wool. The white thread trailed across her black hand as she walked back and forth with the turn of the wheel.

Mistress Ashe was upstairs with Mama. She came almost every day, to sit and talk, to sit and read, to sit and pray. On the days she could not come, Mistress Moseley was there. They brought custards or puddings, to tempt Mama to eat. They changed the bed linens and stuffed the pillows with fresh feathers. They brought all the local gossip. If the two neighbor women had not helped so much, Polly did not know what would have happened to Mama.

And what was going to happen to the baby? Their good, stout, big boy was going to die if Polly could not find something he would eat. She had tried cow's milk first. She cleaned a narrow-necked wine bottle. Over the opening she tied the finger from a soft old leather glove with three tiny holes she punched with a needle. Timothy Charles could nurse just fine from the bottle. But he screamed with stomach pains and flailed the air with his tiny fists.

"I've never seen a child who could not tolerate cow's milk," Mistress Ashe said.

"I have," said Mistress Moseley. "Polly, steam rice and try to get him to drink the rice water."

Polly cooked rice and strained the liquid through cheese cloth to be sure there were no lumps or pieces to choke the baby. He sucked greedily on the rice soup for a few moments before he began to scream. His thrashed wildly about in his cradle, then drew his legs up close to his chest.

Next she tried white potatoes. The baby only got a taste before he turned his head and vomited out the mixture. She tried sweet potatoes, but he refused to suck. The only thing that he had kept down was apple cider mixed with water. And he was starving to death. His lusty cries were now only mews. His bright blue eyes, once so alert, were dull. Mama was right. The boy was going to die.

Through the quiet of the tavern room, a shout came from outside the house. Charlotte leaped from her chair. "What's that?"

"Don't let go!" a voice cried. "Grab the rope! Grab it!"

Polly ran to open the door and was met with a blow to the stomach that knocked her sprawling. A creature tore past her into the room and turned, ready to charge again.

Sephie yelled, "Lord and His angels save us. The pure devil is come to this house." She flung her hands above her head. "Look at the horns on that devil!"

Leah grabbed Charlotte. They jumped up and down, screaming. Cecilia flung herself over the cradle, her head buried against the baby's chest.

From the yard men were yelling. "You let her get away." That voice sounded like Daniel's.

"You had hold of her." Polly knew that voice was Moze's.

"I get her." Polly did not know this voice, but she saw a child standing in the doorway. His ragged shirt came down to his knees, covering his breeches. Water dripped from his hair across his black face, streaking the mud caked on his forehead and cheeks. His feet were bare. But when he spoke, his tones were soft and gentle.

"Ain't nothing but old she-goat," the child crooned. "Ain't nothing but old she-goat that wild and scared. Ain't nothing but old she-goat this boy gonna get his hands on." He shook his head. "Ain't gonna to have old she-goat called a devil, even do she act like one."

As the boy sing-songed, he stepped over Polly's legs, never breaking his stride or stopping his tune. He moved slowly toward the creature. Out before him he carried a short rope. As he reached her, he slipped the rope over her horns and began to scratch the top of her head. "Old goat, no need to run over folks like that. You scare these folks with your wild ways. And we got a job for you to do here. You come on now. Follow me."

The boy began to slowly back toward the door, holding the rope with one hand and still scratching the goat's head with the other. Polly, sitting on the floor, moved her legs out of the way as the child led the goat out of the door.

Daniel looked down at her with a big grin. "Funny place for you to sit. Do you sprawl on the floor often?"

Polly scrambled to her feet. "Only when a she-goat comes knocking at my door," she answered. "What is happening? And who is that half-naked child?"

A maa came from the goat. Polly looked over Daniel's shoulder to see the little boy still backing up, leading the animal. Moze limped beside them as they headed toward the barn. A kid bounced behind, bleating and trying to get to its mother.

Charlotte and Leah crowded to the door to see what was happening in the yard.

"Mercy me, I never thought about goat's milk," Leah said. "Are you gonna be able to milk that wild thing?"

"Why, Leah, I thought you would milk it," Daniel said.

"Not me, Mister Daniel," Leah said, shaking her head. "Sephie is right. Goats is part devil."

Laughing, Daniel turned away and loped toward the barn. Polly closed the door and stood leaning against it. Would the baby drink goat's milk? Where did Daniel find a goat? Who was the small boy in his ragged clothes? She had never seen a goat or that boy before.

When Daniel brought in a small bucket of the warm, frothy milk a little later, Polly had already cleaned a wine bottle and made a fresh tit of leather, ready to try. She held the baby in her arms. He began to suck. He looked up at her with great surprise in his eyes, and then clamped down on the glove finger with force. He did not stop sucking until every drop of the milk was gone. Slowly his eyes closed in sleep — his first natural sleep in days.

Polly held him on her shoulder and patted his back. He gave a burp, and lay heavy in sleep against her chest.

"Whose idea was it to get a goat?" she asked Daniel.

"Do you remember hearing about the old settlement at Town Creek?"

Polly nodded over the baby's head.

"The people had a lot of misfortunes, including Indian attacks. Most of the settlers abandoned the place long before Brunswick was settled. They must have departed in a hurry, because they deserted most of their livestock. There are cows and pigs and even a few sheep wondering around in the woods over there. We went yesterday to look for a goat." Daniel grinned at her. "We found a devil of a she-goat, that's for sure."

Polly grinned back at him. She put Timothy Charles in his cradle and pulled the quilt up to his shoulders. Sephie had gone back to her spinning, and the whir of the wheel sounded like a lullaby in the room. When Mistress Ashe came down from Mama's room Cecilia ran to her to tell about the goat.

"Gracious," Mistress Ashe said. She bent over the baby and watched him sleep. "I've never heard of such. You do know we had all given up on this baby." She straightened up and held her hands to her back, as if she were very tired. "Polly, you are the most stubborn girl I've ever seen in my life."

"Mistress Ashe, I probably am stubborn. I don't give up easily on anything."

"In this case I meant being stubborn as benevolent, Polly. Somebody here had better be stubborn and try to get Henrietta out of that bed." She sighed. "I'm going to say it, even though I probably shouldn't. But there is really nothing wrong with your mother, you know. I mean, nothing wrong with her physical person."

"Mistress Ashe, I do thank you for all you've done for Mama."

Mistress Ashe took her shawl from the peg behind the door and covered her head and shoulders against the sleet. "I haven't given up, Polly." She smiled. "I can be stubborn, too, you know. At least my husband John says I am. I'll be back tomorrow."

After the door closed, Polly turned again to Daniel. "Tell me about this little boy you brought back with the goat."

"He was holed up in an old cabin over at Town Creek. He had a fire going on the hearth of an abandoned house, but I didn't see any food around. I have no idea what he's been living on or how long he's been there. He seemed mighty glad to see us."

"He's been with someone," Polly said. "He talks too well to have been alone long. Didn't you ask him?"

"Ask him what? We were busy catching a goat," Daniel said. He pulled his cape about his shoulders and went out.

Polly could not get the child off her mind. He had looked so cold. His clothes were so scanty. She remembered a trunk that Papa had stored in the attic after a traveler had left it behind at least two years before. She trudged up the stairs to the top floor and pulled the trunk from behind several boxes that were piled there. Inside were clothes for a man and a boy. A pair of woolen britches appeared to be the right size to fit the boy. A blue smock, faded at the lines where it was folded, seemed large but adequate. There was a pair of shoes, the toes curled from wear. She found two pair of woolen socks, both patched.

Toward the bottom of the trunk was a green silk shawl with long tassels of knotted cream silk thread. Polly carefully refolded it and put it back in the trunk. She would give the shawl to Charlotte when there was a need for her to really dress up. She took the clothes for the boy down to the tavern room with her and put them under the counter. It was time to serve the evening meal.

Chapter 7

Hog killing started the next morning. Before light Polly heard the men coming in from the tar pits and sawmill to help with the butchering. She wasn't sure what arrangements Daniel had made with Mister Colston, the overseer of the turpentine and sawmill operations. She did know they would need all of the men for the hog killing.

She called the girls awake. One yellow kitten slept with its face in Cecilia's hair. The other one was curled next to Charlotte's shoulder. Both kittens stretched as the girls began to stir.

Polly dressed as quickly as she could. Timothy Charles whimpered from the bed, where he had slept warm beside her. She changed his napkin and gown, carrying him with her as she went down to the tavern room.

With the fire going and the corn mush bubbling in its pot, Polly unbarred the door and looked out. The sleet had abated in the night, but the chill wind blowing from the river meant the day would stay cold. The men sang from just beyond the barn, where the equipment was set up for the killing.

"Michael, row your boat ashore," a voice rang out. "Hallelujah," a chorus of voices answered. "Jordan's river is deep and wide," another voice declared. "Hallelujah," came the chorus.

Mister Ashe came up the road, nodded to her, and walked on toward the sounds. His hogs were being butchered today, too. Mistress Ashe, if she got here to see Mama at all, probably would not come until late.

The boy from Old Town came toward her lugging a bucket. "Morning, Miss Polly," he said. "Here the goat milk. I be told to do your fetch and carry this day."

"Put the bucket on the counter. Then bring in fire wood," Polly said. She watched him for a minute before she fixed the baby's bottle.

Cecilia, dressed and ready for the day, took the bottle from her and picked up Timothy Charles. She sat on the floor by the cradle and hummed to him as he sucked the goat's milk. "He's smiling, Polly," Cecilia said. "He's really smiling at me."

Polly didn't think babies that young would smile, but she did not dispute her sister. It was so wonderful that their baby was not screaming with pain or mewing with hunger. If the goat was kin to a devil, then she would welcome a devil into this house.

When Moze came in the yard she called to him. She pulled a bench by the hearth and served him a bowl of mush. The boy brought in another armful of oak for the fire and she settled him on the bench to eat with the old man.

"I want some answers," she said. She placed her chair in front of them and sat. "Moze, who is this boy and who does he belong to?"

The child began to tremble. He held the bowl close, as if she would snatch it from his hands, and ate so quickly Polly was afraid he would choke.

"I don't know for sure who he is, Miss Polly." Moze touched the boy's hand to calm him. "Mister Phillip bought several men from the islands a short while back. They was to work in the tar pits, making the turpentine and pitch. There was one ran away. He was caught over near Town

Creek. Mister Phillip sold him off. Somehow I 'spect this boy was with that runaway slave."

Polly looked at the child. Tears stained his cheeks. He rocked on the bench, his arms still surrounding the bowl.

"Is this true?" Polly asked him.

He nodded.

"Was the man your father?"

Again he nodded.

"Where is your mother?"

The boy stilled. "She die. She die of fever in the islands."

"If your father belonged to Papa, then you belong to us, too. That means I have one more person to look after." Polly took a deep breath. "What is your name?"

"Just Boy, Miss Polly."

"Well, that won't do. You think about a name." She went behind the counter and got out the clothes. Taking the empty mush bowl from him, she placed the bundle in his lap. "Go out to the barn and put on these clothes. I will not have a child in my care freezing in this cold. And when you're dressed come back to me. I can use all the help I can get before this hog killing is over."

Moze went out with the boy. Polly set Charlotte to the task of making a stew for their noon meal. She and Leah went to get out every pot and pan they owned to be ready for the preparation of curing the meat that would soon be coming.

Cecilia rocked Timothy Charles. " 'Great A, little a, bouncing B, the Cat's in the Cupboard and can't see me,' " she sang to him. The baby waved his tiny hands and gurgled back at her.

By the third day of hog killing Polly had most of her meat salted down or curing. Two of the men who had come in from the tar pits were excellent workers who did not seem to mind taking orders from a woman. They had matched her step for step as they cured the meat, cleaned the intestines for stuffing, mixed sausage, made souse meat, and boiled the fat for lard.

As the men stirred the huge kettles of bubbling fat with boat oars, they laughed. "Good eating this night, Miss Polly. Does you wants a crackling straight out of the pot?"

Jeremiah, the younger man, reached in the kettle with iron tongs and lifted out several pieces of the fat that had cooked into shriveled hunks. He spilled the cracklings on a huckaback cloth on the table. Jeremiah was the one who brought the wood for the tavern. She was finding that he was not only a good worker but always had a smile and a song or tune to whistle.

The older man, Isaac, nodded confirmation. Isaac was the blackest person that Polly had ever seen. His skin glistened in the light as he moved about his work. He was much shorter than Jeremiah, but they could carry the same weight, she had observed. And while the younger man was merry, Isaac's eyes seemed sad, as if he had come through some great sorrow.

Isaac looked at her now. "This one of the best hog killings I's worked, Miss Polly."

Polly picked up a crackling, still so hot she had to toss it from one hand to the other, and knew that there would indeed be good eating this night and for a long time to come. She had hams and tenderloins from seven shoats, each weighing close to two hundred pounds, salted and hanging from the rafters in the tavern. She had sausage drying in the case and sausage packed down in saltpeter and pepper. She bit into the hot crackling and looked up to see two men riding toward her. Cousin Maurice swung down from his roan and lifted his hat.

With her mouth full, she could only nod a greeting.

She knew her apron was covered with blood from the hog meat. Her disheveled brown hair poked from her mobcap. Her hands were greasy and salt stains blackened her knuckles. This was certainly not the way she had intended to welcome her benefactor on his first visit.

He did not seem to notice her dress. He picked up a crackling from the cloth and bit into it. "Good." He said. "Very good."

He turned to his companion. "Cornelius, you know Polly. She's Phillip's daughter. Get down and try some of this treat."

Jeremiah took another batch of cracklings from the hot grease, spread them on the table and stepped back from the kettle. Isaac hunched down on his heels, his hands resting on his knees.

"Will you come inside?" Polly asked. "Mister Harnett, it is a pleasure to welcome you."

Mister Harnett tipped his hat in greeting.

Still munching on his treat, Maurice tied his horse to the post near the door and walked in. Mister Harnett handed the reins of his horse to Isaac and followed. Polly hurried to draw beer from the barrel and hand the men tankards.

Cecilia rocked the baby by the fire, keeping time with Sephie's spinning wheel. Charlotte stirred a pot hanging over the fire. Leah stuffed the last of the sausage. The fragrance of thyme and sage tarried around the table where she worked.

Cousin Maurice looked up at the hams and slabs of bacon hanging above his head. Then he took in the picture of Cecilia with the baby. "It goes well, then?" he asked.

He would hear no complaints from her. She answered, "Yes, it goes well."

"William Dry sent word of your spring orders." He took

a swallow of beer and looked at her over his tankard. "He tells me that you are paid up so far."

So it was Mister William Dry who was keeping an eye on her to make reports, Polly thought.

"And," Cousin Maurice continued, "I was told the baby was near to death."

"We found a goat," Polly said. "Timothy Charles can drink the goat's milk."

"You also found a boy over at Town Creek."

"Yes, sir. He's a good worker."

Cousin Maurice put his empty tankard on the table. "We came over to Russellborough to see Governor Dobbs. The lieutenant governor is still away visiting. Seems Tryon is going to know this colony well before he has to take up the reins of government from the old man." He glanced again toward the baby. "I just stopped in here to see if you needed anything." He pulled out his gloves.

"As you said, Cousin Maurice, it goes well. The only thing —"

He looked at her. "Speak up. Speak up."

"Where is Papa?"

Maurice finished smoothing on his leather gloves before he answered. "Phillip is in Charleston. He is sober, at least for now. He is working, at least for now. I sent him word of the boy's birth after you wrote to me. Now I can tell him that the child is still living."

"You can tell him, sir, that Timothy Charles is thriving," Polly said.

Cousin Maurice smiled. "We'll be on our way then, little cousin. I think I made a good bargain here."

He and Mister Harnett climbed on their horses and trotted up the road.

As Polly shut the door, Leah let out a whoop. "Oh, Miss Polly, you done so good. 'It goes well.' And you say it so proper. Those men got no idea what we been through here. And the way you talk, they never will know." She pounded at the mixture of sausage. "That baby almost dead. Miss Henrietta upstairs not saying a word or caring if she breathe another breath. Wheee!" Leah nodded, a wide grin on her face.

"Lawdy, Miss Polly, you is something, you is. You got any idea of how strong you is? You got any idea how we looking to you to keep us together?"

Polly's knees gave way and she toppled into the nearest chair. She had passed a test of sorts. Cousin Maurice hadn't even asked about money. He just knew she was paid up on all of her orders.

Her head ached so dreadfully. If only she could stop the throbbing in her temples. She had told no one about the pain that came and went. She never knew when her head would hurt and when it would ease. There was no time to be sick.

And then what Leah had said really got through to her. As quickly as she had slumped in the chair she pulled herself aright. Waving her arms above her head she shouted, as an answer to Leah, to her sisters, to herself, "I am strong! Oh Leah, I am strong. Wheee! Wheee!"

Chapter 8

Winter storms rolled fierce across the Atlantic Ocean. Shipping had almost stopped for several weeks because the vessels could not ride through the gales. The barks and brigs and brigantines were anchored at the islands, or were still moored in England. Not even a sloop had ventured up the river for several days.

Great piles of logs, ready to be loaded for their English ports, waited on skids to be pulled to the docks. Hogsheads of pitch, tar and turpentine sat on the docks, filled the warehouses, and lined Street on the Bay, which ran parallel to the Cape Fear River.

Mister Colston, the foreman at the saw mill and turpentine works, rode his great dun from the woods down to the docks more and more frequently. He spent time in Mister Dry's office or paced the docks, tapping his riding whip against his leather boots. The Negroes avoided him when they could, but reports of harsh treatment reached The Anchor. Was Mister Colston another obligation she was going to have to assume?

Lieutenant Governor Tryon and his family had returned in February from their visits across the colony. Charlotte wanted to go over to Russellborough every day. Polly wasn't sure what she did there, except supervise Cecilia and the Tryon's little girl, Margaret. Since there were so few customers in the tavern, Polly had let her go often.

"They spent Christmas in New Bern," Charlotte reported after the first visit. "The town was decorated with holly and mistletoe. There were balls and parties." Her eyes brightened as she described the activities. "And Mistress Tryon practices her spinet every day. She's teaching Margaret to play."

By the first week of March the chill winds subsided enough that Polly knew she could work outside. At breakfast she announced her intentions.

"Today we make soap. I'll need everybody to work. Charlotte, you will see to the cooking. A stew will be good, I think. Cecilia, the baby is in your care. Leah, Mistress Ashe told me she won't be able to come for several days. She is going to be making soap, too. Mama is all yours. Since the men have caught up in the woods and the tar pits, I'm sending for Isaac and Jeremiah to help with the tubs and lifting."

"Miss Polly, sounds like you got a battle plan," Leah interrupted.

"Maybe I have. As soon as we finish the soap, we have to make candles." She massaged her temples, rubbing at the dull pain gathering there. "And then we're going to clean this house. I mean to clean it from top to bottom. Mama's room is the place I plan to start."

"Polly," Charlotte wailed.

Her sister looked at her and waited.

"Polly, I want to go see Mistress Tryon and Justina."

"Charlotte, I need you here."

"You're not my mother and I do not have to do what you say." Charlotte's voice was bitter. "I'll go up and talk with Mama. She will let me go."

Polly sighed. Charlotte had been so good all winter and had done very little complaining. She couldn't fuss at her for wanting to do other things. "Go talk to Mama. Please do go talk to Mama." She went out to the barn to find Boy. She had errands for him to run.

All winter Polly had been getting ready for the soap making. The wood ashes from the hearth fires were poured into barrels which were suspended over wooden tubs. Every time a new bucket of ashes went in the barrel, she poured half a bucket of water over them. The lye made from this concoction now filled the tubs.

By the time Polly had the fires burning in the yard, Jeremiah and Isaac appeared. They set up the heavy tripods and swung the cooking kettles from chains to suspend them over the fire.

"This won't make good eating like the last time you helped me," Polly said.

"Boy say we making soap when he come for us," Isaac answered. "I won't planning to eat any of it."

Jeremiah smiled. "Cracklins is much better," he said. There was a twinkle in his eye and Polly smiled back him.

She had saved every smidgen of grease that came from the cooking. She now began to ladle scoops of the grease into the kettles. The men lifted the heavy tubs, pouring the lye in to the grease. Then Jeremiah and Isaac, each with an oar, started stirring the mixture. Polly knew the cooking would take hours.

"Boy, you keep up the fires," Polly commanded. "Do whatever Isaac and Jeremiah ask of you." She went in to see about the girls.

Charlotte was wailing. She had her head on the table and sobs shook her shoulders. As Polly came in the door she sat up and screamed at her. "It's not fair. It's not fair." She put her arms over her face.

Timothy Charles began to cry. Cecilia picked him up

and rocked him back and forth in her arms, trying to sing to him. Tears ran down her cheeks and her sobs stopped her song. Polly saw that the baby was getting large enough that it was all the little girl could do to hold him.

She sat down on the bench beside Charlotte. "What's not fair?"

Charlotte flung her arms into the air. Her hand caught a glancing blow across her sister's face and Polly fell backwards to the floor.

"Charlotte, that hurt!" She sat there, her fingers touching her cheek, wondering if she would have a black eye.

Charlotte stopped crying and stared at her. "I didn't mean to hit you." Her tone was defensive.

The baby was making snubbing noises and Cecilia was still trying to comfort him. What Polly wanted to do was grab Charlotte by the hair and pull out every strand of her thick black curls. She wanted to go up to Mama's chamber and yank her from her bed, for she knew that Charlotte's outburst had something to do with their mother. She wanted to go down to the dock and watch for ships. She wanted to sit in the parlor at the governor's house and listen to the spinet. She wanted time to read her books and the newspapers that came in to the tavern.

She knotted her fingers together and turned to her sister. "Let's try this again, Charlotte. What's not fair?"

"Polly, do you know how sick Mama is?" Charlotte sniveled. "Do you know she does not speak a word? Do you know how thin she is?"

"I do know," Polly said. "I see her every day. How long has it been since you went in to see her? Talk with her? Read to her?"

Charlotte began to cry again. "I don't know, Polly. It's been days and days." Polly got up from the floor and gathered Charlotte in her arms, hugging her. "I have a plan about Mama. And I am going to need your help."

She pushed Charlotte away from her and held her by the shoulders. "Do you remember that Leah said I sounded like someone with a battle plan? Well, I do plan battle. A war, if it comes to that."

Charlotte wiped her sleeve across her face. "What kind of war?"

"Today, with the weather right, I have to make the soap. And if the weather holds, we make the candles next. Then, like I said this morning, we're going to clean. That's when we're going to get Mama out of that room."

Charlotte hiccupped.

Polly slapped her between her shoulder blades.

"That hurt!" Charlotte yelled. "And you meant it!" She hiccupped again.

Polly nodded. "I have soap to make."

At the door she met Daniel coming in with milk pails. "This is all from the cow," he said. "The goat is dried up."

"Oh, dear," Polly said. "The baby has to have the milk. You told me you saw a herd of goats at Town Creek. You can go back."

Daniel plopped the buckets on the counter, slashing milk over the rims. He stood with his head bowed.

"There's more," Polly said. "What else, Daniel?"

"Judge Moore sent word that I was to travel with Governor Tryon when he left again. I have to go over there this morning." He looked at her. "Polly, I have to go where I'm sent."

The smell of boiling lye and grease drifted through the open door as if calling her to the job of soap making. Timothy Charles whimpered, hungry for his breakfast. Cecilia was trying to mop up the milk from the counter and had succeeded in spilling more of it on the floor.

Charlotte dropped a pot against the stone hearth and the ring of metal pounded through her head. She pressed her fingers to her temples.

"Polly?" Daniel's voice was so soft and gentle. "Polly, I don't want to go."

She squared her shoulders. "I'll talk to Moze. He will know who to send to fetch a goat. I have soap to make."

She stepped out into the yard and called back. "Charlotte, cook extra. There's a bark sailing up the river. We'll have men to feed before the sun goes down."

Daniel put his hand on her arm. "Polly?"

She shivered, her heart racing from his touch, but she kept her voice low and even. "I know, Daniel. I know. Just a few minutes ago Charlotte was crying that it wasn't fair." She turned to look him in the eye. "If I could do what I wanted to do, right now, I'd get a book and climb up that old oak over there and sit in the arms of its branches all day. I'd read until my eyes hurt. I'd drink in the words and try to digest the meaning of every syllable."

"Some day you'll have leisure for sitting in trees and reading." He patted her arm.

Polly felt the stomach flutter that caused her heart to pound against her throat. She backed a step away from him and thrust her hands in her pockets. "You have a good trip. Get your reports for Cousin Maurice." She willed her voice to stay steady.

Daniel nodded and headed toward the barn. When she was sure that he was far enough away not to hear, she whispered, "But come back, Daniel. Come back."

She sent Boy to find Moze. She checked the soap mixture to make sure the lye and grease were cooking together. She threw corn to the geese and chickens, then grabbed an old hen from the clucking fowls that ran to peck near her feet. She seized the axe from the chopping block and severed the hen's head in one swift blow.

"Get me some water boiling over your fire," she called to Isaac. By the time Moze came in the yard she had scalded, plucked and gutted the hen, ready for Charlotte to put on the spit.

"Goats, Miss Polly? They'll be hard to catch now it's spring," Moze said.

Polly just looked at him. She was far too tired this morning to listen to excuses from anybody, even Moze.

"I'll need to take Boy," Moze said. He thought a moment. "There's Morrow. She can work." Again he was silent. "If we leave before noon, we can be back before dark the next day."

"Come by the tavern before you leave. I'll get food together for you." She watched Moze limp away from her and wondered how he could manage in the woods on his crutch.

By early afternoon the soap mixture was ready for the salt to be added. As the soft soap began to rise to the top of the mixture, the men ladled it out into wooden trays for it to harden. Into one of the kettles Polly added crushed bayberries. She watched as Jeremiah stirred them in and saw the green tint it added to the soap. The fragrance of the bay floated over the harsh grease odor. This was going to be good bathing soap.

Isaac and Jeremiah carried the cooling tray molds into the tavern to stack on the floor in a corner. Tomorrow, before she started making the candles, they would cut the soap from the wooden trays so she could store it in metal boxes to keep the rats away from it.

Polly sat by the door. Her head ached. She felt so tired. Charlotte and Cecilia were discussing how much of the stew broth they could feed the baby. He was watching his sisters as if he could really understand that they were doing all they could to fill his stomach.

Two men from the bark came in, calling for beer. Charlotte served them and slipped the pennies in her apron pocket. Then she began to strain a half cup of broth. Cecilia propped Timothy Charles in his cradle and spooned a sip of broth in his mouth. He waved his arms at her and reached for the spoon.

The little girl laughed. "Charlotte, he likes the broth. He likes your stew broth." She dipped up another spoonful for him to suck.

"That's because I'm such a good cook," Charlotte bragged.

Polly sat on the bench by the door and leaned against the wall. She had never felt so tired. Jeremiah and Isaac had done most of the heavy lifting, but she had not stopped working since the breakfast meal. She heard Leah ask if she wanted a bowl of stew. She shook her head, closed her eyes, and in spite of the activity in the busy tavern room, she dozed.

Chapter 9

Jeremiah already had the fire going in the yard when Polly came down the next morning. He and Isaac reset the tripods, hanging the kettles as they had the day before. Polly scooped the first of the tallow into the kettles and warned the men that she did not want the mixture to boil. She had enough bayberries to give all her candles the sweet perfume that helped to mask the burning animal fat. She gave the jars of crushed, dried berries to Isaac to pour into the kettle.

She twisted the wicks. Jeremiah helped her tie them to the cross sticks and hang them from poles stretched between two chairs. Isaac kept up a constant stirring. As soon as the fat was hot, just short of a boil, she began to dip the wicks in the kettle. Dip, hang, dry. Then dip, hang, dry. Again and again she dipped her growing candles, making sure that they did not harden too fast, or they would crack when they began to burn. If only she had molds to fill. It would make the work so much easier. Candle molds were on her list to purchase if the tavern made a profit.

By dark, after the two men had helped her move her candles into the tavern, Polly was so weary she could barely walk. She tried to eat the stew that Charlotte had made, but she could not swallow.

"Go to bed, Miss Polly," Leah said. "The girls can bolt the door tonight."

Polly looked around the room. Three men, one of them an officer from the bark, were playing cards. An old man and his wife were eating. It should stay quiet. She nodded to Leah and climbed the stairs.

It seemed like minutes later, although the first light was coming in the window, when she woke from a nightmare. She bolted upright in bed, and then had to grab her aching head. She had never felt such a pain. It pierced behind her eyes and stabbed through her temples. What was the horror that had awakened her? She could not remember. With both arms folded on her head to keep it from falling off, she moaned.

"Polly?" Cecilia asked.

"Go back to sleep, sweet Cee. It's early yet," she said.

She dressed, and holding her head, went down to the tavern. She boiled water and made sassafras tea, hoping it would ease the pain. She started the mush, but stirring it made her head ache even more.

"Oh, I can't be sick," Polly said to the simmering mush pot. "There is too much to do." She carried the tea with her to the door and looked out.

Jeremiah already had the tripod set up over the fire in the yard. Two brigantines were anchored in the river and flatboats were going out from the dock to start unloading supplies. A raft from Cross Creek was tied at a pier. Today would be busy.

Dip, hang, dry. Dip, hang, dry. The candles were growing, and with them, Polly's headache worsened. She ran to the necessary to vomit and went back to work on the candles. She hurried into the tavern to supervise the cooking and back to the candles.

She stopped long enough to talk with one of the men from the raft. He had honey for sale and she bought a small cask of it. Several men from the brigantines came up for the noon meal. She went in to help Charlotte and Leah with the serving and brought out plates of food for Jeremiah and Isaac. They sat under the oak while they ate and were ready to help her when she came back out to finish the candles.

Dip. Hang. Clutch her head. Dip. Hang. Clutch her head. As she strung one more candle wick from the pole, someone took her hand and placed a wooden cup in it.

"Drink, child."

Polly took a swallow of the bitter brew and looked up to see Marie.

"It from willow bark. Drink all of it," Marie said.

Polly drank and shuddered at the biting taste.

"Sit here in shade," the woman commanded. "You sit very still."

Polly sat and closed her eyes. She felt a cool cloth placed on the back of her neck and she took a deep breath.

"You drink," Marie said, and again put the cup in her hand.

This taste was spicy. She opened her eyes to look at Marie. "Herbs. You drink herbs. Feel better soon," the woman said.

The next time Polly opened her eyes Marie was gone. So were Jeremiah and Isaac. The kettle had disappeared, although the tripod straddled the dying fire. Her candles were finished, hanging row after gleaming row on the poles.

Cecilia took her hand. "Are you going to be fine now, Polly?"

"Yes, Cee. My head doesn't hurt at all." She hugged her sister. "Where did Jeremiah and Isaac go?"

"Marie sent them down to the river to clean the kettle." Cecilia giggled. "They were sure afraid of her. But she told them that when the kettle was clean, they should fill it up with oysters and cook themselves a feast. Then they were to clean the kettle again."

"Did Marie finish the candles?"

"Between giving you cups of stuff to drink she did. I helped. She showed me lots of things about the candle making. Polly, I like her. She said we have a comely baby and she patted him on the head. He cooed at her so he must like her, too."

When you need her, she will come, Moze had said. Polly had thought it would be for Mama or Timothy Charles. She had never thought she would be the one who would need such help. She wanted to find out about the herbs Marie had used.

She heard a racket of bells and bleats. She looked up the street. Boy was leading a string of goats. The lead nanny had a harness tied around her neck. From it hung a cow bell that clattered with each step she took. Five more nannies and a billy, roped one behind the other, followed. A girl, not as large as Charlotte, walked beside the procession, carrying a tiny kid. Moze brought up the rear of the strange parade.

"Go get Moze a cup of cider, Cecilia," Polly said. She stood and offered the old man her chair.

He smiled at her and sat, heavily. "Thank you, Miss Polly. You can ask Boy for all the details of our 'ventures." He took the cup from Cecilia and held it in both hands.

Boy and the girl disappeared behind the barn. The noise of the bleating goats and clattering bells faded as the children drove the animals into the pen.

"I'm getting too old, Miss Polly. Much too old to go traipsing through the woods looking for goats and such."

He drank from the cup and looked toward Isaac and Jeremiah, coming up from the river. The men were carrying the huge iron kettle between them. Isaac had a string of trout over one shoulder.

"Thought you might enjoy some fish," he said. "We can cook 'em up out here in the yard, if you want us to."

"I'll get salt and meal for you," Polly said. She suddenly realized how hungry she was. "Fresh fish will be most tasty."

According to Locke, Polly read, a good life was a life of pleasure. Pleasure and pain were simple ideas that accompanied almost all of man's experiences.

"Well," Polly said to the pages of the essay, "I don't think those ideas are simple." Sleep eluded her tonight. She knew it was because she had slept that long hour under the influence of Marie's brews. Sitting in the quiet tavern room, with only her one candle for light, she pondered the statement she had just read.

The terrible headache had been an experience of pain she hoped never to repeat. But what of pleasure? What brought her joy and satisfaction?

A smile from Timothy Charles when his stomach was full, an approving nod from Moze, Charlotte and Cecilia giggling together, would be on her list of pleasures. And Daniel. Oh, Daniel, with his merry grin and his wheat-colored hair falling across his forehead. Daniel, with his kind words and his gentle touch on her arm that left her feeling breathless. Her thoughts of Daniel were like treasures stored in her heart.

"Come back, Daniel," she whispered. "Come back safely from your trip." She closed the book and went up to bed.

Chapter 10

With the morning light Polly brought her battle stations together. When Mister Ashe and Mister Moseley arrived, as she had asked them to, Leah had Mama dressed and ready to move.

"No matter what she does, or what she says, if she speaks," Polly said to the men, "you will pick her up and take her down to the tavern."

"Are you sure you know what you're doing?" Mister Moseley asked.

"I only know we have to clean the room. And I have to get her out of it somehow." Polly hid her hands under her apron.

When the men came into her bed chamber, Henrietta looked startled. Then she turned her face to the wall.

"We going down stairs," Leah said to her. "We going down and sit in the tavern for a while." Leah leaned over the prone figure on the bed and rubbed her shoulder. "It will be good to get out of here, Miss Henrietta."

Not a sound or movement did her mother make.

"Pick her up," Polly said to the men.

Mister Moseley scooped up Henrietta in his arms. She went rigid, her legs stiff and poking straight out, her arms tight by her sides.

"She's so light," Mister Moseley said. "Hardly weighs anything at all. John, you and Leah make sure her head doesn't hit the wall as we take the steps."

They made their way down the stairs, where Mister Moseley placed his unwieldy burden in the rocking chair. Leah arranged a shawl about her mistress's shoulders and sat beside her. Henrietta moaned.

"Thank you so much for coming to help," Polly said to the men.

"How do you plan to get her back up the steps?" Mister Ashe asked. "Do we need to come back?"

"She can walk, so I'll manage," Polly said. "But thank you."

Charlotte stirred mush and tended the fire. Boy came in with a pail of goat's milk. Cecilia strained the milk and sat down to feed Timothy Charles. Polly went to the wash house to get her buckets and rags and brooms to begin the house cleaning. As she came back through the tavern, Jeremiah and Isaac following her, she knew that her mother was watching.

Polly leaned over to kiss her cheek but Henrietta clenched her fists. "Stay with her, Leah," Polly said, and went up to begin her work.

She stripped the linens from the feather bed and dragged them to the hallway. She showed Jeremiah how she wanted the bed ropes and boards scrubbed with turpentine. She started Isaac washing down the walls with lye soap. As soon as she had the men working, she dragged the linens and feather bed down the stairs and out to the wash pot to leave them soaking in the first water. Then up she went to strip the quilts and linens in the chamber she shared with her sisters.

By the time for the noon meal Polly sank wearily onto the bench at the large table in the tavern. She was tired, but her head did not ache, thank goodness. Her mother had not moved, as far as she could see, but her eyes followed three men from the docks who came in and asked for ale.

Daniel walked up in the yard in late afternoon. He rolled a coach wheel before him and leaned it against the side of the oak. "Had to get a new rim at the smithy," he said. "We leave for New Bern in two days."

Polly stopped folding the dried linens she had been taking from ropes strung across the yard. "One of the Negroes usually goes to the smithy," she said.

Daniel grinned. "Usually. But then, one of the Negroes wouldn't have an excuse to stop and talk with you."

Polly grabbed a pillow covering from the line and folded her hands in the cloth. "To talk? About what?"

"Just to let you know Mister Tryon is on the move again, to visit in the colony," Daniel said.

"You have a good trip, then."

Daniel grabbed the wheel and started up the street. "I will be back, Polly Moore. I will be back."

Polly smiled.

But he and the Tryons had to come back more quickly than could have been imagined. Governor Dobbs, seventy-five, feeble and sick for months, died only two days after the Tryons left from Brunswick. Justina sent a servant pelting down the road to intercept the Tryon's coach and riders and tell them to turn back. But they could not wait for the new governor to return and went ahead with the funeral.

There was no preacher to conduct the service. Singing from the Church yard a layman led the procession into the Church. " 'I am the resurrection and the life, saith the Lord:he that believeth in me, though he were dead, yet shall he live. . . .' "

Cousin Maurice, as a Clerk of the Church, led the prayers. " 'I heard a voice from heaven, saying unto me, Write, From henceforth blessed are the dead which die in the Lord: even so saith the Spirit: for they rest from their labours.' "

" 'Christ, have mercy upon us,' " replied the assembled congregation.

In spite of all his efforts, Governor Dobbs had never gotten the funds to complete the building of St. Philips, the Parish church at Brunswick. Birds flew through the openings where windows should have hung. Polly's slippers filled with sand from the unfinished floor as she stood near the back of the sanctuary.

Justina was quiet during the short rites for the dead. Polly wondered what she would do now. She was eighteen and a widow. Governor Tryon and his family would live at Russellborough. Where would Justina Davis Dobbs call home?

The men lowered the casket into the ground inside the church, giving the old governor a place of burial near the altar. Outside, a blue jay scolded and breezes from the river rustled through the tall pines. All in all, Polly thought, when he was compared to some of the other governors of the North Carolina colony, Governor Dobbs hadn't been a bad leader. St. Philips would be a good resting place for him.

The tavern was so crowded after the funeral that Polly gave out of food. That had never happened to her before and she was determined it would never happen again. Drinking men needed to eat. It kept trouble from starting. Experiences with Papa had taught her that.

When the last guest had departed and she knew that the girls were tucked away in bed, she pulled her money box from its hiding place in the side of the chimney. She took down the key from the mantel and unlocked the box that Mister Edward had made for her. The coins, spilled out on the table, gleamed in the candlelight. There was a handful of French francs and another of English pennies. There were several Spanish pieces of eight, many broken in bits for change. There were German marks and even two Greek drachmas. There were colonial papers, one a three shilling note from New Jersey. There were several pieces of silver and one of gold. Most of the coins were English shillings.

She counted, added up her ledger and sat, not yet satisfied with the numbers. Less than a hundred pounds lay on the table, and she needed to order twice that amount to replenish the stocks in the store rooms. The girls needed clothes and shoes and hats. Timothy Charles was going to need so many things as he grew.

And what about Papa? Was he working and earning money? Was he gambling and losing any money he got his hands on? Was he coming back here, just as she was beginning to know what she was doing with the tavern? If he came back, would he again begin his destructive behavior?

She unwrapped the two peppercorns from the strip of gauze that she had used to protect the seeds. What she really needed was a money tree. These seeds were worth enough, with a few shillings added, to buy a small parcel of land. Would a peppercorn plant grow in the Carolinas? It might be worth a try. She left one of the seeds in the box and put the other one in her pocket. She would plant it and see if it would sprout.

She was working with Jeremiah and Isaac in the garden when the message from Mister William Dry came the next morning. "He said he needs to talk with you, ma'am," the young apprentice informed her. "I'm to wait and accompany you back to the office."

Polly ran up to her room to wash her face and tuck her long brown hair under her mobcap. She donned a fresh apron and slipped four pennies in her pocket. Sometimes farmers would be on the docks with early produce she could purchase.Mister Dry met her at his office door. His brocaded vest and velveteen breeches, most in fashion, only accented his rotund frame and pouching stomach.

He fawned over Polly's hand until she pulled it from his sweaty clasp and waited for him to tell her what he wanted.

He sat behind his desk. "You haven't paid your taxes, my dear. It's a serious matter to be late with taxes."

Polly sat and slipped her hands under her apron. "Can you explain to me about the taxes?" she asked.

"You own — " He cleared his throat. "Phillip owns quite a bit of property. The evaluation of this property determines the amount of monies to be paid for the on-going efficient operation of the government."

"What are the properties, Mister Dry? I only know about the tavern. And, of course there is the sawmill. I thought Mister Colston would be looking after all of the maritime products."

He glared at her over the paper in his hand. "Maurice should have explained all this to you. But let's see what I can do. There is the five thousand acres of woodland to the west and south of Brunswick. That's the land where the tar pits are set up. There are the tar pit operations themselves, which do tremendous business. I believe there are some three hundred barrels of tar, pitch and turpentine ready for loading with the next shipments. In addition, most of the hewn logs ready for loading are from your forests. And there is the saw mill."

He sat back in his chair. "There are ten slaves that work the pits and the saw mill. There are the two slaves — " He looked at the paper. "Two slaves named Jeremiah and Isaac who are now doing your bidding at the tavern. They are worth two hundred fifty to three hundred pounds each. They each require a tax. Beyond the tax, there is the matter of wages for your overseer."

Polly's stomach curled into knots and she pressed her hands tightly against her middle. She wasn't sure she could speak.

"All together, when you add the tavern into the equation, I'd say you owe one hundred pounds in taxes." Mister Dry put his elbows on the desk to lean closer to her.

She swallowed. "Mister Dry, the overseer is Mister Colston. I thought he would be the one to see about the taxes. And doesn't Mister Colston collect the money when all of those maritime goods are sold?"

"Well, now." Still leaning toward her, the man smiled. "You do get straight to the point. The overseer, Colston, does collect the money."

"What does he do with it?" Polly asked.

"Do with what? The money?" Mister Dry frowned and sat back in his chair. "He sends it to Phillip, I suppose."

Polly's thoughts were racing and she knew she had to take a moment to put these facts together. She walked over to the window to look out at the ships anchored in the river. One or two were arriving each day, now that the winter gales had subsided. A large pontoon, loaded with logs, was tied up to one of the vessels. Shouts from the ship and barge drifted toward the open window as block and tackle wrenches were attached to the logs.

She turned to Mister Dry. "If Mister Colston sends money to Papa, why hasn't he paid the taxes?"

Mister Dry pointed his quill at her. "You signed an agreement with Maurice. The taxes are your responsibility."

"But if all the money is sent to Papa, I don't have accountability of it." She looked back out on the river. Her stomach knotted again in a painful lump and Polly wondered if it was possible to smell the fear that rose inside of her. Pictures of slaves and burning tar pits, of timber and barrels of turpentine, ran through her head like distorted images seen through the wrong end of a spyglass. She did not hear Mister Dry come up behind her, but suddenly his arm was around her waist.

"We can work it out, my dear," he said softly in her ear.

Polly spun away from his grasp so fast she almost knocked him down. She was at the door before he could catch his breath.

"Why, Mister Dry, of course we will work it out," she said. "Thank you for all of your time and instruction."

She walked at a breathless pace away from the office. She did not stop to look at the vegetables in baskets on the dock. She did not look up as a flock of ducks flew overhead. She heard Daniel call to her from the edge of the pier, but she kept walking. She did not stop until she had closed the door of the tavern necessary behind her. She vomited, spewing out the knots of revulsion and fear that clutched at her.

Finally she wiped her mouth with the back of her hand, slumped to the floor and leaned against the rough wall. There was money to be had. There were slaves, timber, and maritime products of vast worth that she could control. She had to find out the details of it all.

She went to the well and drew up a bucket of water to rinse her mouth. She knew little of Mister Colston. He would stride into the tavern, slapping his polished riding boots with his riding whip. He and Papa would hold conferences over a tankard of beer or glass of Madeira. Mister Colston would usually tramp out with a scowl on his face.

She had seen him sitting on his great dun, shouting instructions to the men from the pits as they worked. Sometimes the men drove oxen pulling skids loaded with logs. They rolled barrels tied inside frames built with crude wooden wheels. Colston's riding whip was ever ready to flick toward the back of someone who moved too slowly to satisfy him. Once she had seen him slice off the tip of a man's ear with that whip. How she hated this institution of slavery that kept some in bondage and gave a man like

Colston power. She thought of Daniel, indentured and following orders of where and when he could go or stay. And she herself wasn't really any freer than the two slaves working in her garden. She could be bonded. She could be married off to anyone, if Papa decided that was the best thing to do with her. She could be beaten, as long as it did not cripple her. She could be locked up, denied food, stripped of any possessions. Legally, she had nothing except what a man said she could have. Who gave white men all the power to leave a woman groveling for their charity or living by the mercy of their own wits?

An accumulation of anger roiled through her guts. Polly knew it would destroy her if she did not dominate it first. Men did not care for angry women. Grace and manners, Mama had taught her, would get her through the day. She would not give up as Mama had. She would be gracious. She would speak softly. But she would fight.

She called Isaac from the garden.

"Oh my, no, Miss Polly," Isaac exclaimed when she told him she needed to see Mister Colston. "That ain't a man you wants to traffic with."

"I don't want to traffic with him."

"Miss Polly, I can't go to the woods without a pass," Isaac said. "I be kept there. That man will put me to work in the turpentine pits again."

"You will have your pass, Isaac. And if you are not back before the supper meal, I will come and get you."

Polly wrote out the note of safe passage and watched Isaac plod up the road.

As she showed Jeremiah how to plant beans and pumpkins, Polly watched the sun. Charlotte and Charity played on the see-saw. "See-saw, Marjory Daw," they sang. Up and down they bounced. "Jack shall have a new master."

"But not Isaac," she said. "Isaac will stay with me."

"Who you talking to, Miss Polly?" Jeremiah asked.

"To myself, I guess," she answered. "Go get all of those cracked clay pots I told you to store in the barn. I'm ready to plant the geranium slips. By mosquito time they'll be blooming and will help turn those pesky insects away."

"Never knew 'bout geranium flowers and mosquitoes."

"Geraniums blooming and citronella oil burning in my special candles, Jeremiah, will help to keep the mosquitoes away." She looked at the longer shadows gathering in the yard.

"And I have one very special seed to plant." She took the pepper corn from her pocket and breathed on it before she poked it into the rich dirt of a pot. It might sprout. It just might.

She finally sat on the bench by the door where Leah was churning. She twisted her hands together until the woman reached over and caught both of them between her own.

"Stop fretting, child. Isaac will come back, or he won't. That overseer man will come, or he won't."

"I know, Leah." Polly folded her hands together and took a deep breath.

"I handed Miss Henrietta some yarn and knitting needles this morning. She was always a fast one with the needles." Leah smiled. "She been knitting all the long day."

One of the boys playing in the street caught his hoop. "Look yonder," he called, and pointed. "Look coming yonder."

Mister Colston rode down the street on his great, gray horse. Behind him, a rope around his waist, loped Isaac. The man stopped the dun in the tavern yard and swung down from the saddle. He spat a wad of tobacco juice toward the well and nodded as if satisfied with his aim. He turned and yanked on the rope so that Isaac fell to his knees.

Polly walked toward him. "Mister Colston."

He looked her up and down. "Did you send this nig — "

"And it was so kind of you to come." Polly interrupted so quickly that the man looked startled. "I did send a message to request that you visit me. I think we can let Isaac loose from that rope now so he can finish his chores. Why, all the signs show that it's time to get the seeds in the ground and we've been planting most of the day."

Mister Colston threw the end of the rope to the ground and walked into the tavern. Polly motioned behind her back for Isaac to get up, and then followed the overseer inside.

Mama gave a little squeal when she saw the man. Mister Colston appeared surprised to see her sitting there.

"You know my mother, sir," Polly said.

He nodded at the woman in the rocking chair.

"And may I pour you a drink? We have beer and ale and a very good wine." She went behind the counter.

Mister Colston seemed to relax. "I think a beer would do," he said. He took the tankard she placed on the counter and stood, drinking.

Leah came in carrying the butter churn. She settled on the bench just inside the door and continued the thump-thump of the dasher.

And Polly waited. And waited. And waited. She would make him ask.

Mister Colston drained the last swallow. He slapped down the tankard and wiped the back of his hand across his mouth. He asked. He sneered at her, but he asked. "Well, what did you want? You sent for me."

"Mister Colston, I know how well you manage the tar and turpentine operations. And the saw mill, too. Papa must have had great confidence in you."

The dasher hit an extra hard knock against the churn before Leah returned to her rhythmical slosh-slosh.

"And with Papa gone, I would like to have that same confidence," Polly continued. "I want to do what is most convenient for you. You could bring me the books and records on the first of each month. Or you could give your accounting whenever you send out a shipment. I will accept either arrangement. The money would, of course, be due when I examine the books."

John Ashe and his wife came into the tavern. Mistress Ashe sat down beside Mama and began to exclaim over the socks she was knitting. Mister Ashe came up to the counter.

"Good day, Colston," he said.

"Would you like some wine, Mister Ashe?" Polly asked.

"Why, yes. That would be just the thing."

Mister Moseley strolled in. "Miss Polly, I was thinking about your good apple cider. Have you some on tap?"

Before she could fill the goblet, Moze came in and took his seat by the hearth. An officer from the *Maryanne* poked his head in the door and asked if the supper meal would be ready by dark.

"How many may I expect, sir?" Polly asked.

"Three of us tonight, ma'am," he answered. "We look forward to your hospitality."

Colston's eyebrows were up. It was evident to Polly that he had not expected this support for her. She knew she had the edge and pressed her point.

"Mister Colston, when may I expect you to bring the reports and fees due me?"

He held out his tankard. Polly took it, looking him in

the eye. "The first of the month," he growled.

"The first of each month?" she asked.

"By crackers, that's what I said. Now pour me a beer," he shouted.

Mister Ashe and Mister Moseley were suddenly standing on either side of the overseer. The man looked from one to the other.

"Why, of course, sir. And when you bring the books, I'm sure there will be beer or an ale for you to enjoy while I add the figures." Polly handed him the full tankard.

After he finished his drink, Mister Colston settled his hat on the back of his head and strode out of the tavern without a word.

"I worry about you dealing with that man," Mister Ashe said.

"But there is no one else to deal with him," Polly answered. "I do thank you for coming."

"Polly," Charlotte asked, after they were all gone, "did I do the right thing? Mister Colston looked so fierce, so I sent Charity to get her father and I went to the Ashes."

"Oh, yes, Charlotte. You did exactly the right thing."

"But Polly, weren't you afraid of him?"

"Oh, yes. But I'll never let him know it!"

Leah began to laugh. "Don't even give the man time to say mean words. Just cut off his words 'fore they can leave his mouth."

" 'Request that you visit,' " Moze said. "Is that what you told me, Leah? Miss Polly say she 'request a visit?' " He chuckled.

"That's exactly what she said." Leah was still laughing.

Polly couldn't laugh yet. She would wait until she had the books in her hands and the money in her pocket.

Chapter 11

Polly watched her sisters stroll up the street behind Leah. A soft May breeze ruffled their new striped cotton petticoats. They looked so comely, swinging hands and chatting. She knew they would be fussing at each other by the time they got out of her sight. Timothy Charles rode in the little wagon Leah pulled. He waved his plump arms and his happy gurgles drifted back to her. They would all have such a good time visiting at Russellborough. They would have so many things to tell when they got back.

Polly sighed and looked toward the river. A sloop, the same one that had just delivered the packet of mail from Charleston, bobbed near the dock. The pilot was still on deck, so she knew the ship would be sailing with the tide. There was not another ship in sight. It was rare to have a quiet afternoon to do her paper work, to catch up on orders, to read. She stood for a moment, drinking in the aloneness.

She was startled to hear horses. Cousin Maurice and Cornelius Harnett reined in at the tavern and swung down to greet her. She led the way inside.

Cousin Maurice threw a newspaper on top of the packet of mail, then sailed his hat toward a peg on the wall. Polly poured the men beer before she grabbed up the paper to read the headlines. Parliament had passed a Stamp Act and residents in New Bern were demonstrating against the injustices of it.

Mister Harnett pointed at the pile of mail on the table. "Good King George and his Parliament have gone too far this time. They couldn't get enough revenue with their Sugar Act. So now they're trying this taxing of paper."

The details of items to be taxed were listed. Every kind of paper in use, from official documents in the courts and at the harbors to land transactions, were subject to the new tax. Playing cards and marriage licenses would require a stamp. The very newspaper she was reading would have to have a stamp on it. The paper she had signed with Cousin Maurice would not be legal without paying for a stamp.

"The Sugar Act was bad enough," Polly said to Cousin Maurice, looking at him over the top of the newspaper.

"And what do you know of the Sugar Act?" Mister Harnett asked.

Polly folded the newspaper. "I know, sir, that the act set tariffs on sugar and coffee and wines. It increased the cost of a barrel of molasses by two pounds. The Currency Act last year prohibited the colonies from printing paper money. If we cannot print money, we must use only coins. And coins, any coins from any country, are hard to come by. How then do we pay this tax?"

Mister Harnett raised his eye brows. "Sir, I run a tavern," Polly said. "I order supplies. I buy and sell."

Cousin Maurice grinned. "Cornelius, I told you she would make a go of this tavern."

Mister Harnett shook his head. "Pity Phillip didn't. I don't like the idea of a little girl running a tavern."

Polly drew herself up to her full height, ready to say that she knew that his own parents had run a tavern when they first came to Brunswick, when he was just a little boy. And besides that, she was not a little girl. But before she could speak, Mama began rocking her chair hard enough that Mister Harnett and Cousin Maurice both looked across the room at her.

"Good day, Henrietta," Cousin Maurice said. "I had not seen you sitting there."

Mama gave a half-smile and went back to her knitting.

"Maurice, when we get to Russellborough we may find that Tryon has some information on this Stamp Act that isn't in the newspapers." Mister Harnett picked up the paper to reread the headlines. "He is ready to call his first Assembly. We must be prepared with our arguments."

"I need to talk with Polly first. Then I'll be ready to go. We do need to confer with Tryon though, Cornelius. Communication is going to be more important these next few months than ever before."

Mister Harnett set his hat squarely on his head. "I'll see to my horse."

Polly stirred the stew and put another piece of wood under the fire. Then she sat at the table to wait for whatever Cousin Maurice wanted with her.

The Judge sat, leaning across the board table. He whispered, "Polly, how is Henrietta? Is she well enough to leave the house?"

"Some days Mama is better than others. Why should she have to leave the house?" Polly asked. She, too, spoke quietly.

"I want you to arrange a supper for a group of men. It will be a political meeting, but it must not appear to be anything more than a social gathering. We have to discuss this new tax and make decisions about how to respond. In the Carolinas we have always been given the right to set our own taxes in our own Assembly. That must not change. We must find a resolution for this disgraceful Stamp Act that is being imposed."

Polly leaned forward to catch each word. Taxes had become so important in running the tavern. She wanted to understand everything she could about how they were levied and how they had to be paid.

Cousin Maurice leaned back in his chair. "There must not be any women present."

She felt a flash of anger, but waited for him to continue.

"In Parliament, with all the debates over this Stamp Act, the colonists were recently called 'The Sons Of Liberty.' It might have been meant as an insult. But by God, that is what we are." The judge's voice rose as he warmed to his subject. He stood to pace up and down the room as he talked. "Liberty to make our decisions. Liberty to have representation before taxes are levied. Liberty to govern this new land."

Mister Harnett spoke from the door. "Maurice, your tones carry well."

Cousin Maurice sat down again. "Polly, can you do a supper for us?"

"How many men would you expect?" she asked.

Mister Harnett answered. "Eight or ten, I should think."

"And no women," the Judge said. "You will have to find a man to do the serving. *In nuce*, Polly, a very secret meeting."

"*In nuce*," Polly repeated, trying to remember her Latin lessons. "In a nutshell. You can have a secret meeting, sir. But why no women?"

"They aren't needful," said Mister Harnett.

"They talk," said Cousin Maurice.

Polly stood so quickly her chair scooted away from the table and overturned. She bent to right it, feeling heat from her anger beating in her brain. When she spoke her voice was how-is-the-weather pleasant. "*Necessitas non habet legem*, Cousin Maurice."

"Latin, Polly?" The judge's face showed great surprise. "Necessity has no law?"

"Sir, I studied well when I had a tutor. I do what is necessary for my family. When do you wish for me to arrange this supper meeting for men?"

"Sunday next, I think. It will take that long to get the messages to the right people. Don't you agree, Cornelius?"

Mister Harnett nodded.

"And you will pay the usual supper fee for each person?" Polly asked. The only evidence of her anger was in the clip of her question. Neither of the men seemed to notice.

Cousin Maurice took his hat from the wall peg. "Are you always the proprietor, Polly? You could not give a meal for friends?"

"Sir, you did not ask me to give a meal for friends. You asked me to make a contract in a business proposition. I can only do that for profit. I have to pay taxes, too."

Cousin Maurice turned at the door and gave her a piercing look before he answered. "We will, of course, pay the usual supper fee."

She watched the men ride away before she turned to collect the beer mugs. She slammed one of the heavy mugs on the table. "Liberty!" she screamed. She thudded the mug again. "*Sons* of Liberty!" And for the third time she hit the table. "No women!"

She hurled the mug at the stone fireplace. Shards of pottery clattered to the floor as she picked up the next one, ready to throw it.

Her mother jerked the heavy mug from Polly and set it on the table. Then Henrietta took Polly's hand and pulled her toward the stairs.

Chapter 12

"Mama? What is it, Mama?"

Henrietta shook her head and continued up the steps. Polly followed to the attic room above the bed chambers. Straight to one of the storage trunks Henrietta went. She opened the top of the trunk and kneeling on the floor, began to lift out old clothes. She handed Polly a pair of broadcloth breeches with great silver buckles at the knee. The finish was tarnished with age, but Polly knew that polishing would restore them. Mama continued to sort through other garments. From near the bottom of the trunk she pulled out a man's lawn shirt with great sleeves and a ruffled front piece. She gave the shirt to Polly and began to return the items to the trunk.

When everything was packed to her satisfaction, Henrietta straightened and rubbed her back. Polly turned to leave, but she saw that her mother wasn't yet through. She was searching, with her eyes, across boards that stretched on pegs on the wall. Suddenly she reached up, pulled down a little leather-bound book and put it in Polly's hands. And she was gone, almost running from the room.

Polly followed her, clutching the clothing and book to her chest. When she reached the tavern room, her mother was seated in the rocking chair, knitting. Her face showed not a sign that she had ever moved.

"Mama, what do you want me to do with these clothes?"

Henrietta gave no sign that she had heard.

Polly put the book on the table and held the yellowed shirt up to the light of the window. What was she to do with it? It would fit her, and so would the breeches. She dropped the clothes on the bench to pick up the book. It was the play *Twelfth Night* by Shakespeare. She had read portions of the play with Justina Davis Dobbs when they were in school. She had played the part of Viola, who dressed like a man. Justina had played the part of Viola's brother, Sebastian. The brother and sister traded places for protection. For a long time, in the story, they got away with their charade.

"Is that it, Mama? Do I dress like a man and serve Cousin Maurice at his political supper?" Polly warmed to the idea. "I could. I know I could. Oh, Mama, how did you ever think of something so outrageous!"

Polly knelt by her mother's chair. "Mama, talk to me. Please talk to me. You know what's going on around us. You know how much I value and need your advice."

Her mother picked up her knitting.

"Mama, there is no one I can talk with. There is no one in whom I can confide. Sometimes it gets to be too much, with the cooking and cleaning, the paper work and worrying about money." She waited but her mother did not answer. Nothing on her face showed that she had heard the words.

"The planting is going well," Polly continued. "The men have been doing a good job in the fields. We have the first vegetables for the stew. If the weather holds, we will have a bountiful harvest this year. But will it be enough?

"Mister Colston has brought the first accounting of the maritime products. It doesn't tally with the logs and barrels I see coming by on the road. He's loading more than he's reporting. I don't know what to do about it. Oh, Mama, did Papa ever talk about the business of the tavern? Did he ever share information about the sawmill or the turpentine production?"

Henrietta shook her head and Polly knew that continued questions were futile. She sat at the table with the book. She was still reading when Charlotte and Cecilia returned from their visit. Little Margaret Tryon and her nurse were with them.

"There will be a baby when I go home," Margaret exclaimed.

"She can stay and visit, can't she, Polly?" Cecilia begged.

"Of course she can. Margaret, we are most glad to have you. What about a baby?"

"We are going to have a baby like Timothy Charles. Mother doesn't know exactly when. And it might be a baby girl instead of a baby boy. But if I stay here and I'm good and do what I'm told, when I get home I can hold him like Cecilia does your baby." Little Margaret jumped up and down in her excitement.

Leah spoke quietly. "Miss Polly, things is mighty hectic over to Russellborough. The governor himself suggest Little Miss Margaret come over here with Miss Cecilia."

"There's no problem, Leah. We'll manage."

"And Miss Polly, Daniel be at the barn working. He came back with us just now from the governor's house. He ask you to come out there. He wanted to talk to you about something."

Polly set Leah and Charlotte to the task of fixing the supper meal. She sent Cecilia and Margaret with the nurse, Hattie, out to play. She sorted through the pieces of mail and arranged them on the mantel for folks to pick up. She took the clothes that she had brought from the attic out to the wash house. She stashed *Twelfth Night* under the counter. As she directed the activities of the house, she planned a party in her head. There would need to be at least three meats. Would the new potatoes be ready to dig? Could she send Boy to the swamp to find wild strawberries? Who was she going to find to help with the serving?

She took a deep breath and knew that she had delayed as long as she could. She went to find Daniel.

He was in the lot behind the barn, using straw to brush down a fine chestnut mare. He led the horse into the barn and tied her loosely to a post.

Polly followed. A milk cow lowered softly from her stall. A pigeon cooed from the rafters. Daniel turned from his tasks and stood quietly, just looking at her.

Polly's heart was thudding so loudly that all she wanted to do was run away. She grabbed a wooden bucket from its peg on the wall and set it upside down to sit on.

Mister Ashe's gelding snorted. Daniel grinned at the sound and sat down in the straw, his back against a post.

Polly found her voice. "Leah said you wanted to see me."

"I always want to see you."

Polly pushed her hands into her pockets. She was determined that Daniel would not know the confusion she felt when she looked at him. "And what do you want to see me about?"

"Snippy-snappy are you today, Polly?"

She shook her head. "No. Just busy."

"Then I'll not keep you long." Daniel brushed a piece of straw from his stockings. "Judge Moore told me that he had asked you to give a supper next week. I am to stay here to help you."

"Daniel, who holds your indenture?"

Daniel frowned. "Does it matter?"

"Not really. But when Papa was here you were here. Then when Papa went away you went to Russellborough and stayed with Governor Tryon. Now you say that Cousin Maurice has asked you to come back here for a time. I guess I'm trying to . . ."

"Trying to figure out where I belong?"

"Oh, Daniel, I'm always trying to figure things out."

Daniel moved to kneel beside her. "Polly, I'm indentured to Judge Moore. He sent me to Brunswick to help your father." He reached to touch her cheek, and with his finger began to trace the line of her jaw. "Then he needed to know about the new governor and where he stood on certain issues."

Polly pulled back from the caressing hand. "You're a spy!" she shouted.

Daniel stood. "Tell the town, Polly."

She jumped up from the stool. Back and forth she paced, her petticoats sweeping through the straw. Every time she passed him she beat her fists in the air. On her third turn, he caught her wrists and pulled her to his chest.

For a moment she leaned there, feeling the strength of him. She knew that if she let herself she could rest forever in his brawny arms. Oh, how she wanted to lay down the duties and burdens of her life. Oh, how she wanted to stay here in the security of his embrace. She looked up into his face.

But he had been spying on her! She pushed away from him and ran from the barn.

Chapter 13

The news of demonstrations reached The Anchor with increasing speed. From New Bern, from Edenton, from Cross Creek, the information came into the tavern. The end of May had been quiet for shipping, but June brought brigs and brigantines from England and the islands. A captain and his mate from a Massachusetts sloop brought newspapers from Boston and from New York. The Pennsylvania papers came with information of unrest there. In one colony a government official was burned in effigy. A harbor master's office was ransacked in another. Many people of the colonies resented the Stamp Act passed by Parliament and they wanted King George to know it.

Cousin Maurice sent a rider to tell Polly that the dinner was definitely set. Only the number of participants was changed. She should expect at least fifteen men to be at the tavern by dark on Sunday.

Polly didn't know the young messenger, but his horse had been ridden hard. She suspected that he still had several other destinations before he returned to the judge's home at Rocky Point. She gave him a mug of ale and sent him on his way.

Cousin Maurice had also sent the latest New Bern papers with the young rider. The business of the Assembly was the major news. Governor Tryon, it was reported, asked Assembly Speaker John Ashe what the people would do about the Stamp tax. And Mister Ashe answered firmly, "The people will resist to the death!"

Now the words of rebellion against the tax were officially spoken. They were written in the paper for all to read. And the words had come from a man who lived in their own little port of Brunswick.

When she tried to talk with Mistress Ashe, the good woman cut her short. "Polly, I do not deal with things like that. Taxes and money are best left with the men. I do not understand why you expend one moment even thinking about taxes."

"I want to feed my family," Polly said. "If I don't think about it, there is no one else to do it for me. But, Mistress Ashe, what if something happened so that you had to deal with money? What if you were alone and had to find out about taxes?" Polly pleaded.

But Mistress Ashe refused to say another word on the matter.

To quiet the arguments about the Stamp Act, Governor Tryon cut short the session of the Assembly and dispersed the assemblymen. He could stop the business of the government and he did. He could not stop the news. Every landowner with business in the courts, every merchant reading his newspaper over coffee at his breakfast, every ship master playing cards in a tavern, knew that the hateful tax would become a reality on the first day of November, 1765. It was all that was talked about at The Anchor.

Some men spoke in whispers. Some disagreed loudly. A sailor from a British ship pulled his knife on a young lad from the crew of a Boston sloop before an officer intervened. Polly and Leah bound the cut on the boy's arm and his captain led him away by the ear.

Polly called Leah and sat with her on the bench outside the door to lay out help plans for the supper.

"Lawdy, Miss Polly. We gonna need help. You talking about a lot of extra work."

"What about the girl that helped Moze with the goats?"

"That be little Morrow. She'll be good help." Leah bit her lip while she thought. "She belong to you. You can do what you wants to with her."

"What do you mean, Leah? How does she belong to me?"

"She your slave, Miss Polly. Don't you know that? Her mama died 'bout three years ago. I 'spects that was during the time you was over in Wilmington. Her mama was the Jennie that cooked for Mister Colston. And her papa works at the turpentine mill. You owns all of 'em."

"And with her mother dead, who looks after her?" Polly asked.

"Moze. He cares for all them children who don't have nobody."

Polly looked toward the docks. A brigantine was getting ready to depart and a large sloop was tacking its way toward the middle of the river. She could see sails from two ships that were still out in the ocean. As close as they were hugging the shore line, they were probably making for the Cape Fear entrance. A pair of oxen pulled a skid loaded with lumber down the street. Leah was right. She had to have more help.

"Bring Morrow with you in the morning. We'll see how that works out. Tell Boy I'll need him, too."

"Miss Polly, you gonna make Boy a house boy? He a smart one, that child is."

"We'll see, Leah. We'll see. Please get started now on all the things I told you about. I have to find Daniel. I'm going to need meat for the table."

"He's at the barn," Leah said. "And Miss Polly, while you thinking about food, think fish and crabs. They mighty plentiful this time of year."

Polly found Daniel working with the horses. She had not talked to him since she called him a spy and ran from him. She approached the fence and stood watching as he led a half-grown colt around and around on a rope halter.

At last he set the colt free and walked over, hat in hand, to stand by the fence. "Your servant, ma'am," he said.

"You're not my servant, Daniel."

"Then how may I help a friend?"

"You may help by getting the meat for this supper I'm doing on Sunday. I thought we could have turkey. There is a big flock near the edge of the swamp and it shouldn't be hard to trap a couple of them. We can keep them in the chicken pens until Sunday morning." Polly took a deep breath. "Trout would be good to have. Crab stuffing would taste delicious with fish."

Daniel interrupted her. "You're trying not to go into stores?"

She nodded.

"Then think about roasting a goat," Daniel said. "You have quite a herd now."

"I like that idea. And when you go fishing, can you take Boy so he can gather strawberries and mint?"

Daniel swung his leg up over the top rail of the fence to straddle the log. "Polly, you do know I never meant to hurt you. We had to stop your father. He was selling slaves to get his gambling money. He lost three riding horses. He was in debt to the point that he was going to lose everything he had. The forest lands, the turpentine works and the tavern all were in peril. His gambling started long ago, but he got more and more reckless. Please understand this, Polly."

"But now you're spying on me!"

Daniel chuckled and his blue eyes seemed to darken. "Pauline Moore, I spy on you every chance I get. It is the most pleasant thing I do."

"I'm serious."

"I know you are, Polly." The smile stayed on his face. "I know you are. You're much too serious. You work much too hard. You have the care of your household and the tavern and so many other things as well. And now the judge is drawing you into this political situation."

Daniel jumped down from the fence to stand beside her. "You shall have your goat and your fish and your strawberries and your mint. If I can shoot a deer, you shall have venison as well. You shall have a great fire pit in the yard for roasting, to keep the heat out of the tavern." He took a deep breath. "You should have rubies for your fingers and pearls to string about your neck."

Polly felt her face turn crimson and she knotted her hands over her stomach to still its sudden churning. She backed away from the love she saw shining in Daniel's face.

Very soberly, with not a hint of a smile, he said, "Take care, my pretty Polly. And I shall be spying on you."

"Oh, Daniel," she whispered. She turned and ran as fast as she could move her shaking legs.

Chapter 14

The noises from the yard woke Polly before light on Sunday morning. She dressed and hurried down the stairs to investigate. When she opened the door she saw that Daniel had fires started in both of the fire pits that he had dug during the week. Jeremiah and Isaac spiked the carcass of a deer on an iron pole and swung the heavy burden to rest on tripods fixed at the edges of the pit. Blood dripping on the burning logs sent out a sizzling sound and Polly knew that the deer had been slaughtered during the night.

She watched for a minute before she started the breakfast mush. She put a rasher of bacon in the huge iron spider, and as the grease began to sputter, she slid on a cover.

"Morning, Miss Polly," Morrow said from the door.

"Do those men know what they be doing?" Leah asked, as she came in behind the little girl.

Polly laughed. "Leah, if they don't, I'm not going to ask them at this point. I'm just glad they have all that cooking heat outside." She turned to the girl. "Morrow, keep the mush stirred. And turn the bacon. Those men will be ready to eat soon."

The pungent odor drew townspeople and ships' captains, with members of their crews, to the tavern. Daniel set up sawhorses with boards laid across them to put out the food. He moved a barrel of beer and a cask of ale out to serve under the shade of trees in the yard. Twice he came into the tavern to hand Polly a knotted handkerchief filled with coins.

"Is there going to be enough food for tonight?" Polly asked him, as she returned his handkerchief.

Daniel nodded. "There will be enough."

In the late afternoon Daniel put up a sign:

> Private Party tonight.
> Come partake tomorrow.

As she took her strawberry cobblers and dried peach pies from the outside oven, men tipped their hats to her and began moving toward home or the docks.

The tables in the tavern were set with Mama's best pewter plates laid on red-and-white checked cloths. A candelabra, with seven candles, sat in the center of the long table in the middle of the room. On smaller tables scattered about the room Polly set up games. At one she put Papa's chess set with the scrimshaw pieces. On another table she had playing cards. If this was supposed to be a social event, then it had to look like one. She smiled to herself at the view.

She had only told Charlotte and Cecilia that Cousin Maurice had asked her to serve some of his friends. Mama, of course, knew what the supper was all about. It was John Ashe who had asked his wife to have Mama and the girls at his home for the evening. Nobody had asked her where she would be.

"Charlotte, please come help me," she said now quietly to her sister.

"Now help you do what? I've been working all day for this party that I can't even come to. We're all ready to go to Mistress Ashe's house. Polly, Mistress Ashe is going to have entertainment. We'll sing songs and do recitations."

Charlotte tilted her head and held out her hand as if a partner stood in front of her. " 'Soldier, soldier will you marry me, with your musket, fife and drum?' " She turned her head the other way and answered herself in a deeper voice. " 'Oh, how can I marry such a pretty girl as you, When I have no hat to put on?' "

She turned to Polly and stamped her foot. "I don't want to be late for any of that. I've practiced and practiced my recitation."

"I need you, Charlotte," Polly said.

"It better be important." Charlotte looked around the room. "What? Where?"

"Our bed chamber," Polly answered.

Charlotte muttered as she followed Polly up the stairs. "Workhorse. You treat me like one of the slaves. We never have any fun. Just work, work, work. Higgler. Higgler."

Polly ignored her. She went straight to the clothes press. She took out the shirt and breeches Leah had washed and ironed, and put them on the bed. Quickly she stripped to her shift and bathed with the water she had earlier carried up for the wash basin.

Charlotte had been singing. " 'Musha ringum durum da, there's whiskey in the jar.' " She stopped her tune and picked up the shirt. "This is beautiful. Whose is it?"

"Mine," Polly said. She took the shirt from Charlotte and slipped it on. Sitting on the bed she put on white hose and tied the garters. She pulled on the breeches, fastening the buckles just below the knee.

"Polly, what are you doing?" Charlotte screeched. "You look like a boy!"

"Good. That's the whole idea. 'I prithee conceal me what I am and be my aid for such disguise as haply shall become the form of my intent.' "

"Polly, what are you talking about?" Charlotte asked.

"It's a quote from another girl who dressed up like a

man to get her work done. Now help me with my hair. I need a braid and I don't know how to fix it."

Charlotte plopped down on the bed. "Mama would have a fit!"

"Mama knows. Now please help me with my hair."

"Well, sit down." Charlotte patted the bed beside her. She took the comb and began to work.

Polly felt the tug as Charlotte braided. What if this didn't work? What if she didn't look enough like a boy to carry out her plan?

"Be still, Polly," Charlotte scolded. "If you wiggle around I'll never get this done."

"I'm scared."

"You? Scared? Polly, I didn't know anything scared you." Charlotte turned Polly's head to look at her face. "You're really scared?"

"I'm scared most of the time, Charlotte."

"Well, there is no need to be scared tonight. When I get through with you, it will take Mama to recognize who you are." Charlotte hurried over to the clothes press and began sorting through ribbons. She selected a black cotton one to tie on the end of the braid.

"Now," she finally said. "Stand up. Turn around." She nodded. "A bow, please."

Polly took an imaginary hat from her head and swept it to the floor in a courtly bow. When she straightened, she looked at her sister. "Well?"

"And, my dear sir, what is your name?"

"My name? I hadn't thought of that."

Charlotte crossed her arms and frowned. She walked around her sister, shaking her head. She stepped in front of her and gave a curtsy. "Why, Paul Moore, how kind of you to help us out tonight."

Polly grabbed Charlotte's arms and twirled her about. "Paul is a perfect name."

Horses snorted and men's voices came from the road outside the tavern. Polly tried to twist away, but Charlotte held on to her. "You are the most annoying sister any girl ever had. You're a higgler and sometimes I really, really hate you. But you are the bravest sister any girl every had."

Charlotte threw their hands into the air. "Sister, go be a man!"

Chapter 15

Polly stood at the foot of the stairs, looking about the room. Leah turned from the fireplace to watch Charlotte glide between the tables.

"Miss Charlotte, you look mighty fine tonight. You and your mama will have a nice time with Mistress Ashe," Leah said. "Miss Cecilia already gone with her and the baby. They didn't know what was taking you so long up in the bed chamber."

Charlotte stopped to adjust her shawl and flutter her fan. She swept a deep curtsy to Cousin Maurice as he came through the door.

He bowed to her, then sailed his hat toward the wall peg.

Mister Harnett, coming in on the heels of his friend, shook his head as he watched the hat fly through the air and settle, with a spin, on the peg. "One of these days, Maurice, you'll send that hat out the window."

Charlotte slipped through the door before several more men made their way into the tavern. Polly felt frozen in place, her stomach churning, as she watched the men greet each other. Boy came from behind the counter to offer refreshment and the men accepted the goblets of wine he carried on the huge pewter tray. Leah followed Boy with another tray, filled with warm pasties and cheese biscuits flavored with bits of bacon. Leah was a slave, so she didn't count as a woman to help serve at the supper.

Mister Ashe and Mister Moseley seemed to know all of the other guests. Mister Dry, as commissioner of pilotage for the Cape Fear River, and the customs collector of the Port of Brunswick, knew everyone as well. It seemed strange to Polly that Mister Dry, who would be responsible for collecting monies from the Stamp Act, if they could not stop it, should be present to discuss the very issue of how to stop distribution of the stamps.

Mister Dry was talking with William Hooper, who had not been to the tavern before. They lifted their pewter goblets toward each other. Mister Hooper took a sip as he listened to a comment. He was so young. And he was so pretty, with full smooth lips and beautiful eyes. Polly stifled a giggle, clutched at her stomach and wondered if she would ever again be able to move her feet. She was more afraid than she had ever been in her life. What if someone recognized her.

Then she saw Daniel striding across the yard toward the door. He was dressed in gray linen britches and a brocaded waistcoat. His crimson cravat was tied just so at his throat. His hair was braided and powdered. Polly knew that he belonged with this group of men — lawyers and judges, elected and appointed officials of the colony — as they discussed affairs of state.

Daniel stopped to speak to Jeremiah and Isaac, still working over the cook fires. As he lifted the great wooden tray of sliced venison to bring into the tavern, Polly took a deep breath and finally moved.

An hour later Polly knew the party was going well and she didn't think any one, except Boy, had recognized her. Boy had grinned at her before he continued with his tasks. Leah had looked a little startled when Polly began to dish up the vegetables to serve, but they soon were working together as they had done for years. The men, intent on food and conversation, never looked at them.

They talked of farming. William Moore, who had taken over Orton Plantation from his father, King Roger, went into detail on the rice culture. He had just returned from an inspection visit to the South Carolina islands where rice was also widely grown. Orton was much closer to Brunswick than the judge's plantation across the river, but Polly rarely saw this kinsman. He talked of the new shipment of slaves from Barbados he had received recently.

One of the men discussed tobacco he grew on his plantation. Another had planted great fields of peanuts. Still another belabored the fact that he was having to move further west to tap pines for his turpentine products.

"Gentlemen, King George knows not what he does. If he suppresses trade, he draws the knife to cut his own life line," Mister Hooper said.

"Hear! Hear!" cried out Mister Moseley.

Polly didn't think that the men, now that they had eaten their fill and started into politics, would need more attention for a while. She settled down on a stool behind the counter, leaning her back against the wall. She took a deep breath and let it out silently.

Boy climbed on a stool next to her. "Serving is a powerful lot of work," he said.

"Shhh."

Boy nodded and closed his eyes.

"We must be taxed only with our own consent," Cousin Maurice called down the table. "We must have our own representatives. English law demands it."

"Our voices were stilled only temporarily when Governor Tryon sent us packing from the Assembly in New Bern," said John Ashe. "But we are making ourselves heard.

The people are speaking out. The demonstrations against the Stamp Tax at New Bern and Edenton, at Cross Creek and Wilmington, prove that."

"Is there anyone here who does not know that the appointed distributor of stamps for the province was burned in effigy?" asked Mister Moseley. "That demonstration in New Bern was most serious."

"And the same performances are being repeated in Cross Creek," said one of the men far down the table.

"Wilmington also burned the stamp distributor in effigy. The mood in that town is explosive," said another man.

Mister Hooper spoke. "What I hear from my friends and family in Boston bears out this point of representation, Maurice. People are gathering to find ways to distribute information and pamphlets are being printed. Men are speaking out. This Stamp Act is intolerable."

"You all must have seen the pamphlet our own Maurice published," said John Ashe. "He states eloquently that the colonists are not a conquered people. That we are constitutionally entitled to be taxed only by our own consent. Imposing a stamp duty on us, here in the colonies, is as impossible as it is inconsistent with our rights."

Mister Harnett rose from his seat and raised his goblet. "Gentlemen, to the Sons of Liberty."

Boy shivered.

Every man at the table raised his goblet and drank to the toast. And for a moment there was silence.

"The repeal of portions of the Sugar Act shows that we do have some voice," Mister Moseley said to the group. "We must find ways to speak so that Parliament will listen."

"And that is precisely why we meet here tonight," the judge responded.

"We know the British have to pay for their wars,"

Mister Ashe said. "We know the cost in lives and equipment, in gun powder and horse flesh. Several of us in this very room fought in the French and Indian War." He pointed to Maurice. "You and I rode side by side in the wilderness as we fought." He nodded toward William Dry. "You, sir, rode with us. I felt proud to serve my king and ride with men of distinction." He took a swallow of wine and held the goblet between both hands. "But this tax, that is said to cover the cost of that war, is too encompassing. It assumes that, instead of trade and barter, we have money."

"We cannot issue paper currency. We cannot mint coin. We have only the trade monies that come into the ports." Mister Hooper's voice was grave.

Mister Harnett rose and began to pace about. "The Sugar Act showed us that Parliament could dare to tax the colonies. Taxing trade is one thing. But this is different. The Stamp Act is a direct tax." He slapped the table with the flat of his hand. "A direct tax, gentlemen. Not to be tolerated."

A man shouted, "Representation! Liberty!"

"Liberty," Boy whispered. "Is that freedom, Miss Polly?"

Maurice Moore held up his hand. "Gentlemen, we are Englishmen. We must band with other colonies to inform King George of our opinions and to remind him of our rights. We must be represented. We must push for the liberties that are inalienably ours. But through discussion. With calmness. With clear heads."

He looked down the table. "We will form our committees to begin correspondence with other colonies. We must never allow ourselves to be isolated. We must never allow Parliament to think that they deal with just one severed group. We must know what is happening from the most

northern point of Massachusetts to the southern border of the Georgian colony." He raised his goblet. "*Non sibi sed Patriae.*"

"For country," repeated Mister Hooper.

As the men began to break into groups, forming their committees and taking assignments for correspondence, Boy whispered, "Miss Polly, do they mean liberty for everybody?"

"I'd like to claim it," Polly said.

"You free, Miss Polly."

"Oh, yes," Polly muttered. "Free as an opossum carrying her babies on her back, creeping through the swamp, hoping no water moccasin invades her tree limb, wishing that food were more plentiful. Praying, if creatures pray."

"Didn't know you felt like that, Miss Polly."

Leah hurried over from the bench by the hearth to the counter. "You two be quiet," she admonished in a low voice. She leaned over and glared at them. "The judge looking over this way at you young 'uns. Behave, now." Then she signed. "How much longer they gonna talk, you reckon?"

"Leah, they talking liberty," Boy confided.

"And you better take the liberty to close your mouth, you black imp. You here to serve these white men. Not talk about what they talking about." Leah shook her finger in Boy's face. "Boy, you have to be careful. Take that tray of drinks around again. Mind your manners while you do it."

Several men declined the drinks that Boy served. Mister Hooper reached for his hat, ready to leave. Mister Harnett was again pacing the floor.

Cousin Maurice raised his voice. "As we continue with this important issue, remember discretion, gentlemen. Are we agreed on that?"

Murmurs of compliance arose from each man. They

said their good nights. Leah began to wash dishes in the hot water she had at the ready. Boy dried and stacked the platters and goblets in the center of the table. Polly wrapped and covered the food.

As she turned from stacking the left over pies under the counter, she found Cousin Maurice at her elbow.

"Yes, sir?" she asked. She wrapped the towel she had been holding around her hands.

"I don't know where Polly found you, but you did a credible job here tonight. I might need to use you sometime myself. Your name, lad."

Polly twisted her fingers under the towel and stammered, "P - P - Paul."

"Paul, eh?" Cousin Maurice put his hat on and went to the open door. "Tell Miss Polly I'll see her later in the week."

He was gone. Polly listened as his horse trotted away. She sank down on the floor and hid her face in the towel.

Leah wiped her hands on her apron and burst out laughing. "Miss Polly, I heard tell of them folks who act on the stage and plays parts of other folk's lives. We got us a real live actor right here in this tavern. Lawdy, you plays a good part."

Polly looked over her towel-clasped hands. "When did you know it was me, Leah?"

"Well, at first I wonder who you gave that fine shirt to. That shirt I work over so hard all week." Leah let out another deep belly laugh. "I recognized you when you started serving up the bowls. Lawdy, Lawdy, Miss Polly!"

"I knew before you," Boy said, and grinned at them.

"Did any of the men recognize me, Leah?"

"Not a one, child. Not a one. Not even the judge just now when he was talking to you face to face. And Paul!

How did you come up with that name?" Leah huffed. "That Daniel Cooper hisself didn't even know it was you! Now if we had a room full of women, you wouldn't have fooled a one of 'em."

"Miss Polly, I ask before. Can you tell me now?" Boy pleaded. "Does liberty mean freedom?"

"Liberty! Freedom! Boy, these men think only in terms of their own positions." She wrung the towel between her hands. "Freedom to do business and manage the business of women and children and those who cannot help themselves. I'm not expected to think or understand because I'm a woman. You, Boy, are not expected to think or understand because you're a slave. But we do understand! We do!"

Polly could almost hear Mistress Ashe's view of the discussions that had gone around the table tonight. Why should a woman even think about money or taxes or government? she would say and dismiss any other thought.

"Boy, liberty and freedom are the same, in the way you ask. And as long as I have any control over it . . ." She stopped, remembering she had control only as long as she was declared incompetent. She took a deep breath. "Boy, as long as I have any control over it, you shall be as free as I am."

Chapter 16

Polly was in the fields, that hot August and into September, supervising the men working with the harvest. From the time the first rays of the sun rose over the horizon until it was too dark to see without lighting a candle, she worked. The corn crop was the best that she had seen. She and Jeremiah had rigged giant swaying scarecrows of straw, dressed in bright rags, that danced in the slightest breeze and kept most of the pesky fowl from the ears of ripening grain.

The sweet potatoes were almost ready to dig. A bear had raided the potato field during the earlier part of the summer. Daniel kept watch throughout several nights, waiting for its return. The report of the musket one early morning woke her, and she knew they would feast on bear meat for the next several meals.

She had planted peanuts this year, a crop Papa had never thought to try. When she pulled a bush to try a pea, it was as sweet as any she had ever tasted. And she had planted two acres of tobacco that had a most beautiful yellow leaf. Most of the men from the sawmill and tree tapping were pressed into the fields and there were days when she picked up a hoe and worked along side them to set the pace.

Isaac understood the soil. Polly found herself relying more and more on his judgment. "Is the corn ready for picking?" she would ask.

"No, ma'am. It needs 'bout two more weeks 'fore we sends it to the grist mill."

"See to it," she said, and went off to some other task.

Today she had worked in the house garden, gathering beans and peas. She brought a basket of beans to the house and set Cecilia to shelling them. Then she sank down on the bench by the hearth

"The bounty will kill me, Leah." Polly wiped her face with the tail of her apron.

"I never see a white woman work like you do, Miss Polly." Leah handed her a tankard of ale and sat beside her.

Polly took a sip of the liquid and sighed. "I can't keep up with it all. I can't!"

"You just tired, child." Leah put her arms around her and rocked them both back and forth. "You been working in those fields right along with the men. You been keeping this tavern running. You got Miss Henrietta and the girls and Timothy Charles to see to. You just tired. You need some time to yourself."

"Time is what I don't have."

Leah straightened up. "You smells like a field hand, Miss Polly. I gonna fix you a bath in the wash house. We gonna find some of that perfumed soap to wash your hair. We gonna change your clothes from the shift out. You gonna feel better."

Polly sat on the bench as Leah bustled about. The bag of mail lay unopened on a table by the door. She knew it would contain instructions from Cousin Maurice about people she needed to get messages to, for he had made her an intermediator between several of the groups. The newspapers from Charleston and Boston, from Philadelphia and New York, would be filled with news of the conflict over the Stamp Act. Committees in every colony would be sending messages of the antagonism between the spokesmen here and the insistence from Parliament in England that the tax on paper would be paid. The stamps were due to arrive on November the first. That was only a few weeks away. She needed to read all of the mail. She needed to answer letters. She went over to open the pouch.

"No, ma'am, Miss Polly." Leah interrupted her. "You gonna take a bath. And then you gonna eat. Now you just follow me out to the wash house and put yourself in the tub."

"Someone has to watch for customers, Leah."

"I sent Morrow to fetch Miss Charlotte. She be down to the Moseleys talking to Miss Charity. Miss Henrietta in her room. And Boy be round some place. I sent him out to gather the eggs, so he be back directly. Now you stop fretting and come on."

Polly submitted to Leah's care. As the woman poured water over her head and began to work lather into her hair, Polly leaned back in the tin tub. She closed her eyes to keep out the soap and felt her muscles twitch before they began to relax. It was almost too soon before Leah told her to stand up. She wrapped a linen sheet around her and began toweling her hair dry.

The warmth from the fire and the care of Leah's hands tugged the last of the tiredness from her bones. She even let the woman dress her.

"Now you gonna eat. You so skinny, Miss Polly."

"But I'm not hungry."

"Hungry or not, you will eat. Lawdy, Miss Polly, don't you know that you runs this place. Don't you know that without you, we'd all be gone some place else, sold off to Lord knows where, into Lord knows what. You the center. You the man of this tavern and the fields and all that bounty you be fussing about." Leah reached out to straighten a fold in Polly's petticoat. "You got to eat and stay well and strong."

"If Papa came back —"

"Don't even mention that, child. It was while you was studying over in Wilmington that your papa almost lost this place. He sold off Cook. He sold most of the Negroes, 'specially the ones that would bring any kind of a price. He seem to go through his books, picking off every slave that would pay his debts, 'cept the ones down in the turpentine woods. He gambled away his finest riding horse and sold the work horse. He talked to Miss Henrietta about selling me, and I be with her since she was a little girl living in Edenton where your papa first met her."

Leah slumped down on a bench. "Miss Cecilia was sick with the fever. Your papa was drinking himself into a stupor most every night. Miss Charlotte was so lost she stayed angry all the time. Your mama was grieving over all of it. And nobody seem able to do nothing. The Lord might strike me down for saying it, but Miss Polly, you don't want Mister Phillip back."

Polly nodded and reached to pick up her dirty clothes.

"I'll do that, child. You go get your something-to-eat. There's squirrel stew in the pot. And some rice cakes left from noon."

Polly walked slowly across the yard. Charlotte and Boy were sitting at the table outside, a basket of eggs and a book between them. Neither of them looked up as she went in the tavern. Mama sat in her rocking chair, knitting. Cecilia played with her dolls near Mama's feet. Timothy Charles crawled in and around the rockers of the chair, petting one of the yellow cats and gurgling happy sounds.

She served herself a bowl of stew and spooned portions of it into her mouth with a rice cake. She was munching on the second rice cake when she heard shouts from the yard. She ran to the door.

"Lawdy, Miss Polly, come quick. Mister Colston took Boy!" Leah cried.

"What do you mean?" Polly asked. "Took him where?"

"I don't know where. He drag him up from the bench and drag him off toward the barn."

Polly hurried out into the yard. Charlotte sat crying at the sawhorse table.

"Charlotte, what happened?" she asked.

Her sister lifted her tear stained face toward Polly. "Boy and I were just sitting here. I was reading and he was listening. And then Mister Colston came up and started screaming at us."

Polly ran toward the barn. As she turned into the space near the horse lot she saw a group of men from the sawmill standing near the fence. Colston's back was to her. It took a moment to realize that he was tying Boy's wrists to the limb of a sapling. The full weight of Boy's body hung from his arms. Not even his toes touched the ground.

Colston stepped back, nodding, as if a job had been done to his satisfaction. From his belt he pulled the short whip that he always carried with him.

Polly screamed, "No!"

The blow from the whip ate into Boy's back. The force of the lash spun the child's body against the tree.

Polly ran to grab Colston's elbow. He flung her to the ground.

She heard a mumbling from the men and a soft moaning from Boy. She heard Leah pleading. "Miss Polly! Lawdy, Miss Polly! Is you hurt?"

Polly scrambled to her feet and faced the man. "Mister Colston, do not do this."

He looked over her shoulder at the figure swinging by

his arms from the tree limb. Again he raised the whip.

Polly turned and covered Boy's body with her own. The blow of the whip ripped her gown and shredded into her flesh. The pain seared through her and she held on to the limb to keep from falling. From behind her there was a silence so deep that she wondered if she had lost her hearing. Then Boy's voice reached her.

"Though I walk through the valley of the shadow of death, Lord," the child recited. "Though I walk through the valley of the shadow of death."

"I will fear no evil," Polly whispered. She felt blood from Boy's back soaking into the front of her gown.

"Though I walk through the valley of the shadow of death," he said again.

"I will fear no evil," Polly answered him.

She let go of the tree limb. She turned to face the overseer.

The whip lay at his feet. He stood, hands on his hips, looking at her.

Polly staggered to keep her balance, but she held out her hand. "Your knife, sir," she said. "Give me your knife."

He pulled his hunting knife from the belt at his waist and handed it to her.

"Jeremiah," she called.

Jeremiah stepped from the group of men and walked to her.

Polly extended the knife toward him. "Cut him loose." She took a deep breath as pain shot through her. "Cut Boy loose, Jeremiah. Take him to Moze."

Leah put her hand under Polly's elbow as Jeremiah took the knife but she shook off the help. "Not yet, Leah. Not yet. This isn't over."

Colston glared at her, apprehension and defiance open on his face. "Mister Colston, you are dismissed." Polly fought to keep her balance as pain coursed through her. She struggled against nausea that threatened to double her to her knees, but she never took her eyes from the overseer's face. "You will bring the books to the tavern within the hour. You will leave after that and never set foot on my property again."

"I don't think you can get rid of me, ma'am," Colston said.

"Try me, Mister Colston. Please try me, sir."

"You ain't nothing but a nigger-loving woman."

"Mister Colston, you are absolutely right." Polly allowed herself to put her hand on Leah's shoulder. Without turning she called, "Isaac, are you there?"

"Yes, ma'am."

"Get these men back to work, please. They were moving hogsheads down to the dock and they need to get on with it. If there is any trouble, send for me."

"Yes, Miss Polly."

"Mister Colston, I believe I gave you an order." She still had not taken her eyes from the man's face.

He picked up his whip. Snaking it against his boots, he walked to his horse and swung himself into the saddle. Then he gave a shout and galloped from the barn lot.

Polly leaned heavily on Leah's shoulder and dared to look around the yard. Henrietta stood with Timothy Charles in her arms. It was the first time Polly had ever seen her mother touch the baby. Cecilia was clutching Mama's petticoat with one hand and her doll with the other. Charlotte and Morrow stood just behind them, their eyes wide.

As Polly walked toward the house, she gave orders. "Morrow, fill a jug with rum and take it down to Moze. Find out what else he will need to treat Boy and come straight back to let me know.

"Charlotte, find Mister Ashe or Mister Moseley. Ask them to come to help me. But Charlotte, don't tell them yet what happened here. I don't want a vigilante group going after Mister Colston before I have the record books."

"Miss Polly," Leah interrupted. "We got to get you taken care of. You bleeding mighty bad."

"We will." She felt her bodice slip from her shoulders and reached to clutch the fabric to her chest. "Cecilia, you and Mama walk ahead of me, please."

She watched Morrow run in the tavern door and Charlotte hurry down the road toward the Ashes. Her head felt light. She put a hand on her forehead and cried out at the pain that seared across her back as she moved her arms. It seemed forever before Leah helped her to sit down on the bench at the huge tavern table.

It was Mama who reached for the scissors and cut away the material from the wound. It was Mama who bathed her back in rum. It was Mama who wrapped the bandages across her shoulder, under her arm, and down her back. All Polly could do was hold her gown to her chest and suppress her groans.

Mister Moseley gave a great gasp as he came in to see Mama tying the bandage.

Polly, with interruptions from everyone, told him of Mister Colston's actions. "He is to leave and never return, Mister Moseley. But I must have the record books to show how many barrels of rosin he has ready for shipment. I need to know the amount of pitch he's made and the hogs-heads of turpentine he was moving to load on board the brigantine. He may even have monies he hasn't yet turned over to me."

Without a word, Mister Moseley strode from the room. He almost knocked down Morrow, who was hurrying in the door.

"Moze say he need cloth for bandages. And he need salve," Morrow said. "Miss Polly, I never see Moze cry afore."

"Why is Moze crying, Morrow?" Leah asked. "Is Boy hurt that bad?"

"He don't cry over Boy. He cry over what I told him 'bout Miss Polly." Morrow warmed to her message. "He say there be some hateful men is this world. He say —"

"That's enough, Morrow," Polly said, as Mama thrust a basket in the girl's hands. "Take that to Moze. If you can help him, you stay. If not, come back. We have to get ready for the men who will be here tonight."

"What men?" Leah asked. "Miss Polly, you don't plan to serve here tonight!"

"Of course I do." Polly took a deep breath. "Charlotte, please find me a bodice to wear. This one has lost its back."

Leah sighed. "Lawdy, what is you thinking about?" When Polly did not answer, she turned to the hearth. "Guess I better stir up this cook fire."

Chapter 17

Polly could not lie down. After the supper meal, and the last patron had left the tavern, she changed to her night clothes. But when she slipped under the covers of her bed she cried out at the pain in her back.

"What can I do, Polly?" Charlotte asked.

"Nothing."

Cecilia began to cry. Through her sobs, she stammered, "Polly, how did you get so b-b-brave. I could n-never, never have done — " She hiccupped.

"I'm not so brave, Cecilia. Sometimes I feel I'm weaving a rope of sand. It will crumble at the first touch and we will all be left with nothing." She sat in the feather bed, twisting her hands as if she could weave a structure to keep them all safe.

The baby whimpered and turned his head restlessly. Charlotte wrapped Cecilia and Timothy Charles in her arms and started singing. "Michael row the boat ashore, hallelujah. Michael row the boat ashore, hallelujah."

Polly had heard the slaves singing that tune so many times. The words were comforting.

"Jordan's river is deep and wide, hallelujah," Charlotte almost whispered. "Jordan's river is deep and wide, hallelujah."

When they were finally asleep, Polly crawled from her bed and pulled a wrapper over her gown. She took the quilt and trailed it behind her as she crept down the stairs. In the tavern room she lit a candle from the coals in the fireplace. She spilled the contents of the mail pouch across the table. Sitting on the bench, with the quilt wrapped about her legs, she began to sort through letters and papers.

A drum began to beat from down toward the slaves' quarters. The low-pitched thudding was different from drums she had heard in the past. It was talking. She wished she knew the language of its message. A second drum sounded from farther away. This one seemed to come from the northwest, toward Orton Plantation. This sound was also deep and steady. With a short ruffle the first drum stilled and a third, far toward the west, took up the message. The candle burned low before the sound of the drums stopped.

An owl whoo, hoo-hoo, whooed near the house. The scream of a rabbit a few seconds later let her know the hooded bird had found its prey.

Twice she dragged herself from the bench to add wood to the fire. She lit another candle when the first one began to sputter. She read the newspapers from Charleston and Boston, noting the information she needed to pass on to the men in Wilmington. When she had finished the correspondence, she went behind the counter and got the books for the tavern. She wrote out lists for orders. She needed three hundred pounds of rice from Orton. She would need to send the wagon over to Cousin William this week, for her rice supply was low. Six barrels of molasses, six barrels of rum, a pipe of wine and Madeira in those newer necked bottles, cloth for napkins, a new cook pot. She tabulated.

She started a second list of items the family needed. She wrote down calico for petticoats and linen for shifts. They needed shoes and gloves, caps and hats. She had to find a way to send Charlotte to Wilmington. It was only fair that her sister have at least that advantage. And she would need so many things when she went. Polly took out another piece of paper and wrote a letter to Cousin Maurice.

The agitations of the day ebbed with the writing. She searched for the right words to let her kinsman understand how important it was for Charlotte to have her turn at seeing something outside their little village of Brunswick. Less than a dozen families lived here. Wilmington, just up the river, was growing rapidly. Especially after the events of the day, it seemed more important than ever for Charlotte to understand how people in other places lived. She finished the letter and still sitting upright to ease the terrible pain, she dozed.

The sounds of horses roused her. There was a pounding on the door and a voice called out, "Polly? John Ashe here."

Polly unwrapped her legs from the quilt and stumbled over to unbar the door.

Three men sat their prancing horses in the road in front of the tavern. They carried torches, which they held high as Polly looked toward them. Mister Moseley and Daniel nodded to her. Mister Colston, on his horse between them, did not acknowledge that she was there.

Mister Ashe stood at the door, holding a ledger and a wooden box in his hands. He thrust the book toward Polly. "Take a look and see if these are the records you asked for," he said.

Polly turned slowly and put the book on the table. She opened it to the last page. September '65 was written at the top of the page. Lists — barrels of rosin, pitch and turpentine — filled one side of the ledger. The numbers of pine and hardwood logs, ready for loading, were also listed.

She reached for the box. It was so heavy she almost dropped it before she could set it on the table. Inside were crumpled bills of lading. She lifted out a wad of papers to see coins gleaming in the candlelight.

She closed the box lid. "Mister Ashe, I don't know if everything is here. It is more than I had hoped you'd recover. I thought Mister Colston would have taken all the monies and run by now."

"He tried to." Mister Ashe adjusted his hat and started for the door.

"What are you going to do with him?"

"We're escorting him to the Haulover ferry. He will be long gone by sunup."

Mister Ashe turned at the door. "Polly, you need a good foreman out there. You have a wealth of trees and some good slaves. You should be getting much more production than Colston shows in the ledger." He held up his hand. "I know. I probably shouldn't have read it. But I did."

"Why, Mister Ashe, you had to know if you had the correct book." She tried to give a short curtsy, but the pain in her back prevented it. "I thank you, sir, for all your kindness."

"Take care," he said, and was gone.

Polly watched the men ride toward the docks near the ferry landing before she barred the door and turned to look at the papers that Mister Ashe had handed her. It was quickly evident that the foreman had not given her full reports on any of the productivity from the turpentine operations. It was also obvious that the men who worked the woods had not been fed or clothed well. And there was an order for the purchase of another three slaves on the next ship to dock at Brunswick. This order was in a letter, written from Charleston just recently, to Mister Colston. Her father's signature was scrawled across the bottom of the paper. Buying slaves meant that much of the profit shown in the ledger would be wiped out immediately.

"Oh, Papa, what do you get from this?" she whispered. "What have you and Colston devised between you? How does buying slaves add to your profits?"

Her wrath against Mister Colston grew as she sorted the bills of lading from imports and exports made in the last few months. And nowhere did she see proof that the man had sent money to her father. That had been Mister Colston's excuse to Mister Dry for not paying the taxes.

She placed all of the papers in the back of the ledger and opened the box. She sorted the coins by denomination. There were farthings and pennies and shillings, but many of the coins were Spanish gold pieces. She counted them. There was well over three hundred pounds in the box. At least she had this much.

Polly built up the fire and put on water to boil. From the top of the dresser she got down Mama's best china tea pot. She fought against the pain in her back as she brought her arms down, the precious china clutched in both hands. From under the counter she took out the tea tin and measured leaves. As soon as the water boiled she poured it and set the pot on a pewter tray. Carefully she laid a folded linen napkin over the lid. Back at the dresser she again reached up to the top shelf, determined that the agony from the whip lash would not deter her. She selected one of the two china cups that had come from Charleston when they moved here to Brunswick.

Now she had the money to send Charlotte to Wilmington, if she could work out the details. Now she could place her orders and have the money to pay on delivery. Now she could pay the last of the taxes for this year.

Seated at the table she savored the aroma of the tea. Maybe, just maybe, she thought, she could weave together substantial plans. A brief passage from Locke came to mind: "I know that the soul always thinks." She went to get the little book from behind the counter and flipped through the pages.

". . . actual thinking," she read, "is as inseparable from the soul as actual extension is from the body." She suddenly knew who would be in charge of the sawmill and maritime operations. The foreman she had in mind would be controversial, but he would do a good job.

"To show how the understanding proceeds . . ." Oh yes, Mister John Locke, she thought, you are again helping me find answers.

She continued reading. "If mine prove a castle in the air, I will endeavour it shall be all of a piece and hang together."

She raised her tea cup in a salute to herself. "To making it all of a piece," she said. "No matter what I have to do, I will make it all hang together." And she drank her tea.

Chapter 18

At first light, Polly slipped into her bed chamber and got her clothes. She chose heavy clogs for walking and a cloak hanging on the peg by the press. She dressed by the fire in the tavern, leaving her night clothes behind the counter.

The walk to the quarters wasn't far, but at every step she felt that the wound across her back would split open. She was exhausted by the time she reached Moze's log house. Standing at the bottom of the steps that led to the porch, she called softly.

Leah came out on the porch of her cabin next door. "Lawdy, Miss Polly, what you doing here at this hour? Are you all right?"

"I had to see Boy," she said.

"He mighty bad hurt." Her bare feet raised little dust clouds in the yard as she walked over to Polly. "Bad hurt." She raised her voice and called, "Moze? Miss Polly want to see you."

"Come," he answered.

Moze sat on a bench by the fire. In the corner of the room, Boy lay propped in a small bed. From the door Polly could hear his labored breathing. She walked over and laid the back of her hand on his forehead. The heat from his parched skin frightened her as much as the sounds from his troubled breathing. There was a gash on the side of his head that had stopped bleeding, but she could tell that it was deep.

She turned to Moze. "It's more than the lash he took. What else is wrong?"

"He got ribs broke. They crush up from where he hit the tree. Had he taken that second blow, Miss Polly, Jeremiah would have cut down his dead body."

Polly felt the anger building inside her again. "He will not die." She walked to the door and looked out as the sun climbed its slow way through the trees. "How do we find Marie?"

"We have called her."

"The drums —"

"We have called her," Moze said again.

Over and over she hit the door lintel with her fist, feeling the blood ooze from her cut with each blow. "Moze, send for me if you need anything."

"I will, Miss Polly." The old man's voice sounded so tired.

She went carefully down the steps. Leah was waiting for her and they walked toward the tavern.

"You save his life, Miss Polly. Don't you start having regrets 'bout nothing. No matter what happens. You hear me, child?" She turned to look back and called, "Morrow, you hurry up now. We got a day ahead of us. There be a death coming and we got to prepare."

"Whose death, Leah? Boy? He must not die," Polly said in a firm voice.

"I don't know who, Miss Polly. But the signs say we got to prepare. Didn't you hear the owl crying in the yard last night?" She swung her arms as if to scatter a flock of birds. "And the crows been visiting. Them pests not just in the cornfield. Crows visiting be generally bad news for somebody."

Daniel was stirring mush over the tavern fire. The wood pile had been replenished. The tray with her tea service was on the counter and bowls for breakfast were stacked on the table. He looked up with a frown on his face as the three of them came in the door.

"Where have you been?" he demanded.

"Why, Daniel? You don't usually venture into The Anchor so early in the morning. How could I know you would be here this morning?" Polly took off her cloak and hung it on a wall peg.

"But where have you been?" he insisted. He stood, his back to the fire, the long wooden spoon still in his hand. A measure of soft meal dripped from the spoon to the hearth.

Leah muttered something about needing more than corn mush to eat and climbed on a stool to lift down a slab of bacon from the rafters. She sliced thick strips of the meat and laid them in the iron skillet over hot coals. She measured out flour and butter to begin biscuits. "That mush gonna scorch, Mister Daniel, don't you stir it some. You got a mighty roaring fire for just a pot of mush."

Daniel continued to stare at Polly.

Her hands covered with dough, Leah swung the pot away from the heat and reached to take the spoon from Daniel's hand.

Polly walked out the door. Daniel followed her into the yard. He caught her arm and turned her toward him. She gasped at the pain that coursed through her back. Quickly she moved away from him.

"We all have been so worried. How could you have done something so foolish!" He reached again to take her arm.

"Don't touch me, Daniel," she cried out. "Don't touch me."

He let his hand fall to his side.

"I wasn't being foolish, Daniel. We do what we have to do."

"And what if Colston had not stopped. Polly, have you thought of that? What if he had brought that whip down again? What if —"

"I've thought of many things, Daniel." She looked toward the river, its waters gleaming streaks of golds and yellows in the morning light. "I've thought of the beauty of this place we live. I thought of the harshness of the life here. I've thought of free and slave. Of master and servant. Of men who rule and women who serve."

She looked at the man who still stared at her. "Do you really want to know how I think, Daniel?"

He nodded.

"I think slavery is wrong. No person should own another person. Whether it's a black brought in chains from Africa or a cane worker bought up in the islands to work the rice fields. We own his work, but we cannot own his soul. Whether it's a child who must obey the manners of the house. We care for the child, but we cannot own his spirit. Whether it's a woman who must live under the laws set up by men who aren't sure what she'll do if they let her think too much. You cannot own the self of a woman."

Daniel sat down on the bench by the door. He hugged his arms to his chest and shivered. If a north wind, blowing across winter waters, had suddenly wrapped itself about him, he would not have looked more cold. Over and over he softly said her name.

"Do I so shock you, Daniel? So frighten you?"

"Shock? No, you do not shock me. But you do frighten me, Polly. You frighten me far more than you can know. You are asking for —" He held up his hands. "You are asking for —" He again hugged his arms about himself.

"I'm asking for trouble. I know." She sat on the bench

beside him. "Gratis pro Deo, Daniel. Nothing is free of cost."

She stood, hoping to ease the dreadful pain in her back, and spoke sternly. "You can care for me. You can worry about me. But you cannot demand of me."

Daniel looked at her and grinned. "That I have always known." The grin faded. "But if you don't temper your acts, you are in for far more trouble than you have had up to now."

"Temper my acts? Daniel, if I hadn't —"

"I was born in London."

Polly grew very still. Daniel had never talked about himself. And this was so abrupt a statement. She waited.

"My father was a groom in a small manor house owned by Mister Defoe. My mother worked in the kitchen. When I was very small I remember the laughter and warmth of them." He gazed toward the barn. "Before my feet could reach the stirrups my father swung me on the back of a horse and led me around the stable yard."

Daniel held out his work-worn hands and turned them over from front to back. "Father's hands were so strong and gentle. He would touch Mother's face and she would smile up at him. Then they would pull me close. At night, in the loft over the barn which we called home, Mother taught me my letters. Servants cannot usually read but she had a horn book, 'from another lifetime' she told me once when I plied her with questions."

Polly put her hand over her mouth to make herself stay quiet. She wanted to reach out, to hold his hand, to feel the touch of him. She wanted more to hear his story.

"Then Father grew sick of a fever." Daniel's fists rested on his knees. "Mother did everything she knew to do for him." One fist hit his knee. "Even Mister Defoe came to the loft to see about him." The other fist struck his knee. "Father died."

Leah peered from the tavern door. When Polly put a finger to her lips and shook her head, she went back inside. A commotion broke out on the docks. Angry voices carried up the street and Daniel began to beat his fists against his knees.

Polly caught his hands in both of hers. "Daniel," she whispered. "Daniel, what happened to your mother?"

He grew still. "She died, too. Mister Defoe bound me as an apprentice and sent me to the colonies. 'What she wanted,' he told me. And so I landed in Charleston and found that my passage was paid by Maurice Moore."

He finally looked at her. "I know about freedom. I know about losing it. I know how a world can change in an instant. I was bought for the cost of my passage. I will serve until I am twenty-one. I only have a short time more and then I will be my own man."

"Oh, Daniel," she breathed.

"I have been treated well. I've had the opportunity to read and write and cipher. Judge Moore saw to that and I am most grateful. But Polly, don't you understand that if you cause trouble, all you have can be taken from you?"

"I understand very well. I also understand that it can be taken whether I act or not. It is only with the power of that same judge who helped you that I can act at all."

He hung his head, as if he had no more words.

"I will not look for trouble, Daniel. But I will not accept cruelty as long as I can amend it."

He rose from the bench and began to walk away.

"Daniel, thank you for your story," she whispered.

He plodded on toward the barn as if he had not heard.

Late in the morning a rider from Russellborough brought the news that Governor Tryon's son was very ill. "Mistress Tryon asked if you could come to see him," the servant said. "She has heard how you tended your brother and how well and healthy he is."

"How does Mistress Tryon know about me?"

"Little Miss Margaret's nurse, Hattie, told her. The infant is fevered, Miss Polly. A hot fever. And his mouth is blue, Hattie says."

"Is there a rash?" Polly asked.

"Yes, ma'am The baby is covered with a rash. Miss Margaret's got a rash, too. And, ma'am, there is no doctor in Wilmington or anywhere else close by."

"Charlotte," Polly said, turning to her sister, "fetch me a basket. Leah, I need willow bark. Come with me to the attic."

Strings of dried willow bark hung from the rafters. Polly took down a long strip and put it in the basket Leah held. She reached for a string of sassafras root. She gathered a small cloth-wrapped bundle of thyme and another of marigold. "Leah, can you think of anything else to bring down fever or help with a rash?"

"No. But Miss Polly, how you know what you walking into over there?" Leah's face was wrinkled in worry.

"If I find contagion, then I'll have to stay. But there were several cases of measles on one of the ships that docked here about two weeks ago. Everybody here, except for Timothy Charles, has had the measles."

"Miss Polly, it might not be measles. It could be anything."

"I don't know how I got the reputation of being able to help the sick. But I'm going because a neighbor has asked. Say your prayers, Leah."

"Ain't just a neighbor. It be the governor of the whole colony. Miss Polly, that man could send for anybody. It don't have to be you!"

"But he did send for me. I'm going. I will do the best I can."

As Leah followed her down the stairs, she muttered, "You be the most stubborn child. Miss Polly, you always was a stubborn child. You is gonna be stubborn when you old and gray, if you manages to live that long. Stubborn and willful. Stubborn and willful."

"Leah, hush and listen. You have to keep things going here at the tavern. I'm taking Charlotte with me to Russellborough."

As she and Charlotte walked out the door, Leah was still fussing. "Stubborn. Don't you bring back no fever to this house. Willful!" She shouted at their retreating backs, "Lawdy, Miss Polly, you be so willful! Please take care."

Chapter 19

Charlotte did her own share of fussing as they walked through the woods on the path toward the governor's house. "When did you get to be a nurse, big sister? And just when did you decide to make me one, too? And making me carry the basket like a servant. When I'm grown up, I'll have a thing or two to say about what I carry. I'll have a thing or two to say about where I go and when I go."

"Charlotte, I do hope that's possible." Polly wanted to think of Daniel and his story. He had looked so sad as he talked of his parents. Why couldn't Charlotte be quiet, just for a little while. "Now please hush," she said. "Please hush."

"Hush! You say anything you want to say and I'm supposed to be quiet!"

"Mister Locke says that —"

"Who is Mister Locke? Does he live in Wilmington?"

"Oh, Charlotte, how remiss I've been about your education. John Locke is a writer and philosopher. His books are world famous."

"Is that one of those little books with the tiny print that you're always squinting over?"

"Do I squint over books?"

"Yes, you do. And squinting makes wrinkles. Mama told me that when I was a little girl. I try never to squint. I don't want wrinkles."

"Would you like to go to Wilmington?"

"To Wilmington?" Charlotte stopped walking. "Polly, could I? It's getting to be a big town now, with lots of things to do. There are at least fifty families living there. Where would I live? Do we have the money for me to go?"

"I've written to Cousin Maurice. The main reason, and the one I presented to our cousin, is that you'd be going to study. Wrinkles or no wrinkles, Charlotte, there are many uses of ruses. You have to study and read and think to find that out."

"Uses of ruses!" Charlotte started walking, swinging the basket between them. "Polly, half the time I don't know what you're talking about, but I like the sound of that. Uses of ruses. What does it mean?"

"Well, it's the way I get around many of the impositions placed on me. Leah calls it my play acting. But it's far more than that. A ruse is a plan. But you have to know what you really want. And you have to plan carefully."

"So what does your Mister Locke say in his books?"

Polly held up her hand to count off fingers. "Well, he talks about three different kinds of law. The first has to do with the divine, which is the law of God. Then there is civil law made by man. And then there is the law of opinion or reputation. I guess we're obeying both the divine and opinion ones by going to help the Tryons."

They had reached the tall steps of the stately house where the governor lived. Charlotte stopped. "I love coming here. Old Captain Russell knew how to build a house. And some day I'm going to live in a place like this." She made a face. "Not in some smelly tavern with every sailor in the world asking for drinks."

Mister Tryon appeared on the lower gallery. "Charlotte, how good to see you again," he said. "Little Margaret has sorely missed seeing you and playing with Cecilia these past days."

As they started up the steps to the railed porch, he turned to Polly. "You must be the older sister we have heard so much about."

In spite of the pain she knew she would feel, Polly gave a short curtsy.

"Come in. Please come in," the governor urged.

Mistress Tryon hurried toward them as they entered the great hallway. "How good of you to come."

Before Polly could speak, Little Margaret ran down the steps and grabbed her mother's gown. "Where's Cecilia? I want to play with Cecilia."

Polly sat on a step beside the little girl. The child's skin was blotched with measles, but she did not seem to have much fever. Polly stuck out her tongue and made a face. "Now you stick out your tongue at me," she said to the child.

Margaret stuck out her tongue and wiggled it up and down. Then she giggled.

"Do you know you have bumps in your mouth?" Polly said with a smile. "You have the very same kind of bumps that you have on your arms. Now isn't that funny?"

Margaret nodded.

"They are called measles bumps. Why don't we go look in the mirror? You can stick out your tongue and see for yourself. Then you can show me your baby. I bet he has measles bumps, too." Polly stood up and took Margaret's hand.

The child's room was so elegantly furnished that Polly wondered if she was allowed to play there. Margaret ran to the looking glass, built into a walnut frame, that stood next to the clothes press. She stuck out her tongue at herself. "I do have bumps!" she said. "Oh, Polly, I do have bumps on my tongue."

A doll with a lovely painted porcelain face and shiny eyes sat in a high chair next to a table set with china ready for tea. A canopy bed for her fashionably dressed doll stood in a doll house designed as a miniature Russellborough. Beside the bed was a tiny cradle. The dining room was furnished with mahogany table and chairs. The sitting room furniture appeared to be replicas of the pieces she had glimpsed as she was going up the stairs.

Justina had married and moved in with Governor Dobbs when the house was not yet finished. While she had decorated some of the house, she had never had the grandeur now on display.

Mistress Tryon followed them into Margaret's room. "Little William's cradle has been moved to my bed chamber, Polly. Would you come with me?"

From the door of the baby's room Polly could hear the rattles in his chest. She had only heard those sounds once before, when a slave was dying with some form of lung distress. She would fight with everything she had, but she feared, as she lifted the infant from his cradle, that it would not be enough. She forgot the luxury that surrounded her and turned to Mistress Tryon.

"Put a kettle of water on the fire to boil. I've brought willow bark for a tea to help bring down the fever," Polly said. "We'll mix the marigold with it. Then make up a tepid bath with thick oatmeal water. That will help to soothe the rash on his skin."

As she waited for the willow tea, Polly walked back and forth, rocking the baby gently in her arms. She felt the cut on her back open but the child seemed to breathe easier with the rhythm of her steps. She would not stop moving if she could save the child. She kept up the cadence until the water had boiled. She spooned several drops of the tea in the baby's mouth, then began rocking him again.

When the oatmeal bath was ready Mistress Tryon helped her take off the child's clothing. They placed him in the warm water and patted the oatmeal over his tiny body. Then they wrapped him in a soft cotton blanket.

Mistress Tryon picked up the baby to walk with him as Polly had done. Then she gasped. "Your back! Polly, your back! You are bleeding across your shoulders!"

"Yes, I know," Polly said.

"But what is wrong with you?" She clutched the baby tightly to her chest. He gave a weak cry.

"I received an injury just yesterday. The wound has not yet healed. It is nothing to be alarmed about." Polly picked up the cup that held the willow bark tea. "Let me give him another drop or two. I hope it will bring down the fever."

Through the afternoon Polly and Mistress Tryon took turns walking and rocking the baby. At first the child seemed to breathe a little better. For a while he fell into a light sleep. By the time the first star appeared in the sky, they both knew that nothing more could be done. Mistress Tryon laid Little William in his cradle and stood, her head bowed.

Polly thought of the words that Boy, hanging from a tree limb, had recited. She didn't know she had said the words aloud until Governor Tryon spoke from the open door. "The Lord is a shepherd. He will watch over this tiny lamb now."

She stood looking at the still body and remembered the emptiness of her arms after she had laid her baby brother down in his casket. Her back throbbed and the beginning of a headache threatened.

She turned her tearstained face to Mistress Tryon. "I am so sorry."

Governor Tryon patted her hand. "You did all you could. We knew Little William was very ill when we sent for you."

Polly gathered her things together and packed the basket. She woke Charlotte, who was sleeping with Little Margaret. She asked for a pitch torch to give them light on the path home. She refused the servant that the governor wanted to send with them.

As they walked, Charlotte began to cry. "It's not fair, Polly," she whimpered between sobs. "It's not fair."

"Find me something in this world that is," Polly answered.

"You are so cold." Charlotte's anger stopped her tears. "You are the coldest person I have ever known. You are cold and mean. You are cold and completely unfeeling. You don't even care that Little William is dead."

"I am cold," Polly answered. "I am so unfeeling that I rocked a dying baby in my arms until my back bled. I am so mean that I did not remember my own little brothers lying ready for the grave. I have no feelings about anything."

"Oh, Polly." Charlotte was crying again.

"Charlotte, please learn to think before you blurt."

"I don't blurt!"

From just ahead Polly saw the lights from the tavern shining out through the open door, and knew that someone had waited up for them. "Sister, fair or not, you are home. And we cannot go into the house wearing these clothes. We'll have to bathe and wash everything we're wearing."

"I've had measles," Charlotte said.

"You and I have. So has Cecilia. Timothy Charles has not. We will not take the contagion in to him."

Leah had solved the problem. She had the fire going in the wash house, hot water ready and clean clothes in a basket for them.

Charlotte took her bath first. "Leah, this water is too hot," she fussed. "Don't get soap in my eyes. I really didn't want to wash my hair."

Leah scolded back at her. "Miss Charlotte, your chattering don't change nothing. You will not carry measles into our house. Now wash yourself."

Polly took off her shift and put it in a pail of cold water to soak out the blood. Ruining two outfits in two days left her with few changes. Leah cut the blood-soaked bandage from her back. When Charlotte saw the angry wound she finally grew silent.

"How did you know to have the hot water ready?" Polly asked.

"We be getting messages back and forth from Russellborough all day," Leah said. "I knew when the little baby died that you'd come home tonight."

"Thank you, Leah. I thought we'd have to bathe in cold water and change in a room with no heat."

"Now that you're bathed, Miss Polly, I gonna clean this wound. Miss Henrietta needed to pull it tighter when she bandaged it." Leah packed the cut with lint and pulled adhesive plaster across the wound in several places before she began to wind the bandage.

Polly gritted her teeth and endured.

"Was it just the measles, Miss Polly?" Leah asked as she worked. "Just the measles that carried off the child?"

Polly nodded. "As far as I could tell, just the measles. He didn't have anything to fight with. He was so tiny."

"Like Miss Henrietta's babies." Leah gathered their clothes and put them in the bath water to soak. "I think

I'll finish this up in the morning. Now that you and Miss Charlotte are here, I'm going down to my place."

When they walked into the tavern Daniel was sitting at the table.

"And what are you doing here?" Charlotte demanded.

"Hello, Charlotte," he answered, and presented her a formal bow.

She flounced toward the stairs. Polly heard her slam the door to the bed chamber. Timothy Charles began to cry.

Polly sat at the table. The weariness of the last few days washed over her and she brushed angrily at the tears trickling down her checks.

Daniel put a bowl of hot stew in front of her. He placed a spoon in her hand. "Eat," he said. "I know you too well. You haven't eaten all day."

While she ate he banked the fire and blew out the candles in the wall sconces, leaving a single candle burning on the counter. He took the empty bowl from her when she had finished.

"Now sleep, Polly. Sleep."

He went out into the night, closing the door behind him.

Despite the pain in her back, Polly put her head on her arms and closed her eyes.

Chapter 20

When Polly opened the door the next morning, Moze was limping across the road toward the tavern. She pulled a chair near the fire for him and began the morning meal while he settled in.

"How is Boy?" she asked as she sliced bacon.

"Tolerable, Miss Polly. Just tolerable. Marie be with him."

Shouts from the road drew her to the door. Several men were walking up from the docks. Out in the river the schooner, *Nancy*, was dropping anchor and furling her sails. She meant to stay for a while. A sloop was moving in with the tide. That made seven ships anchored at the port. During the night two rafts, loaded with barrels from up river, had also tied up to a pier.

"Wouldn't it be wonderful if a wagon load of fresh apples arrived?" Polly said.

"It's the right time of year," Moze said. "I'd sure enjoy a nice ripe apple."

Morrow took the knife from Polly's hand and continued to slice the bacon. Leah, muttering under her breath, stirred the mush with the long wooden spoon.

"This place gonna be busy this morning," she said. "Miss Cecilia and her little friend picked scuppernong grapes yesterday. I thought to make some preserves but I 'spect we best use 'um now to fill up these hungry men."

And up to The Anchor they came. As she served,

Polly listened. "Price of tobacco is down," said a man from Cross Creek who had brought the rafts down river. "Said we're flooding the market." He spooned mush in his mouth with a rice cake that Leah had just taken from the skillet. He blew on the cake to cool it, then dipped another mouthful from his bowl. "Beats me how you can have a good crop and get less money."

"Tar and pitch," advised another. "Tar and pitch and logs. That's what they want. The British will always need naval stores."

Cecilia was moving about collecting coins, putting them in her pocket as the men paid her. She reached a bearded man sitting near the door. He scooped her up on his lap. "You are pretty as an angel, little girl."

Polly hurried toward them, but the man put Cecilia down and shook his head. "Forgive me, child. I miss my own."

He paid his pennies and went out. In a minute Polly heard the axe and looked out to see the man chopping wood. She smiled at the thought that he might be atoning for some sin. She did need the wood.

Daniel came in while the room was still filled with men from the rafts and several officers from the ships. He stood with his back to the fire, scooping up his mush with a crisp strip of fried pork.

Polly gathered Timothy Charles from under a table and swung him on her hip. How good it felt to hold a healthy, heavy child in her arms. She could understand how the bearded man might want to have the same weight against him. She made her way across the room to Daniel.

"We need meat," she said to him.

He nodded. "I was thinking the same. I spotted a deer run last week. And I think I can get some trout, too." He handed Polly his empty bowl and reached up to take down the Brown Bess musket hanging over the mantel.

As he went out Mister William Dry came in, looking for an officer from the *Nancy*. He asked for a mug of ale and sat talking with the captain, papers spread out on the table between them. When Polly served him Mister Dry nodded as if he approved of all he saw. "You are doing a good business here," he said.

"Yes, sir. We are," Polly answered.

Midmorning, when most of the men were gone, Polly realized that Mama was not in her chair. Wearily she made her way up the stairs to the bed chambers. Mama was lying in the bed, her face as blank as it had been after Timothy Charles was born.

Polly opened the clothes press and took out an outer petticoat of light blue linen. She found a print jacket with blue lacing down the front. She took out stockings and new blue garters Mama had knitted recently. She laid the clothes on the bench at the foot of the bed.

"Mama, we need you down stairs," she said.

Henrietta shook her head.

"Mama, the Tryons' son died. That is a fact. But you have a living son crawling under tables in the tavern." Polly sighed. "Mama, he has Charlotte and Cecilia. He has Leah and Morrow. But no matter how many others there are to look after him, he needs you, too."

Henrietta did not move.

"Mama, Timothy Charles may live to be an old man with gray in his beard. He may die of fever today. Whether or not you lie in that bed will not change what happens to him." She opened the door and turned back to the still figure with covers pulled to her chin. "Mama, if it means anything to you at all, I need you." She went down the stairs and into the yard.

The *Stamford*, which had anchored in the early morning, was moving her human cargo from the ship. As the chained men struggled from the flatboats to the dock, Polly remembered that Papa had ordered three of them. She went inside to find the papers recovered from Mister Colston's reports. She did not want more responsibility. She did not want to traffic in buying and selling slaves. By the time the last of the cargo disembarked, the first slaves were standing in the road in front of the tavern.

The captain and his mate from the *Stamford* came into the tavern. "P. Moore?" the captain asked. "Is there a P. Moore here?"

"Yes," Polly answered. "My father left the papers with me. I'm Pauline Moore."

The mate looked her up and down. "A handsome maid, sir."

"Yes. I agree," the captain said. "Now, Miss Moore, we have three of these wretches for you. The others go to plantations along the road here, I understand. I need to get directions from you. And I want my money before we move on."

"I want to see the men you brought," Polly said. Clutching the papers in her hand, she went out to the street.

The captain, who had followed her, pointed to the first men in the line of chained blacks. "This one is from Barbados. Worked cane. These two are from Charleston way. Worked rice, the seller told me."

"Cut them loose," Polly said.

"Well, ma'am, they are loose from the others that we're moving on. You surely don't want them unchained until they know whose in charge," the captain said.

"Loose them." The mate took a key from his belt, unfastened the locks and yanked at the chains wrapped about the men's ankles. As the chains slashed against their flesh, all three fell to the ground. The mate pulled his whip from his belt.

"No," Polly said. "There is no need for that." She looked toward the tavern yard where Moze sat whittling by the door. "Moze, please come stay here," she called.

"A crippled old Negro?" The captain seemed astonished. "You're leaving a crippled old Negro in charge?"

Polly nodded. Back in the tavern they discussed the price for the men. Papa's papers said 100 pounds for each man, but Polly bargained. "Why, one of those men has sores all over his legs. It will be days before he can work."

"They always get sores in the rice fields," the mate argued.

"And they look half starved," Polly continued, ignoring the mate. "They certainly have not been fed on the voyage."

"It's just two days up from Charleston," the captain said. "For such a short trip we do not carry provisions for slaves. Waste of money and effort."

Polly clamped her lips together. Protesting about the treatment of slaves on a ship would get her nowhere. She concentrated on bargaining.

When the captain and his mate, over a glass of Madeira, had finally agreed to her price of 200 pounds for all three slaves, Polly went behind the counter so they could not see her money box. She carefully counted out the coins. She thought of all the expenses she had, especially if she could send Charlotte to Wilmington. She put the coins for the captain in a small cloth bag and for a moment held it in her hands. Then she walked over to place the bag on the table.

She followed the men out the door. Moze sat on his bench under the tree, talking to the slaves she had just bought. Morrow was serving them rice and rabbit stew. She had drawn a bucket of well water and the men were passing a gourd dipper back and forth to drink from as they ate.

"How goes it?" she asked.

"I am discomposed," Moze said. He did not look at her.

"In the men? In me?"

"I did not expect you to take on more misery, Miss Polly."

"Papa placed the order with the captain of the *Stamford*. I had to honor the contract. And Moze, I really do not owe you an explanation."

"No, Miss Polly, you do not." He pulled himself up and leaned on his crutch. Then suddenly he slumped heavily on the bench.

"Morrow, go quickly and get rum."

As the girl ran toward the tavern Polly said, "You don't have to be my conscience, Moze. If I had not bought these men, who were under contract, they would be heading for a rice or indigo plantation somewhere. The captain would have his money. I would not have help. It's all wrong, but I can't change it. I can only do the little I can here."

She took a deep breath. "The chains are off their legs. Their bellies are filled. They will have time to rest. They will be taught how to work the trees. They will not know the whip. If I set them free right now, they would have no place to go or food to eat. Someone would snatch them up and enslave them somewhere else. What more can I do?"

Moze looked at her with anger burning in his eyes. He reached for the mug that Morrow held out to him and drank deeply before he spoke. "Miss Polly, I told these new men that you be a good woman. I told them they should do your bidding. They will make good workers for you." He drained the rum and pushed himself up. Slowly he made his way toward the barn.

Polly watched him out of sight. She turned to the men sitting under the tree and threw up her hands. "What more can I do?" she yelled at them.

She ran to the tavern, stomped up the stairs to her bed chamber, and grabbed her copy of Locke. The passage on the three laws was marked with a goose feather. These were the same laws Polly had quoted to Charlotte on the walk to Russellborough.

"The civil law," Polly read. "The rule by the common-wealth to the actions of those who belong to it, . . . this law nobody overlooks . . . and it has power to take away life, liberty, or goods, from him who disobeys."

What was she expected to understand about these laws? "Men judge whether their actions are sins or duties; whether they be criminal or innocent; whether they be virtues or vices."

Papa had signed the contract for the slaves. That was civil law. She had honored it. She had obeyed the civil law. Obeying the law was considered a virtue.

It was the moral law that ate at her heart. No matter the law of man. Slavery was wrong. Neither Moze nor any-one else had to disapprove of it for her to know that.

She stood up, leaving the book on the bed, and went downstairs. There was work to be done. Her questions were not going to be answered today. She had three new slaves. She couldn't leave them sitting under a tree. She had to figure out what to do with them.

Chapter 21

Mama had decided to attend the funeral service for Little William. She had dressed in her best gown and bonnet. She waited at the tavern door for Polly and Charlotte to pull on their gloves. She reached up to tuck a wisp of stray hair under Polly's cap.

"Oh, Mama," was all Polly could say.

They walked down the street to St. Philips Church. New windows that Governor Tryon had ordered from England were installed. New altar furniture stood inside the railing. No longer did she need to worry about sand filling her slippers, for the stone floor was laid. There was still no preacher.

Governor Tryon himself led the service. His voice broke once as he recited from the Prayer Book. " 'We brought nothing into this world, and it is certain we can carry nothing out.' " He cleared his throat and lifted his chin to an intolerable stretching point. Then he continued to read. " 'The Lord gave, and the Lord hath taken away; blessed be the Name of the Lord.' "

Many of the Wilmington families had come to pay their respects. Polly left Jeremiah and Isaac tending fires in the tavern yard. She did not know how many of the visitors would go to Russellborough and how many would stop at The Anchor, but she had two deer and a goat roasting on the open spits. Little Margaret and her nurse, Hattie, were there to stay with Cecilia. Leah and Morrow, she knew, would be taking bread from the oven about now. They would be checking the sweet potatoes baking in the coals and stirring the great pots of beans and peas. She mentally set out the plates on the tables and counted napkins. Purple James grapes and amber Scuppernongs were piled high on the pewter platters on the counters, where she had arranged them early this morning.

She glanced over at Charlotte, dressed in her blue dimity frock, with a pair of bright blue sandals on her feet. Her sister was a beauty, with her black curls and dimples.

Governor Tryon began reading from the Twenty-third Psalm. Polly, as she was pulled back into the service, gritted her teeth until they ached. She would not cry. After the first verse of the psalm he stopped and looked at her. "We had a young woman from here at Brunswick to tend our infant during his last hours," the governor said.

Polly shook her head. "No, no," she whispered.

The governor went on. "As Pauline Moore walked with our dear sick child she said the words of this very scripture. I think it would be fitting if we all prayed them together."

It was such a departure from custom that several people turned to stare at her, but as Governor Tryon began the words again, the congregation joined with him. "The Lord is my shepherd," they recited, some quite clearly, others mumbling. Charlotte, standing next to her, knew all of the words, and Polly remembered that was the scripture she had been reading when Mister Colston grabbed Boy. Then she realized that Mama was saying the words aloud. "Surely goodness and mercy shall follow me all the days of my life; and I will dwell in the house of the Lord for ever."

Polly took Mama's hand and gave it a squeeze.

With the final prayer of service, Mama stayed standing in place. She motioned for Polly and Charlotte to leave.

Polly saw the Davises nearby and walked over to speak to them. She had enjoyed the months she had lived in their home and she wanted to ask about Justina. Several people she had known in Wilmington nodded to her, but before she could reach Mister and Mistress Davis, Mama ran from the church.

Polly followed her as quickly as she could. People tried to speak to her, but Polly kept Mama in sight. Past the tavern Mama fled. Polly caught up with her in the wash house. She was tugging at the spinning wheel that hung from the wall.

"Mama, wait. You're going to break the spokes."

Henrietta yanked at the wheel again.

Polly pulled a bench over to the wall and stood on it. She lifted the wheel over the pegs and handed it down. Mama took the wheel and leaned it against the wall. Polly took the niddy-noddy from its pegs and bent to set it on the floor. She felt the cut on her back pull around the plasters and bit her lip to keep from crying out with the pain.

"Where do you want this set up, Mama?"

Henrietta picked up the finger-shaped wheel-peg and hurried toward the tavern. Polly followed her, carrying the heavy wheel. She moved through a crowd of people sitting at make-shift sawhorse tables in the yard. Mister Harnett was sampling the venison. He hacked off a piece of the meat, filled his birch bark plate with pumpkin, mixed in field peas, and ate with his hunting knife. Mister Hooper tipped his hat to her as she went by. He swung himself in the saddle and trotted toward the ferry landing.

Cousin Maurice entered the tavern just ahead of her and made his way to the counter. Four officers were playing loo at a small table. One shuffled the cards and began to deal. She had seen two of them at the church, so the game had just started. Other tables were filled with couples who had come for the services, with sailors from the ships, with men from the several rafts that were tied at the docks.

Leah and Morrow were serving and clearing as quickly as they could. Hattie had been pressed into service. Dipping with a ladle, she filled a tureen with peas and carried it to a table. Margaret followed Cecilia to lay out napkins, to carry drinks and to collect coins. Polly could tell that Cecilia kept a careful tally on who had paid and who was ordering another drink.

Polly set the wheel against a back wall, out of the way. She watched Mama go up the stairs, the wheel-peg still in her hand. Polly pinned on her apron and picked up a carving knife.

When Governor and Mistress Tryon entered a few minutes later, the officers at the card table jumped up to offer their seats. Charlotte came in just behind them. She tied her apron about her waist and served them. Polly caught Cecilia's hand and whispered to her, "Get Mama. The Tryons are here and she must come down. She must."

Cecilia and Little Margaret went up the stairs.

"And the Stamp Act, sir." A captain out of Connecticut stood at Governor Tryon's side, speaking in a voice that could have carried to the top of the masts on his ship. "We are not going to tolerate this internal tax."

The governor indicated an empty chair at the table. "Sit with me, good captain. Explain your views."

The man spun about and walked out. But his loud remark set everyone in the tavern talking politics. "We will not accept this intrusion," came from a gentleman from Wilmington.

"Taxes are a way of the world," said the mate of an English ship.

"Surely there will be no tax on playing cards," said one

of the men who had brought a raft of goods from Cross Creek. "A man does need his pleasures!"

Cecilia pulled at Polly's petticoat. "Mama won't come down."

Polly gave her a hug. "Thank you for trying, sweet Cee. Get back to collecting money. I think a captain just went out without paying."

Margaret leaned against Polly's side. She reached down to give her a hug, too. "And you help Cecilia, please. You are one of the best helpers I've ever had."

The little girl smiled at her. Three dried measles bumps dotted her chin like freckles. Why did some people have such simple cases of the dread disease while others died, Polly wondered. Margaret skipped across the room toward Cecilia.

Two men, seated at the long table in the center of the room, raised their voices. "That Boston crowd didn't go far enough. They should have burned the man himself. Burning a dummy doesn't carry a sufficient message. We will not pay this tax. We will not purchase stamps. King George has to see the reasons against this Stamp Act."

"Parliament has the power to raise taxes. It has been so for generations," said the second man. "You colonists must pay for your protection."

"We don't need that kind of protection. We can very well take care of ourselves."

The men were standing now, almost nose to nose as they leaned across the table.

Polly hurried over to them. "Take your quarrel outside," she said quietly.

Neither man responded to her as they continued to glare at each other.

"Sirs," Polly said a little louder.

The man from the raft pulled his hunting knife from his belt. Several men in the room began to rise from their seats. Polly picked up the pitcher of beer from the table and emptied it over his head. He sputtered and stepped back.

"Now out," Polly yelled at them. "Out of my house, both of you."

The man put his knife back in his belt and wiped his sleeve across his face. He scowled at his opponent before walking from the tavern. The other man, who had supported the tax, sat down heavily on the bench. Then he looked at Polly. "A fiery bunch, you colonists."

"Indeed we are, sir. Most fiery. Set in our own ways. Opposed to oppressive taxes. Ready to stand up for what we believe," Polly answered. "Now I would ask you to pay your bill and leave."

The man handed her a Spanish milled dollar. When Polly reached in her pocket for change he shook his head. "No, it has been worth it." He laughed. "I never saw a man drowned so effectively. A good use of beer." He settled his hat on his head and went out.

"I, too, say you acted effectively," Governor Tryon said. "I would not have suspected a mere girl could break up a potential fight so surely and swiftly."

Not knowing what to answer, Polly dropped a short curtsy and went out in the yard to make sure both men were gone. Daniel was carving away the last meat from the carcass of a deer. Jeremiah was throwing the last of the plates of birch bark on the dying fire and raking up scattered debris. There were no more guests outside.

"Jeremiah, you and Isaac take what's left of the meat for yourselves. I'm sure you can find a way to make use of it." Polly smiled at him.

"Yes, ma'am. Thank you, ma'am," Jeremiah answered. "Won't be wasted."

"Tell me about the three new men," Polly said. "How are they faring?"

"They slow, Miss Polly."

"Slow? Slow in what way?" Polly asked.

"They never work pines afore. It new to them."

"Well, Jeremiah, I have put you in charge. Train the new men. Get the most you can from them. Treat them kindly."

"Miss Polly, some don't think . . ." He paused. "Some don't think a African should be acting like a foreman."

"I see." She frowned. "Who has said this?"

He raked an already clean patch of the yard and said over his shoulder, "Mister Dry want to know who do the paperwork now. Told him I sure couldn't read." He turned to face her. "I never told him you teaching me to tally and count, so I can keep up with the barrels and such."

She nodded. "Jeremiah, I'll speak to Mister Dry."

She looked down toward the river where the masts of a dozen ships crisscrossed the sky. Yes, she would speak to Mister Dry.

Polly left the tavern yard and walked down to the cabins. She found Boy sitting in a chair on Moze's porch. "How are you feeling today?" she asked him.

"Tolerable, Miss Polly," Boy answered her. He swallowed and stammered, "M-miss Polly, thank you. Moze —" He shifted slightly in the rocking chair. "Moze told me —"

"And who is looking after you, Boy?"

"The Healer be here. She said I was to sit up for my insides to heal quick."

"The Healer? You mean Marie?"

"Yes, ma'am. She be looking after me."

"Boy, have you thought about a name for yourself?

"I be studying on it. I think I found one."

Polly waited.

Boy's words ran together he spoke so quickly. "I wants my name to be Solomon and I won't never cut no babies in half and I wants to learn to read."

"Solomon." Polly said the name aloud. "Yes, that's a good name for you. You know the Bible story of the King Solomon who was a judge?"

"Yes, ma'am. I knows lots of Bible stories."

"Solomon, what were you and Charlotte doing when Mister Colston rode up in the yard and grabbed you?"

The child began to shake and his breathing came in great gasps. Marie walked out on the cabin porch and placed her hand on his head. She murmured words that Polly could not understand, but he quieted.

"Tell," Marie said aloud. "Tell her."

"Reading," Solomon whispered. "We reading."

Polly's thoughts whirled. "You and Charlotte? Reading?"

No wonder Mister Colston had gotten so angry. As far as she knew, there was no law against teaching slaves to read, but it certainly was not common practice. She walked out into the yard to collect her thoughts. Withered calabash vines, heavy with ripened gourds, hung from the side of Moze's cabin. Corn shocks were stacked in pyramids at the ends of rows in the garden. A hen stuck her head from the base of a shock and inspected her world.

Polly looked at the child who sat so still in his chair, waiting to find out what would happen to him. "Solomon, you shall learn to read. I don't know how much Charlotte has taught you, but that will be easy to find out. You can study with the girls after the chores are done. And you must learn to cipher, too. Numbers, and how they work, is an important part of education."

The boy closed his eyes and his lips moved silently.

"Solomon?" Polly asked. "What are you doing?"

He looked up at her. "I praying, Miss Polly. I saying prayers of thanksgiving."

"And I will say prayers of thanksgiving when you are well enough to come back to The Anchor. You do what Marie tells you to, so you can mend quickly."

Solomon nodded and closed his eyes.

Marie came to the steps and took Polly's hand in both of hers for a brief moment. They did not speak.

Polly walked slowly back to the tavern. The governor's coach stood just outside the door. Governor Tryon came up to her. "Thank you for all you've done for us," he said.

"Do you work this hard all of the time, Pauline?" Mistress Tryon asked.

"I do work hard. Charlotte and Cecilia are a big help. And Little Margaret gave a hand today, too. She is an agreeable child. We love having her here."

"And your mother?" asked Mistress Tryon. "I gather she is not well."

Polly sighed. "Mama does have problems, but we think she's getting better."

"I hope so, my dear." Mistress Tryon smoothed on her gloves as Margaret ran up to them. Hattie helped the little girl into the coach. Polly waved as they pulled away.

Daniel handed Polly a small cloth sack heavy with coins. "I know it was a sad day, but you made money. When your father was here, running horse races and betting on the outcome, or standing drinks for everyone who came in the door, there was not such a crowd as you've handled today."

Polly hefted the sack. The weight was most satisfying. She sat on the bench, holding the sack of coins on her lap.

Daniel sat beside her. "Will there ever be time for us?"

Polly's stomach flipped. Shouts came from the dock as a brig made preparations to sail. "Weigh, boys. It's out into the channel to catch the tide." The voices drifted up toward them as the tops'l mainsheet caught the light breeze and the ship moved slowly into the river channel.

"A beautiful sight," Polly said. "I love to watch the sails go up."

"A beautiful sight," Daniel said. Somehow Polly knew he wasn't talking about ships and sails.

After a moment he spoke again. "Polly, my apprenticeship is almost over. Within a few weeks I'll have my twenty-first birthday. Then I'll be my own man."

"You have always been your own man, Daniel." Her hands trembled but she kept her voice steady.

"Not always, Polly." He hugged his arms about himself. "Judge Moore has been good to me. I was only ten years old when he lifted me off a crate on the dock in Charleston and took me home with him. He gave me a good education. He gave me the opportunity to learn several trades. I've had advantages that most apprentices never have. In many ways, I owe him my life."

She turned her head to look at him. "What will you do now?"

He was staring at the edge of the woods. "I'm going west, toward the mountains."

Her stomach hit her backbone and she uttered a stifled "Oh!"

Daniel seemed not to have heard. "I'll leave as soon as I have my papers and can finish putting together my provisions."

She gathered her strength and tried to think ahead to a time when he would not be here. "Daniel, before you go, will you teach Jeremiah and Isaac to shoot? I will need hunters."

"Yes, you will. I had not thought of that. I'll start lessons in the morning."

He put a finger under her chin and tilted her face up as if to study her every feature. He kissed her forehead, his lips as soft as the wings of a moth. Then he was gone, striding across the yard.

Polly watched until the barn hid him from her and wondered if Marie had herbs for a bruised heart.

Chapter 22

A fall nor'easter blew in, bringing freezing rains and icy winds that cut through the warmest cloak. Polly stood at the window and watched the swaying trees. The ships in the river seemed hunkered down against the blow. No one was moving up or down the street.

Charlotte sat hemming an apron, making tiny stitches as she turned the fabric. Cecilia worked on a column of figures, solving an arithmetic problem that Polly had set out for her. Solomon wrote his alphabet on Cecilia's old slate. His tongue curled against the corner of his mouth as he concentrated on his task. He still favored his side where the ribs were healing, but she had heard no word of complaint from him. Her own back ached at times so badly that she wanted to sit and cry, but the gash no longer bled with every movement of her arms.

The whir of the spinning wheel filled the tavern. Mama had not stopped her back-and-forth pacing all morning. And she sang as she walked. "Niddy Noddy, Niddy Noddy, two heads and one body. 'Tis one, t'ain't one. But soon will be." The measure of thread was finished with the end of the verse. She began again.

"Niddy Noddy, Niddy Noddy, two heads and one body. 'Tis two, t'ain't two. But soon will be." The count of forty-five would bring her to one hank of thread to twist into a skein. Surely her mother had walked five miles this morning in her back-and-forth pacing at the wheel.

Leah walked up to stand beside Polly at the window. "She grieving," Leah said softly, nodding toward Henrietta. "She grieving so hard she don't know how to handle herself. And she so thin she wouldn't cast a shadow if she walk out in bright sunlight."

"I know," Polly said. "I'm worried, too. If only I could figure out what she's grieving about. Is it Papa being gone? That she is, and at the same time, is not a widow? Is she so afraid that something will happen to Timothy Charles? Is it money? Oh, Leah, if she would only talk!"

A rider, so wrapped against the rain that Polly did not recognize him, came into view. He headed his horse toward the barn and a few minutes later came out to walk to the tavern. Moze limped beside him.

"Leah, how old is Moze?" Polly asked.

"Lawdy, Miss Polly, I don't know. He already a old man when I come into this family."

Leah opened the door and stood aside for the two men to enter. Moze went straight to the bench by the hearth and settled his back against the wall. The man pulled off his hat and sailed it toward the wall peg. He took off his cloak and shook it. Water flew everywhere.

Polly giggled. "Cousin Maurice, you are like a shaggy dog this morning."

He grinned at her. "I guess I did shake water on your floor."

"It will wipe up. Come in by the fire. Would you like a drink or some hot stew?"

Cousin Maurice pulled off his leather gloves. "Something hot."

Timothy Charles, playing near the hearth, banged his wooden spoons on the floor. "Hot. Powee. Hot."

"Powee?" Cousin Maurice repeated.

Polly laughed. "He can't say the 'L' sound yet. Powee is

his version of my name and he's asking for something hot to eat."

She served a bowl of the squirrel stew, set it in front of her guest and poured a mug of sassafras tea from the kettle hanging over the fire. Then she dipped up liquid from the stew into a shallow silver porringer and pulled the baby on her lap. As Cousin Maurice ate, Polly spooned the warm pot liquor for Timothy Charles. He waved his arms in the air and cooed between each spoonful.

"That is the happiest, healthiest baby I've ever seen," the man said.

"He is a good child." She wiped the baby's face with a napkin and put him on the floor. "What brings you out on such a stormy day?"

"Several things, actually. I had papers to bring over for Tryon. You know that the Stamp Act was to take effect on November 1, which was last week. The ship bringing the stamps is still at sea, so we had to know just what the legal status is. We don't know when the ship will arrive."

Cousin Maurice held out his mug and Polly poured him more tea. "Most of the merchants have said they will not pay the stamp tax, so we have a real problem. At least one newspaper that I've seen has printed a skull and crossbones in the space where the stamp is to be affixed. The defiance has begun in a very concrete way over this act." He tossed the paper on the table. "You can read it all."

"Where do you stand, sir?"

"As a judge, I'm an official of the crown, Polly."

"I know that, Cousin Maurice. So are most of the leaders in this area. That does not tell me where you stand over the Stamp Act. Will we pay this tax?"

"No." He got up to pace back and forth across the floor. "By God, no!"

"And what will we do? If we do not pay the tax, we are breaking the law."

"We will argue. We will hold court. We will call for assembly meetings where the people can speak. We will talk to the governors throughout the colonies. We will try to make Parliament see reason." He shook his fist in the air. "There are some reasonable men in government."

He stopped his frantic pacing and turned to face her. "We will not see our colonial assemblies stripped of power where we have the right and the obligation to raise our own taxes. We will be heard!"

"And will our own Governor Tryon listen?"

Cousin Maurice slumped down at the table. "Maybe. He did hear me out this morning. He does seem to understand how strongly we feel against this Stamp Act. But in many ways his hands are tied. He is governor at the pleasure of King George. He can be removed at the same pleasure."

Cecilia began to cry.

"And just what is wrong with you, young lady?" Cousin Maurice asked.

"It's Margaret," Cecilia sobbed. "If you don't like her father, I can't play with her. Margaret is my most special friend in all the world."

"It's not personal, child," Cousin Maurice said.

"It *is* personal, sir," Polly answered. "It's all very personal when it matters what happens to you. That's why the stamp tax is so important. It's a very personal tax to a lot of very personal people."

Cecilia hiccupped.

"Go wash your face, Cee," Polly said. "And stop your crying. I will not stop you from playing with Margaret."

Cecilia ran up the stairs, still snubbing.

"Well!" exclaimed Cousin Maurice. "I didn't mean to cause that. But I do have other news. And this is for Charlotte."

Charlotte, who had seemed to pay no attention to the conversation up to that point, settled her sewing in her lap and looked at her cousin.

"Times are most turbulent just now. I'm sure you've heard of the riots in the streets. A harlequin spirit seems to have descended on the people. The jester and the clown are holding court and I fear events may get out of control. Charlotte, it is not a good time for you to go to Wilmington."

Charlotte clutched her sewing to her chest and fled up the stairs.

Cousin Maurice looked toward the door where Charlotte had disappeared. "I seem to be upsetting everyone. And now I guess you will run away, too." He reached into his coat pocket and handed Polly a letter. She recognized her father's handwriting.

"This letter to you from Phillip was included in a packet to me, Polly. He's asking you to send him money. Don't send him any. Not one penny. As your guardian, I'm making that a stipulation. I will inform Phillip that I have so told you."

"You sound like a lawyer and a judge now, sir," Polly said. "But Papa just sent three slaves here recently. If he needed money, why didn't he keep them and sell them?"

Polly realized that her mother had stopped her spinning and was listening intently to the conversation. She did so wish Mama would speak. If only she knew what her mother thought of the situation with Papa.

"Polly, you know Phillip. He has money one week and the next he is in debt," Cousin Maurice said. "I did a good day's work when I put you in charge of The Anchor. You are managing the tavern and have the oversight of everything else as well. You're sending out your maritime products and placing orders most prudently. Don't jeopardize your position here by sending money to Barbados or Charleston or some other place Phillip has decided to try out his gambling schemes."

He tapped the letter with his finger. "I have not given you any orders about running the tavern, or about what you do with the operation of the turpentine processes, or how you handle and ship your forest products. I haven't even talked to you about putting that slave in charge of the sawmill. As long as it works, I'll let you run it your way. But this is an order, Pauline Moore. Send no money to Phillip."

Polly walked behind the counter to put the letter with other papers she had stored there. She almost fell over Solomon, hunkered down in hiding with his slate. She stood looking at him, and at Timothy Charles as he played on the floor. "Sir, I will not send Papa money."

Mama walked out of the tavern room and up the steps.

Cousin Maurice took his heavy cloak from the peg and fastened it at the throat. "I seem to have emptied your tavern," he said. "Take care, little cousin. I'm sorry my news was not more cheerful."

"Cheerful or not, it is always good to have you come. I truly mean that, big cousin. Have a good ride home."

He nodded and went out into the cold.

For a few minutes the only sounds left in the room were Moze's snores, where he dozed by the hearth, and the baby's gurgles, as he played under a table. Slowly, one by one, Cecilia and Charlotte and Mama came back to hear the news from the papers that Cousin Maurice had left.

"The colony has gone mad," Polly exclaimed, as she read sections of the paper aloud for them all. "It says here that in New Bern the people have tried, condemned, hanged and burned Doctor William Houston in effigy!"

"What's effigy, Polly?" Cecilia asked.

"Who's Doctor Houston?" Charlotte asked.

"Doctor William Houston was appointed by the king as distributor of stamps for the province," Polly read. She looked up. "That's what the article says, anyway. It seems the people don't think too much of his position. And an effigy, Cee, is like a mannequin or a dummy."

"Is that like a scarecrow, Miss Polly?" Solomon asked, poking his head around the edge of the counter.

Polly nodded. "Exactly like a scarecrow."

"So they burned a dummy," Cecilia said. "That's play acting. I didn't know grown men would do things like that."

"It's very serious play acting, Cee. If they can't send their business letters or get their newspapers or buy a deck of cards to have a friendly game, I guess they would get mad enough to burn the King's representative in effigy," Polly said. "They might get angry enough to do even more."

During the last week of October, the paper said, a drunken crowd, right in the middle of a Wilmington street, built tar-barrel bonfires and incinerated the absent stamp distributor. On Halloween night, with the muffled ringing of the town bell, the crowd held a funeral for "Liberty." The funeral procession bore the coffin toward the church. But before they buried the body in the ground, someone felt its pulse and declared there was some life remaining in the mannequin, after all.

"Liberty lives," someone cried out. "She still lives."

"They talking about liberty again, Miss Polly," Solomon said from behind the counter. "Oh, liberty and freedom."

"The procession returned to the bonfire," Polly read, "placed the effigy in a large chair and rejoiced on finding that 'Liberty' still had an existence in the colonies." She looked up. "This is why Cousin Maurice doesn't think it is the right time for you to go to Wilmington, Charlotte. I do agree."

"They say liberty be living," Solomon said.

"Sounds like to me those gentlemens was most liquored up," Leah commented. "Or they a little bit crazy."

"I feel crazy," said Polly. "Crazy with worry. I am desperate for supplies. The rum and beer reserves are both crucially low. My last purchase order included dress fabric and shoes, tea and molasses, wine and pottery. Even if the ships come in, they cannot be unloaded without stamps."

No ships bearing the hated stamps arrived. The business of government, and the business of business was, for all intents and purposes, shut down.

News reached them that sometime in mid-November Doctor Houston, who did not seem to understand the fury of the people, visited Wilmington. He was spotted and before long a crowd gathered. The men bodily carried Doctor Houston to the courthouse. He was forced, in the presence of the mayor and aldermen, to resign his commission of stamp distributor.

The crowd, having taken care of the distributor, took over the newspaper. From the newspaper press came an issue dictated by the crowd. And a skull and bones in printer's ink was placed on the spot where the stamp should have been affixed.

"I don't know what will happen next," Cornelius Harnett said, when he stopped by The Anchor on his way to Russellborough. He brought a copy of the illegal newspaper for Polly to read. "We must keep clear heads in this matter."

"How serious are these demonstrations?" Polly asked him.

"Serious enough that I'm concerned," he said. "The people manhandled an official of the crown. They forced their way into the *Gazette* office, took over the presses and printed a newspaper without stamps. The governor did not call the Assembly in New Bern this fall because he wanted to avoid just these kinds of acts. Now he's asking for a meeting of merchants. That's why I'm on my way over to Russellborough."

"What kind of meeting, Mister Harnett?"

"The merchants are the ones most immediately and directly confronted by the stamp tax. If Governor Tryon can come to an understanding with the merchants, they can help to control the populace."

"I'm a merchant. And a tavern owner. I am most directly confronted." Polly's mind was racing. If there was going to be a meeting, she wanted to be there.

"Mister Harnett, can you wait long enough for me to write a note to Cousin Maurice? I will be very brief."

Mister Harnett threw up his hands. "Maurice did ask me to find out how you are faring."

Polly wrote quickly: Sir, the servant, Paul, who helped at the party in the summer is available to assist at the governor's meeting with the merchants.

She folded, sealed and handed the paper to Mister Harnett.

He nodded and strode out. Polly watched him stuff the letter in his saddle bag before he mounted and rode off. One way or another, she was determined to be at the meeting at the Governor's House to hear the discussions between Tryon and the Wilmington merchants.

"Miss Polly, you got that stubborn look on your face," Leah said.

"Leah, I do think we should make sure Paul's clothing is ready to wear."

"Lawdy," the woman whispered. "Miss Polly, you is so willful."

Chapter 23

Governor Tryon's kitchen bustled with activity. The large room, built in the yard at the back of the house at Russellborough, was dominated by a huge fireplace. Simmering pots filled every available hook on the lugbar. For a moment Polly, with Solomon close by her side, stood at the door and watched the flurry of men cooking vegetables, roasting a pig, polishing pewter.

A tall dark-haired man turned from the hearth and spotted them. "*Comment vous appelez-vous, Monsieur?*" he asked.

"P-P-Paul," Polly stammered. "*Je m'appelle* Paul Moore. And this is my —" She took a deep breath and put her hand on Solomon's shoulder. "This is my apprentice, come with me to help."

The man broke into a spiel of French which Polly could not understand. She could only look at him and shake her head.

"In the house. They want you inside the house. Carry this as you go," he commanded. He handed her a silver tray polished to such a shine that she could see her reflection on its surface.

The commotion extended into the house. As she climbed the stairs to the second floor she saw servants polishing furniture, waxing floors and moving furniture about. Mistress Tryon stood in the doorway of the second floor dining room.

"Ma'am," Polly said.

Mistress Tryon whirled toward her. "Who are you?"

"Paul, ma'am."

"Oh, yes. Paul. Judge Maurice did say he was sending someone. Do you know how to lay a table?"

Polly looked at the two long tables that dominated the dining room. "I understood there would be fifty to serve," she answered. "Each of those tables will seat about twenty."

"Each will seat twenty-five, if you lay it correctly. The china is in the wall cabinets. The forks and spoons and knives are stored in the drawers there. Do you need any other instructions?"

"No, ma'am."

Mistress Tryon hurried out. Polly could hear her heels clicking on the polished floor as she started down the stairs.

"Linens first, Solomon," she said. She thought of the dinners at the Davis home. She remembered the few times Mama had brought out their china plates and crystal goblets. Mama had grown up in Edenton with the very best of everything and now it was all packed away in boxes in the attic. A tavern was no place for china and crystal.

The India Huckaback table cloths, long enough to cover the surface of the central tables, were spread first. Then Polly went about the room, rearranging tables, moving chairs, placing napkins, counting and counting, until she had seating for fifty. Solomon, following close behind her, counted aloud.

"First time I counted that high, Miss —"

"My name is Paul. Don't forget that tonight, Solomon. Not for a minute."

"First time I count that high, Paul," the boy said. His face was wreathed in smiles.

Polly smiled back. "Go around and count again. Do it out loud so I can hear you."

While he was counting, Polly opened the cabinet and took out a china plate. It felt so fragile in her hands after handling the pottery ware and wooden bowls they used at the tavern. She took a deep breath and began to show Solomon how she wanted the plates set, with the forks and spoons just so on either side of the plate. "After ten is eleven, Solomon. Ten, then eleven. Say it."

Solomon dutifully repeated the numbers.

She set the crystal goblets at the tip of the knife and left room for a cup and saucer on the right side of each place. "And after eleven is twelve. Say it."

In the late afternoon she and Solomon went to the kitchen to eat. As they sat together at a small work table, a bowl of beans and corn between them, Polly heard the first riders coming into the yard.

"Put on that clean apron I brought for you," Polly said to Solomon. "And get ready to work."

"I thought I be working."

"I thought I had been working," Polly corrected, as she tied her own short apron over her breeches. "Let's go serve and hear some thoughts from these merchants about King George and taxes."

Governor Tryon led the dinner conversation at first. There were many there that Polly had not seen before, but the governor knew each man by name. Through the meal the conversation was so general that Polly wondered why they were all sitting in the governor's dining room, drinking his wine. But as she took the last plate from the table and stacked it on a tray in the corner of the room, Cornelius Harnett got them down to business.

"Sir, you know this stamp tax is abominable," Mister Harnett said.

There was a stir of agreement around the tables.

The governor stood at his place. "Gentlemen, that is

why we have come together. I, too, feel that this tax is a burden. I understand the drain of coin from the colony. So I have a proposal, if you will hear me out."

The room stilled. Solomon started toward a table with a wine bottle, but Polly shook her head at him. He moved back to the wall and stood quietly.

"Gentlemen, I am appointed by the crown. I must uphold the laws until we can reason with Parliament to amend or change them. So we must confront this tax situation in that context."

Several men nodded. Others frowned. But they were all listening.

These were men, Polly knew, who felt at home at a governor's table. They sat down, every day, to tables like it, spread with damask or linen cloths and napkins, in their own houses. They traded in Chinese silks and South American coffee. They owned the ships that brought goods from the West Indies and Barbados, and carried naval stores back to merchants in England. Many of them had family of distinction and wealth in Boston and New York, in Philadelphia and Charleston. They were landowners with vast acreage in corn and tobacco, rice and indigo. Much was at stake in this room.

The governor continued. "I am entitled to fees on many of the duties included in the Stamp Act. I will waiver those fees. I offer to pay the tax on tavern licenses in the principal towns and on those legal documents which would have fees coming to the governor's office. Until we can come to a resolution of this matter of duties, I will pay those taxes myself." He sat down, heavily, in his chair.

The men muttered among themselves. One or two seemed to be ready to agree to accept the governor's proposal. Most of the men, however, were growing angry. Their voices reached a shouting pitch.

John Ashe rose. He had been elected speaker of the Assembly by these same men arguing at the tables. He spoke now, not for the government, but as a neighbor and friend.

"Gentlemen." He nodded at the group and they grew quiet.

"Governor." Governor Tryon turned his full attention to Mister Ashe.

"You have made a most generous offer, sir." Mister Ashe held up his hands. "But we cannot accept. It would put it out of our power to refuse, with any propriety, a submission to the whole."

Several men, including Cousin Maurice, nodded in agreement.

"Sir," continued Mister Ashe, "let me speak more plainly. If we submit to any part of the tax, we will be saying that the tax can and should be required. Will we not then be required to submit to any other part of the tax? If we allow you to pay a part of the duties for us, we allow you the power to refuse to pay any part of the tax later. And if you do pay for us, as a father caring for his children, we have said to you that the tax should be paid."

Mister Ashe raised his right hand as if he were taking an oath. "This tax shall not be paid, in part or in whole."

Now all of the men were agreeing.

"We respect your office, sir. We respect that you have tried to find a peaceful solution to the problem here in Carolina. We respect your intention to uphold the law even as we must defy it. But sir, defy it we will." John Ashe sat down.

A profound silence enveloped the room. Several men sat with bowed heads, as if in prayer. Others gazed thoughtfully at their plates. One leaned his elbows on the table, his chin resting on his knuckles, while another clutched his head. John Ashe's words were treasonable. Treason carried severe penalties, including imprisonment or death.

Mister Tryon's voice was soft as he spoke to the quiet room. "I can only hope that Parliament is not too slow to understand the situation here and that members of that body will act soon. This Stamp Act is folly. They must see that."

He took a swallow of wine. "I do plead with you to keep the demonstrations to a minimum. I do plead with you for caution."

There was some quiet discussion among groups at the tables, but the main reason for the meeting had been addressed. These men would not consent to payment, in any part, of duties imposed by the Stamp Act. On that note the men, quietly and politely, began to depart.

As Cousin Maurice passed her, he paused. "Paul, eh. How do you think it went?"

"The meal or the meeting, sir?" Polly asked.

Cousin Maurice stared at her for a moment and then threw back his head in a great burst of laughter. When he could speak, there was still laughter in his voice. "You do make a fine boy. I've said all along that's what you should have been. I will send your money to The Anchor, if that is agreeable with you."

Polly nodded, afraid to speak.

"Paul, eh! Well, Paul, I do admire initiative. That is what was always lacking in your father." Cousin Maurice walked over to join a group of men who were saying their farewells to the governor.

"Paul?" Solomon whispered. "He knows?"

"He knows," Polly answered.

"Are we in trouble?"

"Solomon, you should know by now that I'm always in some kind of trouble. Come on and let's get to washing up.

All these plates have to be back in the cabinets before we can leave."

"One question, please, Miss Polly."

She raised her eye brows and waited.

"Did you understand what these mens talking about tonight?"

"Solomon, it's men, not mens." She sighed. "And yes, I did understand. These men will fight before they will pay the tax."

Her thoughts were filled by the confrontation that had taken place around these tables. She knew exactly how these men felt. They had been given no say in the making of the law. If only she could explain to them that she felt that way about her own situation. Of all the women she knew, she was the most free. Even so, she was bound. A word from a judge, or a marriage that was either welcome or unwelcome, could end her running of the tavern and caring for her family. Oh, what would she have done if Cousin Maurice had not approved of her initiative? She knew she would do anything she had to do to keep what freedom she had.

These men might well have to fight before problems with King George were resolved. They would use guns if needed. She had only her wiles — those ruses she had tried to tell Charlotte about.

Mistress Tryon came to stand at the door, looking first at the tables and then at her.

"To work, Solomon," she said. "I want to get to bed before the rooster wakes the sun."

Chapter 24

A few days later Polly saw the *Diligence* dropping anchor in the Cape Fear River. The stamps had arrived. The date was November 28th, 1765.

Captain Phipps, captain of the *Diligence*, came to the tavern, asking for directions to Russellborough. He must have had a long talk with the governor, because it was several hours later when Polly saw him at the docks, waiting for a boat to row him out to the sloop. The packets of dark-blue, foil-attached stamps stayed on board the ship. For want of stamps, no shipping could legally enter or clear any port.

At Christmas time, the governor and his family went into Wilmington for church services and spent several days visiting friends. Cornelius Harnett and Maurice Moore, joined by a few other men of position, came to Brunswick. Together with John Ashe and Edward Moseley, they forced the opening of the Cape Fear to shipping without stamps. Ships sailed out. Tryon could do nothing, for he had no way to police the ports.

Then Captain Lobb of the sloop, *Viper*, seized three other sloops which had arrived at Brunswick without stamped papers. By January 20th he had been so criticized by those opposing the stamps that he promised to seize no more vessels. While Polly waited and wondered about her supplies, there was little business at the tavern. Cousin Maurice, on his way to and from Russellborough, stopped by when he could, to catch her up on the news. Mister Ashe or Mister Moseley came in each afternoon to make sure her household was not in need.

She sent Isaac and Jeremiah hunting, so that she did not have to kill a chicken or slaughter a goat. There was food in plenty, if she was careful.

Mistress Ashe still visited often. On one afternoon she sat at a table near the hearth and motioned for Polly to sit with her. "You have to watch out for your reputation," she said to open the conversation.

"Ma'am?"

"Polly, Henrietta isn't herself, you know. She doesn't seem to understand some of the things you are doing. So I feel that I have to speak to you."

"What am I doing, Mistress Ashe?"

"Well, for one, you are with that little Negro boy much too much. I've even seen him walking beside you when he's carrying baskets for you at the docks. Now, Polly, you know he should walk behind you. And he runs in and out of this place like he belongs. You have your sisters to think about."

"Yes, ma'am. What else?" Polly was holding herself as still as possible.

"You have made that tall slave, the one who is so light-skinned, an overseer down at the sawmill. There is much talk about that, you know. You simply must hire a white man as foreman."

"Yes, ma'am," Polly said again.

"You talk politics with the men here. Last night John told me of a conversation with you about the tax and those dreadful stamps. Polly, it is not a woman's place to discuss, or even understand, politics. We leave that to the men."

When Polly did not answer, Mistress Ashe sighed. "It was bad enough that Phillip left so abruptly, walking out when Henrietta needed him here. It was bad enough that

Maurice said you could take over the tavern and run it. It's even worse that you've made a success of it." She sat back in her chair, as if she had made her point, and seemed to be waiting for Polly to answer.

"Yes, ma'am," Polly said.

"Are you going to do anything about any of this?"

"No, ma'am," Polly said respectfully.

"Pauline Moore!"

"Mistress Ashe, thank you for caring enough to talk with me. I'm truly sorry if I've upset you." She leaned across the table. "Solomon is a little boy who needs much guidance and I've found that reason goes far in dealing with him. Jeremiah is a slave, but he's getting more work from the men, and making more profit for me, than Mister Colston ever did. As for politics, we seem to be pulled into it whether we want to be or not. And I don't know why Papa left."

She sat back in her chair. "Mistress Ashe, you have been so kind to Mama. I don't know what I would have done without your help."

Mistress Ashe pulled her cloak about her shoulders. "I had a letter from the Rhetts in Charleston. You know, William's wife's family. They have so much influence." She smoothed on her gloves. "They were appalled that a Moore girl was getting involved in business." She headed for the door. There she turned. "Polly, I think you're a good girl. People are talking, however. You must be careful."

As Mistress Ashe went out Polly thought how much easier it was to run the tavern, and be involved with business, than to deal with people.

On the 18th of February a group of merchants from Wilmington marched on Tryon himself for an interview with Captain Lobb. During the discussions somehow the papers of the three seized sloops mysteriously disappeared from the house of the customs collector at Brunswick. The ships, with their papers, sailed down the river.

"Whose side is Mister Dry on?" Polly asked John Ashe, when he stopped by for a cup of cider.

"William Dry? Why, William opposes the Stamp Act as much as I do," Mister Ashe answered.

"But he is the customs collector."

"True," said Mister Ashe. "Make no mistake, Polly. William Dry, while he may hem and haw, will defy the King over this issue, though it means his job. He may, at times, take excesses with drink or women. He is not always as polite in public as he could be. But he will stand with us. He will fight, if it comes to that. William Dry is a good man."

Mister Ashe finished his cider. "There is something else, Polly. I understand my wife talked with you recently." He turned the cup around and around on the counter. "She is right about your foreman. Would you like for me to look for someone for you?"

Polly answered carefully. "Thank you for your concern, sir. Jeremiah is doing a good job for me. I think I'll let the situation stay as it is."

"It's potentially dangerous, Polly. That's all I'll say now."

With so few people stopping in, and no newspapers, Polly felt very isolated. She wished she had someone to send to Wilmington to bring back information. She wished for the busy days when the tavern was full. She walked to the docks to peer at the ships anchored there and wished them unloaded, with her own barrels of rosin and turpentine secure in their holds for the voyage to England.

On the morning of February 21st a rider from Cousin Maurice appeared on her door step with a note.

"There will be much movement of men in your area in the next day or two. Take especial care of your household,"

Polly read.

"What kind of movement?" Polly asked the boy who had delivered the note.

The boy took a sip of cider that Polly had poured for him and wiped his mouth with the back of his hand. "There's men from Edenton and Bath, up to the north. There's men from Hillsborough in the west. There's men from every plantation and farm on the river clear up to Cross Creek." He took a drink of cider. "Maybe beyond Cross Creek."

"There are men where?"

"Why, moving into Wilmington. They gonna march on the gov."

"The gov? You mean the governor?"

"That's what I said, ma'am. They gonna get that stamp man who's staying there." The boy frowned. "Judge Moore said something about signing papers."

Polly looked out of the window at the idle ships. "When does this march on 'the gov' take place?"

"Tonight, ma'am. And I tell you 'cause Judge Moore said you could be trusted." He set his empty tankard on the table and stood. "I thank you for the drink. I got to deliver more messages." He was gone.

Polly sat at the table in the empty tavern room and tried to figure out how she could witness the confrontation. She had as much at risk in this business as any man who would convene at the governor's residence.

With so little trade, she had given Leah and Morrow the day off. Mama and the girls, with Timothy Charles, were up in their chambers. She paced about the table. If only Daniel were here. He would be in the thick of things. He would tell her exactly what was going on. But Daniel was somewhere to the west. She had not heard from him since he left in the fall.

She was going to Russellborough, that she knew. But Cousin Maurice would not have sent her the message if he didn't think there was some danger involved. If she were a man —

Polly grabbed her cloak from its peg and ran across the street, down toward the cabins. In front of Moze's place she stopped and called. "Solomon? Are you there, Solomon?"

The boy popped his head out of the door. "Yes, ma'am. We got trouble, Miss Polly?"

"No, Solomon. Well, no trouble yet. But I want you to dress in your warmest clothes and be at the tavern by late afternoon. I need you to go with me over to the governor's house."

Solomon looked at her for a moment. "I guess we won't be serving a supper meal, because if I wear my warmest clothes then we must be outside."

"Absolutely, young man."

"Yes, ma'am. I'll be there."

Charlotte helped her fix her hair, fussing all the while. Cecilia cried herself into a fit of hiccups which sent Timothy Charles into spasms of wails.

"Powee, no. Powee, no," he screamed.

"You and Cee didn't speak this early," Polly commented, gathering the baby in her arms. "You gurgled, but you didn't say words."

"That's probably because you wouldn't let us talk," Charlotte spat.

"Polly, you're going to get hurt," Cecilia cried.

"I'm not going to get hurt. I'm going to hide and sit very still and listen to what the men have to say. Now hush, please."

The baby grabbed a handful of her hair and pulled.

"Now he's undone the whole braid," Charlotte complained. "I'll have to start all over again."

Polly gave the crying baby to a sobbing Cecilia and tried to hold still while Charlotte redid the braid. She knew the girls were afraid for her, but she had to go. She had to. When she walked into the tavern room a few minutes later, dressed in her breeches and leather shoes, Mama handed her a man's heavy woolen cloak.

"Mama, this is beautiful. Where did it come from?"

"It was my father's cloak. You must stay warm."

"Oh, Mama." She fought back the tears.

"Mama talked!" Cecilia exclaimed. "Oh, Mama, Mama, Mama." She hurled herself at Henrietta and snugged her arms about her mother's waist.

Henrietta hugged her back. Over the child's head she said, very softly, "Mistress Ashe is wrong. Be careful, but do what has to be done."

"Mama, I told you we need you," Polly said.

She wrapped the cloak about her shoulders and thrust her arms through the side slits. "Bolt the door. Don't let anyone in unless you know them."

And to Solomon, who stood near the hearth, she said, "Let's go."

Mama caught at Polly's sleeve and handed her a pair of woolen gloves. Then she held out a pair of gloves to Solomon.

"Thank you, ma'am," the child said. "I never had gloves to warm my hands afore." He pulled them on as they went out the door.

Polly heard the bolt slide home behind them.

Chapter 25

She set a brisk pace through the path toward the governor's house. Though she listened, she heard no sounds coming from the woods — not a bird call or the rustle of an animal moving. Even the wind was still. The feeling of solitude turned into isolation. It was almost as if she and the boy who walked with her were the last two people on earth.

Solomon suddenly dropped to his knees and groaned.

"What's wrong?" Polly pleaded.

"It's my side, Miss Polly. When I walk fast, it's like a fire burning inside me."

Polly knelt beside Solomon and waited for his breathing to ease. When she knew he was all right, and his breathing steady, she helped him to his feet. This time she walked more slowly.

Then the governor's stately house came into view. Polly stopped so quickly that Solomon bumped into her.

" 'Scuse me, Miss —"

"Shhh." She pointed toward a huge live oak that grew in the edge of the house yard. The lowest limbs were close to the ground. Polly thought that the twisted limbs of the tree could hide them.

"We gonna climb that tree?" Solomon whispered.

Polly nodded. She caught hold of a limb and kinked her legs up until she was sitting. She motioned for Solomon to climb, too. Slowly, carefully, they moved up until Polly found a crotch near the trunk that was big enough for them both.

Solomon looked down and covered his eyes with both hands.

Polly giggled. "If you fall and get killed, then you'll never have to listen to me again."

"It's not falling I scared of. It be the men."

Looking down, she saw two men at the edge of the clearing. One had a musket over his shoulder. Another carried a flint lock on his arm. As she watched, the two were joined by several more and she realized Solomon was counting.

A man rode past and stopped his horse a few feet from the nearest tree. A second joined him. More men on foot walked from the woods and began to form double, then triple, lines across the yard.

"Miss Polly, I counted to fifty and there's more coming," Solomon whispered.

"Count to fifty again," Polly said. "Just remember how many fifties you had."

She was awed by the sight of the orderliness and the silence with which the men moved, without a single recognizable signal. These were the merchants that deployed commerce across the Atlantic, and up and down the coast to other colonies. Many of them had sat at the governor's table not so long ago and vowed to defy the Stamp tax. These were Assembly representatives who took an active role in government. They supported law and expected taxes, but rebelled when taxes were levied without their consent. These were landowners, wealthy in property and slaves. They had fought with the crown, often at their own expense, in the French and Indian War to secure the frontier. These men meant serious business.

Cornelius Harnett walked his horse across the front of the line and turned to face the assemblage gathered on the lawn in front of the governor's house. Behind Mister Harnett rode Cousin Maurice. She saw John Ashe and Edward Moseley and William Dry. There were other men she had served in the tavern or had seen on the streets of Wilmington. Many of the faces she did not know.

"I counted fifty at least five times, Miss Polly." Solomon's whisper was so close to her ear that his breath tickled her check.

But Polly wasn't paying attention to him. There were more men moving through the trees onto the yard, taking their places in the ranks before Mister Harnett. A man with a torch began to move about the edges of the lines, igniting other torches, until light circled the entire group. It was beautifully premeditated, deliberate in execution. Not even the deep shadows cast by the torches concealed the intensity with which the men waited.

For centuries Englishmen had stood up to the king for their rights. No laws and no taxes, without representation, had been an ideal since Magna Carta. "Here again," Polly whispered. "Here again the leaders confront their king." She shivered.

Then Mister Harnett raised his arm. One great cry went up from the lines. "Ho!" Then again the silence.

Governor Tryon appeared on the balcony of the second floor of his house. He stood, feet apart, hands resting on the railing. "Who addresses the Governor?" he called.

"Men of the Cape Fear and the colony of Carolina," Mister Harnett answered.

"And what is your business, sir?" asked Governor Tryon.

"We would see the Comptroller of Port Brunswick. He has the authority to issue the stamps. He can repeal the order. He resides in your house."

Governor Tryon nodded and turned back inside.

Not a sound or motion that she could detect came from the lines in the yard.

After several minutes the governor appeared on the lower porch. "I will receive your spokesman," he called.

Cornelius Harnett and John Ashe dismounted, walked across the short distance to the house, and went inside. No one else moved or made a sound.

Lights blazed now from every room in the big house. Polly saw Mistress Tryon pass a window. Little Margaret peered out of the door on the second floor and was hastily pulled back inside.

Polly's foot was going to sleep, and in spite of the warm gloves, her hands were so cold she had trouble feeling them. What was going on in the house?

After long minutes that seemed hours, the governor came out to stand on the porch. Mister Harnett and Mister Ashe, the Comptroller between them, stood at his side. "The Comptroller would choose to go with the gentlemen," Governor Tryon said. "The stamps will be returned to England. Shipping is cleared."

Mister Harnett raised his arm and a mighty "ho!" again sounded from the assemblage. The men, lead by Harnett and Ashe, moved toward Brunswick.

When the last man was out of sight on the woods path and the last light had been extinguished in the house, Polly let out a deep breath. "When I am old and gray-haired, and all my teeth are gone, and the aches in my knees make it hard to walk, I will still remember this night."

"There were more than seven fifties of men, Miss Polly," Solomon said.

"Tomorrow I will have to teach you how to count that high." She scrambled down to the ground and stamped her foot to make it wake up. "Come on, Solomon. They will be worried about us at the tavern if we don't get back soon. Many of these men will walk right past our front door."

Solomon landed on the ground beside her and stood, clutching at his side. Through the obvious pain, he whispered, "Why did we come here tonight, Miss Polly? Did we come just to count these men?"

Again she felt amazement at the men's audacity. "There were four to five hundred armed men in that yard. Anything could have happened. Just anything. And not a shot was fired. Not a knife left its sheaf. Not one man raised his voice in anger."

She shook her head. "Why did we come, Solomon? I wanted to see and hear what was happening. I wanted to know about the stamps. I wanted to know when shipping would clear the port. I have a tavern to maintain and I need my supplies. What was decided here was important to my business."

She began walking, Solomon by her side. "I wanted to know how Englishmen confront the king, or his representative, to get laws changed. It takes a collective voice, with a show of force to back up the words. Women do not yet have that unity. We do not yet know how to speak together. Solomon, I wonder if we ever will."

From the west a mockingbird began to sing.

Chapter 26

Shipping was moving again. The hogsheads of turpentine and rosin, the sleds of logs, the bundles of tobacco, were being loaded on the ships that dropped anchor in the river. Every plantation in the area was sending produce of one kind or another. Many of the ships sent flatboats or barges across the sandbars to Wilmington for produce to balance off their shipments. That port, just a few miles up river from them, was growing while Brunswick seemed to be declining. Already, several families had moved, either into Wilmington or out to begin new plantations. Even Mistress Ashe had talked of moving.

What cheered Polly as much as sending out and receiving supplies was that her faith in the two men she had chosen as foremen was well placed. Jeremiah's production of maritime products outdid anything that Colston had gotten from the men. Each week he brought his tallies done in crude scratches on bark. He and Isaac, who was now in charge of the farm produce, sat across from her at a small table in the tavern to give their reports.

"Got some sickness, Miss Polly," Jeremiah said this morning of early spring.

"Contagion? Fever?"

"No, ma'am. Seems to be the changing weather. Sniffles and coughs and such."

"Leah and I will mix herbs. You can send someone to the tavern this afternoon to pick up the bottles. Some of it will taste bitter, but see that they drink it anyway."

He nodded. "We need a new saw blade."

"The old one cannot be sharpened?"

"No, ma'am, not again. It be mighty thin in the middle and like to break do we keep using it."

"I'll see Mister Edward this morning about making a new one. Jeremiah, don't endanger the men if the blade is not safe."

"Yes ma'am, Miss Polly."

"Isaac? Do we plant this week? You've got two fields plowed and ready."

"We needs another week 'fore we sure of no more frost." Isaac paused and Polly waited for him to speak his mind.

"Sweet 'tatoes takes a heap of good ground up in 'um. Do we move the sweet 'tatoes to the new ground and plant 'um there, they do better. Then we takes the muck from the hogs and plows it in the ground where the 'tatoes was. Then we plants the beans there."

"And the corn? We need extra corn this year."

Isaac rubbed his chin. "We plants the corn in two different places. One field where we be planting afore and one field where you plant the beans last year. And Miss Polly, we needs . . ." He stopped.

"Go on, Isaac."

"Miss Polly, the seed corn got mold in it. We can't plant it like that. We needs a plow horse. The 'quipment needs fixing. We needs a point on that old plow."

She took a deep breath, thinking of how much money she would have to expend. "Isaac, you are in charge. I will give you a pass and I will send Solomon with you when there is a reason for it. Buy the horse. Find the seed. See Mister Edward at the blacksmith's shop about putting a new point on the plow. Do it. Bring me the bills so I can pay for everything."

She got up from the table to get quill and paper to write a pass for Isaac.

"And I needs men to work the fields, Miss Polly."

"That I will see to," she answered him. "For now use anyone from the woods that Jeremiah can spare. I want those corn fields ready for planting by the time the last frost is gone."

"Yes, ma'am."

"Start today, Isaac." She went behind the counter to get the small bags she had prepared for each man. She had been paying them seven pennies a week since she had put them in charge.

"Thank you, Miss Polly," Jeremiah said.

"It be a pleasure to work for you, Miss Polly," Isaac said.

After they were gone she sat at the table, holding her dead peppercorn plant. There was no money tree. There never had been. This plant, born in the tropics, had not been able to survive a Carolina winter. Hard work and caring for the crops and tending the forests were all she had to bring in money. "I'm as bad a gambler as Papa," she said to the black leaves lying in the soil of the pot.

An hour later Mister Edward stomped in the door of The Anchor. "Did you send that insolent slave to me to fix your plow?" he demanded.

"If Isaac was rude, Mister Edward, I will deal with him. But I did send him to you." She placed a tankard of ale on the counter. "Can the plow be repaired or must I have a new one?"

He looked at the tankard and then at her. "For me?"

"Of course for you. Now please tell me about the plow."

"I can fix it," he said, and raised the tankard to drink.

"Will you fix it, sir?" she asked, thinking that talking with this man took as much diplomacy as dealing with Charlotte.

"Who pays me?" Mister Edward asked.

"Mister Edward, I told you that I would pay for any work I requested. I really thought that problem had been settled. Now Isaac is acting as my farm manager. If he requests work, it comes from me." Polly took a deep breath. "Can we work with this arrangement, sir? Or do you expect your money before you do the work?"

The blacksmith finished his drink and answered. "I do my work and then I get paid." He put the tankard on the counter. "I will repair the plow."

"And I need a new saw blade, Mister Edward. I was going to come to the blacksmith shop later this morning to tell you about it. Will you make me a saw blade for the mill?"

"I will do it. The plow first. Be ready in the morning. The blade will take all week." He started to leave and then turned back. "But I never heard tell of a slave being a farm manager. That will take some getting use to."

"The blacksmith told me about Isaac and the plow. Wish I could get that kind of fruitful labor from most of my slaves," Mister Ashe said to her about Jeremiah and Isaac. He had stopped by the tavern for a beer. "Maybe it will work out for you."

"Mister Ashe, I need some warehouse space. I've ordered more and more for the tavern. I'm shipping extra goods. I need storage."

"Warehouse space? Polly, one of those smaller buildings on the docks belongs to Phillip. And how is your father? I haven't heard Maurice say anything about him lately."

"I don't know, Mister Ashe. I haven't heard anything either."

"Well, check up on the warehouse. It's the one next to mine, I think. Go down and ask William about it."

Mister Dry was away, but the young clerk knew exactly which warehouse building belonged to The Anchor. He fitted a key in the heavy lock on the door and swung it open. Several barrels of molasses were stacked against the back wall. A split bag of rice leaned against a post. As Polly took a step into the room a wharf rat scurried from the bag to disappear through a hole near the door.

Polly squeaked and jumped back, right into the young man who had followed her inside. They both fell in a heap on the dusty floor.

She scrambled up, shaking out her petticoats.

"I don't much like rats myself," the clerk said. He sat on the floor.

"Are you hurt?" Polly asked.

"No, ma'am. Just resting." He looked about the almost empty space. "Really isn't much here. There are some bundles stacked on those tall shelves at the back."

The boy got up from his resting place on the floor to help her move a ladder over to the shelves. She climbed up to inspect the merchandise. The bundles she had seen from the floor were yards and yards of canvas in a plain weave. Polly rolled a corner of the cloth through her fingers. This material wasn't heavy enough for sails. Papa must have meant for it to be used for clothing for the slaves.

There was a small burlap-wrapped bag of tobacco. There was a wooden box of cigars and another of clay pipes.

At a far corner of the wide shelf, almost hidden by the bags and boxes, was a bulging saddle bag.

"I can't reach it," she said to the boy. "Please get down that saddle bag for me."

The boy scrambled up and tossed the bag to the floor. "Do you want anything else from up here?" he asked.

"Not now," she answered. "Thank you for unlocking the door. Please take all of the rats with you when you go."

"I'll stay and help."

"Thank you, but no. Just give me the key and I'll return it to the office when I'm through."

She watched him leave before she turned to a desk that sat in the center of the room. The drawers were filled with papers of different kinds. She wiped the surface of the desk with her handkerchief and began to pile the papers there.

There was a bill for a slave, a receipt for 500 pounds due from a bet on a horse race, the papers for the sale of two slaves, a debit of 1000 pounds on another bet, the sale of Cook, an order for two pipes of wine. Polly tried to make some kind of order of the monies coming in and monies going out.

She found so many unpaid bills that she stopped adding when she reached one thousand pounds. There were letters from creditors from New York to Charleston asking for their money. Some of the debts had been paid. Most had not.

Cousin Maurice had loaned Papa money. So had Mister Harnett. Mister Dry had advanced money, and Polly saw no evidence that it had ever been repaid. Evidently Papa had gambled it all away.

Polly's stomach ached and she swallowed bile. To think that Papa had lost so much money, and betrayed so many friends, was horrible. She stacked the papers and weighted them with a small ballast stone from a pile in the corner of the warehouse. Then she lifted the saddlebag from the floor and emptied it on the desk.

And finally she understood why Cousin Maurice had sent Papa away. Papers and money — quantities of paper money and coins of every denomination — were there. Papa had broken into the custom house. He had stolen money and government papers from William Dry's office. The official government seals on some of the papers had not even been broken.

Her father was banished. Cousin Maurice had not just sent Papa out of Brunswick to stop his gambling. He had gotten him out to protect him. He would never be able to return to the colony without being arrested and tried in court. If he were tried, he would be convicted and sent to prison, probably in England. It went far beyond money. Papa had stolen government documents. That's why Judge Maurice Moore had made out a paper putting her in charge of The Anchor. If she was running the tavern, people could believe Papa would come back. Did her cousin really think she could be successful? Or had he just been covering to gain time to get Papa away?

Carefully she gathered the papers and put them in an empty sack. She put all of the government papers back in the saddlebag and slung it over her arm. She locked the door of the warehouse. She trudged up the street to The Anchor.

In the necessary she threw up until she was weak. Her back ached and her head felt as if rats scurried through her brain. She beat on the saddlebag in anger. "I will repay every debt. To the last farthing." She shook the bag. "To the very last farthing, Papa. I will take this money to

William Dry and tell him where I found it. I will tell Maurice Moore of my discovery and find out how much he has repaid. I will . . ."

"Polly? What are you doing, Polly?" Charlotte yelled from outside the door. "Who are you talking to in the necessary?"

"I need a horse," Polly said to herself. "Mister Moseley knows horses. I'll talk to him. He can tell me where to find a good horse."

"Polly, open the door!" Charlotte yelled.

"Maybe his groom can teach Solomon about horses."

"Polly, we need you in the tavern. There is too much to do there without you." Charlotte banged on the necessary door again. "You come out of there right now. Please, Polly. Come out."

"And I have to go to Wilmington. I have to . . ."

"Polly, if you don't come out I'm going to break down this door. I'll get the axe and chop and chop and chop 'til that door is open. Polly, do you hear me?"

Polly picked up the saddlebag and sack, squared her shoulders and opened the door.

Chapter 27

Governor Tryon called the Assembly to session at New Bern in the fall of 1766. It was the first time the Assembly had met in eighteen months. There was a cordiality towards the crown administrator. Tryon was felt to have acted well in the matter of the Stamp Act and other political controversies that affected the colony. Now Tryon, with this feeling of approval, requested an appropriation for public buildings that would fix the capital of the colony in New Bern.

Mistress Ashe, with her husband at the Assembly, came up to The Anchor every day. "Do you know that if the governor lives in New Bern, and John stays in politics, he'll be gone half of every year?" she complained to Mama.

Mama nodded and continued with her knitting.

Polly read aloud from the New Bern newspaper: " 'Can you see the Public Records carted from Place to Place and your Properties and Estates trusted to the Mercy of a Shower of Rain, and at the Discretion of a Cart Driver? Forbid it Heaven!' " Looking up, she said, "James Davis is right. There are many in the colony who read his newspaper and many who will agree. And Andrew Steuart's new paper in Wilmington says that we must have a place for the government to call a permanent home. We've moved from place to place so much and never had a permanent capital here in the North Carolina colony."

"Do they really take the records around in a cart?" asked Charlotte. She lifted a kettle of hot water from its hook over the fire and carried it behind the counter.

"They probably do," Polly answered. "Every governor seems to have a preference for a different town for the capital. From Bath in the north, sitting on the Pamlico River that was so good to pirates, to New Bern on the Neuse where the Assembly has met for the last several sessions, the records have traveled. There was one meeting here in Brunswick when many of the papers could not be found. I remember the men talking about it here in the tavern."

"Why can't the capital be Wilmington?" Mistress Ashe asked.

"I would like that better, too," Polly said. "But I do think that both the governor and Mistress Tryon have wanted to move for some while." Then she grinned. "Mistress Ashe, I thought you didn't worry about politics."

"I'm not worried about politics," she said. "I want my John closer home."

Polly went back to the newspaper. "The town of New Bern is judged to be the best place for the governor's residence and the seat of government. Plans for these structures are being drawn up." She put the paper down and looked at the women. "All of the men who have business with the courts, or were involved with the Assembly, will be in New Bern for the next few days, I guess."

"I know the honor John feels of being speaker. If they would only meet in the dead of winter it would make it much easier," she said to Mama. She held up the piece of needlepoint she was working on to inspect the threads.

"The overseer at the plantation hasn't sent a report since Edward left for New Bern," Mistress Moseley said. "I know they must have harvested the corn. Certainly they have finished cropping the tobacco." She dropped the napkin she was hemming and reached for another length of thread. "But not a word. Not one word. Sometimes I wonder just how hard that overseer works. Or works those slaves."

"Mistress Moseley, aren't you at all interested in what the Assembly is doing?"

"That's all business for men. I need to know when my cornmeal will be delivered. That should concern you, too, Polly."

"It does. But the business is not just for men. The laws influence how I run the tavern and what taxes I have to pay."

Mistress Ashe looked up from her sewing. "Polly, you should be worrying about what ball gown to wear to the Assembly parties. It is certainly time for you to be going. You should be worrying about an escort to plays or gatherings. Instead you worry about laws and taxes. It is not natural for a young girl." She shook her finger. "It's time you began thinking about marriage."

Polly thought she would scream if the complaining and reproaching didn't stop. She had moved a small table near Mama's rocker and had seated the women there out of the tavern traffic. The last of her noon trade had left only a short time ago. Soon she would have to put down the paper and begin preparations for the next meal. If she only had a parlor, where she could get the nattering women completely out of her way.

Charlotte, from behind the counter where she was washing dishes, caught Polly's eye and made a face.

Two men appeared at the tavern door. "Miss Polly, I got some fine apples," said one. "Just down from Cross Creek way."

She went out to bargain with the men about the price.

"Polly, how do you manage it?" asked Mistress Ashe, when she came back in carrying a basket of apples.

"Manage what?"

"Why, manage the tradesmen who come to the door. Manage those slaves who work for you."

"I give the orders. I pay the bills," she said. "I treat them with kindness, as much as possible. I listen to them about the work and what their needs are. I respect their labor."

If she had just fallen off the moon the two women would not have looked more shaken.

"Listen to them!" said Mistress Ashe.

"Respect!" said Mistress Moseley.

Leah slammed a lid on a pot. The noise sent shivers through Polly, and the dull pain in her head, that had bothered her all morning, ached even worse. "Excuse me, please. I have an errand to run. Charlotte, would you like to come with me?"

Polly didn't wait to be excused. She stepped out into the yard. Charlotte ran to catch up with her and Polly screamed at her. "How would they look at me if I said how much I hate slavery?"

"I haven't said a word," Charlotte huffed. "Don't take it out on me."

"Miss Polly, you all right?" Solomon had come out of the barn and was keeping pace with their long strides.

Polly stopped to look at him. "Speak in complete sentences, Solomon. I don't know where you're going or what you will become. But I promise you that you will not always be a slave."

"Yes, ma'am," he said. "Miss Polly? Miss Charlotte?"

She waited.

"Moze is mighty bad off today."

She tried to remember the last time she had seen

Moze. He had spoken to her, since she bought the slaves, only when he had to. But he did still come to the tavern to sit and whittle, or just listen and doze near the hearth. He was so old.

"Miss Polly, did you hear me, or are you talking to yourself inside your head?"

"Solomon, you are too smart by half. Don't you sass me."

"Lawdy, Miss Polly, I would never sass you."

"Right now, let's go pay a visit to Moze."

The inside of the cabin was tidy and a fire burned on the hearth. Moze lay propped in bed, his eyes closed.

"Moze?"

He looked toward her. "That you, Miss Polly?"

His voice was so weak that Polly hardly recognized it. "Oh, Moze, I did not know that you were this ill."

"Not ill, Miss Polly. I still got all my wits 'bout me, 'specially the memory ones." He sighed. "Mostly I still got the memories."

"Are they good ones, Moze?"

"Some."

"Tell me a good memory."

He closed his rheumy eyes and was quiet for so long that Polly thought he had drifted into sleep. Then slowly he lifted his hand to trace an image in the air. "You got that jutting jaw from old Colonel Maurice, what was the judge's daddy. You stubborn like he always was. You got those eyes set deep in your forehead just like him. You got a strength like the Colonel. Like the judge, too."

His hand fell to the bed. "It don't make you a pretty girl, but you is becoming a handsome woman."

Moze opened his eyes. "Colonel Maurice dreamed about this land here. When he come to survey, I be with him. I pull the survey chains and slash the trees to mark the boundaries. Lost my leg. Got caught in vines and thorny bushes. All the bones in my foot was broke. Colonel cut it off to save my life. I never could pull the chains again."

"Oh, Moze."

"But my leg was all I lost. Found me a place here. And the Colonel freed me. I be a free man these years I live here." He nodded slightly. "Freedom be worth a leg."

She could feel the tears wet on her cheeks. "Moze, being free would be the most wonderful of all memories, I think."

"Miss Polly?" Moze said.

"Yes, Moze. I'm here."

He did not answer. Soon he was asleep. She knelt by the bed, her elbows resting on the torn cotton mattress. She gazed into his face, memorizing the lines of strength and courage written there. She knew, in her heart, that she had talked with him for the last time.

Freedom, she thought. Such a simple word. Such a powerful word. To have the room to move about. To have an independence to make choices.

"Freedom," she said. "Moze, I'm glad to know you are not a slave."

Charlotte was waiting on the porch when she finally moved away from the sick bed. On the walk back to the tavern, Charlotte said, "It is important, isn't it?"

When Polly didn't answer she went on. "It is important to be free."

"Yes, Charlotte, I think it is very important." She slipped her arm about her sister's waist in a firm hug. Charlotte hugged her back.

Chapter 28

By the time the Assembly adjourned that fall, Polly had made her plans. Families were moving out of Brunswick. Many of the tradesmen no longer brought their goods across the sandbars to the port, but stopped instead at the Wilmington docks. Even the large ships moved their merchandise up to the larger port. Economically, she had to move with the trade. For weeks she had been writing back and forth to Cousin Maurice about her decision.

She had still not found a horse that was both a good mount and a price that she wanted to pay. The day after the simple services for Moze, she swallowed her grief and began to make plans to move. She went to Mister Edward at the blacksmith shop to talk about borrowing a horse.

"Yes, ma'am. I got a horse that will pull a wagon. It's no good for riding but it will do you for a trip across the river," Mister Edward said.

Polly had Isaac hitch the horse to the farm wagon to drive her across the Haulover. She told the household only that she had business in Wilmington. She met Cousin Maurice at the courthouse as they had arranged.

Cousin Maurice offered her tea and a young clerk brought the tray in to place it on the desk. "You have served me many times, little cousin. I am glad to have the opportunity to offer refreshment to you."

"Thank you, big cousin," she answered. She tried not

to fidget as she took a sip of the liquid. She didn't want a drink. She wanted to get down to business.

Cousin Maurice must have felt her agitation, for he leaned back in his chair and laced his hands across his stomach. "Polly, some other business first, before we get down to this move you want to make. I want to thank you for letting me know about the papers you found in the warehouse. Phillip would never tell me what he'd done with them. William Dry knows all he needs to know about the situation, as I told you in my last letter."

He leaned forward and pointed his finger at her. "You have done all that is required on this matter. You have helped your father and there is no more you can do. I have taken care of everything else. Now you must let it go."

Polly breathed a huge sigh. "Thank you, sir."

"Now to this new business. Polly, you have done well in Brunswick. Are you sure that moving to Wilmington is the best thing for you to do?"

"Yes, Cousin Maurice." She set down her cup and held up her hand to count off, on her fingers, the points she wanted to make. "Trade is shifting here. Business from the interior counties is moving here. The town is growing and the center of wealth is in Wilmington. Brunswick is not growing."

"In Brunswick you know everyone. You have protection because of that," the judge said.

"Yes, sir. But I know many people here, too. The same tradesmen stop here at these docks. I think I have earned their regard and will find the same treatment that I have received from them at Brunswick."

"Your farm land and the maritime products? Do you have an overseer that you can trust?"

"Cousin Maurice, I have been openly criticized for having Jeremiah and Isaac as foremen. But I can trust them.

The men work well for them. I am not concerned about either the farm produce or the maritime production."

"Polly, when we signed that paper two years ago, I had no idea this would be one of the results." He stood and gave a courtly bow. "If you will come with me, I'll show you the two properties that are available and that I think can be used for your purposes."

By late afternoon the papers were signed. She was again declared incompetent, to meet the requirements of the court. Judge Maurice Moore was the guardian of the property. But she had a deed for a structure on Front Street, just a block south of Market Street, that could be used as both a house and a tavern. The main room was much larger than the tavern room at the The Anchor. There were four rooms above for bed chambers and a great attic space. She had the deed to a warehouse on the busy docks to store her supplies for the tavern and the produce coming in from her woodlands.

"I will plan the move for the first of the year, Cousin Maurice." She paused as the thought occurred to her. "Timothy Charles will be two years old."

"You shouldered difficult responsibilities, Polly. The tasks have not ended. If I have not told you before, let me do so now. It is a pleasure to be associated with you." He reached to shake her hand, before he helped her up on the wagon seat beside Isaac. She felt most competent.

Now, only two days later, she sat in the dusk on the bench outside The Anchor, wrapped in her grandfather's woolen cloak. She held the letter from Daniel. She had read and reread the words. She didn't need light to read it tonight. Each syllable of the letter was etched in her memory.

Come to me, he had written. Come and marry me.

She had felt, since she first read the letter, that she was running out of her edges. No decisions that she had made held so many consequences. She could not marry Daniel and open a tavern in Wilmington. She could not marry Daniel, or any other man, and keep her incompetent status. That was the law.

Now, sitting here in the dark, she had decided. Her stomach was still, and her hands on the paper were calm. With the letter clutched to her heart, she looked up at the brilliant stars that filled the sky.

Leah sat down beside her. "I thought you be pleased to hear from that young man. I know how you care for him. I see it shining in your face when you look at him. I see how he look at you."

"He wants me to marry him."

"Lawdy!"

They were both silent for a long time. Then Leah peered into Polly's face. "You gonna marry him?"

"No."

"Lawdy." This time when Leah said the word it was a prayer.

"I love Daniel. Leah, I love him so much that it tears at my heart. He loves me. If he loves me enough he will come back. I know he will."

"Then what are you gonna do?"

"Leah, when Papa had to leave and Cousin Maurice signed the paper that put me in charge here, it was all thrust at me. Nobody can begin to know how scared I was. Mama was sick, Charlotte resented me, Cecilia was much too young to know what was happening. Then the baby came and we almost lost him. Oh, Leah, I coped the best I could."

"Yes, you did, child. You never act scared, even from

the beginning. 'Cept you not a child any longer. Miss Polly, what are you gonna do now?"

She leaped from the bench and grabbed Leah's hands to pull her up, too. "We are going to Wilmington. You and I will run the finest tavern the port city of Wilmington has ever seen."

From inside The Anchor Cecilia called, "Polly? Where are you, Polly?"

"I can't find the extra candles," Charlotte yelled. "Polly, where did you put the candles?"

"That Miss Charlotte got to learn some patience," Leah said.

Polly whirled about and raised her arms above her head, as if to gather stars from the sky. Then, with her hands thrust deep in her pockets, she hurried in to her sisters.

★　★　★